AF720373

GOING TO STRASBOURG

Going to Strasbourg

An Oral History of Sexual Orientation Discrimination and the European Convention on Human Rights

PAUL JOHNSON
Professor of Sociology, University of York

OXFORD
UNIVERSITY PRESS

OXFORD
UNIVERSITY PRESS

Great Clarendon Street, Oxford, OX2 6DP,
United Kingdom

Oxford University Press is a department of the University of Oxford. It furthers the University's objective of excellence in research, scholarship, and education by publishing worldwide. Oxford is a registered trade mark of Oxford University Press in the UK and in certain other countries

© P. Johnson 2016

The moral rights of the author have been asserted

First Edition published in 2016

Impression: 1

All rights reserved. No part of this publication may be reproduced, stored in a retrieval system, or transmitted, in any form or by any means, without the prior permission in writing of Oxford University Press, or as expressly permitted by law, by licence or under terms agreed with the appropriate reprographics rights organization. Enquiries concerning reproduction outside the scope of the above should be sent to the Rights Department, Oxford University Press, at the address above

You must not circulate this work in any other form and you must impose this same condition on any acquirer

Crown copyright material is reproduced under Class Licence Number C01P0000148 with the permission of OPSI and the Queen's Printer for Scotland

Published in the United States of America by Oxford University Press
198 Madison Avenue, New York, NY 10016, United States of America

British Library Cataloguing in Publication Data
Data available

Library of Congress Control Number: 2016943989

ISBN 978–0–19–877761–8

Printed and bound by
CPI Group (UK) Ltd, Croydon, CR0 4YY

Links to third party websites are provided by Oxford in good faith and for information only. Oxford disclaims any responsibility for the materials contained in any third party website referenced in this work.

for

Marilyn Jane and Terence Alexander Bedford

Acknowledgements

I am extremely grateful to the research participants for the time they spent talking to me about their experiences of going to Strasbourg. I am equally grateful to the Leverhulme Trust for the award of a Research Fellowship (RF-2015-105) that enabled me to carry out the research and to Ed Kirby at the University of York for encouraging me to apply for it. I am indebted to Alex Flach and Elinor Shields at Oxford University Press for the encouragement they have given me. I am very grateful to Albert Stewart for his skilful and careful proofreading. A number of colleagues and friends have been supportive in recent years, and this is my opportunity to thank them: Ellen Annandale, David Ashley, David Beer, Sam de Boise, Nik Brown, Karen Bullock, Kate Burningham, Nick Ellison, Emanuel and Luciana Gloor, Damian Gonzalez-Salzberg, Lesley Hall, Laurie Hanquinet, Laurence Helfer, Loveday Hodson, Stevi Jackson, Lynn Kilgallon, Michael Kirby, Steph Lawler, Murray Lee, Xiaodong Lin, Gail Mason, Andy Nercessian, Sarah Nettleton, Les Moran, Jo Moran-Ellis, Carole Nicolson, Mike Savage, Eric Taffyn, Alison Taylor, Imogen Tyler, Katharine Tyler, Amanda Waggett, and Marc de Werd. My heartfelt thanks to Mary Burden Castiglione for all the love and encouragement she has given me during our long friendship. I am also very grateful to Geoff Cooper for many years of treasured friendship. I am similarly appreciative of my long and close friendship with David Pringle and all that flows from it. I owe an enormous debt to my family for the constant love and support that they provide. My greatest debt is to my husband for the love and intellectual support that he gives.

Contents

Table of Cases

EUROPEAN COMMISSION OF HUMAN RIGHTS, EUROPEAN COURT OF HUMAN RIGHTS, AND COMMITTEE OF MINISTERS OF THE COUNCIL OF EUROPE

NATIONAL COURTS

Table of Legislation

COUNCIL OF EUROPE

EUROPEAN UNION

UNITED KINGDOM OF GREAT BRITAIN AND NORTHERN IRELAND

JURISDICTIONS OUTSIDE THE UNITED KINGDOM

Introduction

When, in 1949, Winston Churchill expressed his 'hope that a European Court might be set up'[1] it is unlikely that he would have envisioned it as a judicial body that would receive, let alone entertain, applications from individuals complaining about discrimination on the grounds of what is now commonly referred to as 'sexual orientation'. If ever such an idea crossed the minds of those who created the European Convention on Human Rights (hereinafter 'the Convention'),[2] then it is probable that it did so only in relation to the question of whether granting individuals the right to petition an international human rights body would lead to its abuse by 'cranks and evilly-disposed persons'.[3] Yet, just three months after the European Commission of Human Rights (hereinafter 'the Commission') became competent to receive individual petitions in 1955, an individual submitted the first application concerning discrimination related to sexual orientation.[4] Since then, the Strasbourg organs—the Commission (which ceased to function in 1999), the European Court of Human Rights (hereinafter 'the Court'), and the Committee of Ministers of the Council of Europe—have dealt with a considerable volume of applications submitted by individuals complaining about sexual orientation discrimination.[5]

This book tells the story of those individuals who have challenged sexual orientation discrimination in the UK by 'going to Strasbourg'. It does so at a time when there is widespread and growing mistrust of the Court in the UK. Recent high-profile judgments against the UK on issues such as the disfranchisement of offenders in prison[6] and the irreducibility of 'whole life orders' imposed on prisoners[7] have led senior politicians to claim that the Court has 'distorted' and 'discredited' the

[1] Council of Europe, First Session of the Consultative Assembly, Sixth Sitting (17 August 1949) in *Reports, Part 1, Sittings 1 to 6* (Council of Europe 1949) 284.

[2] Convention for the Protection of Human Rights and Fundamental Freedoms (4 November 1950) ETS No 005.

[3] Sir David Maxwell Fyfe, Council of Europe, First Part of the Second Session of the Consultative Assembly, Sixth Sitting (14 August 1950) in *Reports, Part 1, Sittings 1 to 12* (Council of Europe 1950) 174.

[4] For a discussion, see Part 1 of this book.

[5] For a complete survey, see Paul Johnson, *Homosexuality and the European Court of Human Rights* (Routledge 2013).

[6] *Hirst v the United Kingdom (no 2)* [GC] ECHR 2005-IX.

[7] *Vinter and Others v the United Kingdom* [GC] App Nos 66069/09, 130/10 and 3896/10 (ECtHR, 9 July 2013).

Going to Strasbourg: An Oral History of Sexual Orientation Discrimination and the European Convention on Human Rights. First Edition. Paul Johnson. © Paul Johnson 2016. Published 2016 by Oxford University Press.

concept of human rights[8] in ways that would have the founders of the Convention 'turning in their graves'.[9] This sentiment has found popular support as shown, for example, by a 2014 YouGov survey, which reported that 41 per cent of those adults polled favoured the withdrawal of the UK from the Convention.[10] Within this context, the UK used its chairmanship of the Committee of Ministers of the Council of Europe to attempt to limit the scope and function of the Court.[11] Since then, the Conservative Party has gone on to propose fundamental changes to the UK's relationship with the Court that include making its judgments 'advisory' rather than 'binding'.[12] It has pledged to 'scrap the Human Rights Act, and introduce a British Bill of Rights' that would 'break the formal link between British courts and the European Court of Human Rights'.[13] The Conservative Party has also stated that if the Council of Europe does not agree to such changes, then the UK 'would be left with no alternative but to withdraw' from the Convention.[14] In sum, the relationship between the UK and the Strasbourg organs can be characterized as highly strained.[15]

In telling the story of how individuals in the UK have utilized the Convention system to challenge sexual orientation discrimination, this book rebuts many of the now popular myths that circulate about the Court. One such myth is that the Court is, as Lord Sumption argues, 'the international flag-bearer for judge-made fundamental law extending well beyond the text which it is charged with applying'.[16] The idea that Strasbourg judges routinely exceed their authority in

[8] David Cameron MP, quoted in BBC News, 'Concept of human rights being distorted, warns Cameron' (25 January 2012) <www.bbc.co.uk/news/uk-politics-16708845> (accessed 19 February 2016).

[9] Chris Grayling MP, quoted in Nicholas Watt and Alan Travis, 'Tory ministers condemn ECHR ruling on whole-life prison sentences' *The Guardian* (9 July 2013) <www.theguardian.com/law/2013/jul/09/whole-life-sentences-david-cameron-human-rights> (accessed 19 February 2016).

[10] YouGov, 'Scepticism about human rights as well as the ECHR' (20 July 2014) <https://yougov.co.uk/news/2014/07/20/scepticism-about-human-rights-well-echr> (accessed 19 February 2016).

[11] See 'High level conference on the future of the European Court of Human Rights: Brighton declaration' (Council of Europe 2012) <www.echr.coe.int/Documents/2012_Brighton_FinalDeclaration_ENG.pdf> (accessed 19 February 2016) and Protocol No. 15 amending the Convention for the Protection of Human Rights and Fundamental Freedoms (24 June 2013) CETS 213. For claims by the UK government that the 'Brighton Declaration' and Prot No 15 will significantly change and limit the scope and function of the Court, see Ministry of Justice, 'UK delivers European court reform' (20 April 2012) <www.gov.uk/government/news/uk-delivers-european-court-reform> (accessed 19 February 2016). For a contrary view, see European Court of Human Rights, 'Opinion of the Court on Draft Protocol No. 15 to the European Convention on Human Rights' (6 February 2013) <www.echr.coe.int/Documents/2013_Protocol_15_Court_Opinion_ENG.pdf> (accessed 19 February 2016).

[12] Conservative Party, 'Protecting Human Rights in the UK: The Conservatives' Proposals for Changing Britain's Human Rights Laws' (2014) 6. For a critical discussion of this, see Kanstantsin Dzehtsiarou, Tobias Lock, Paul Johnson, Fiona de Londras, Alan Greene, and Ed Bates, *The Legal Implications of a Repeal of the Human Rights Act 1998 and Withdrawal from the European Convention on Human Rights* (2015) <http://ssrn.com/abstract=2605487> (accessed 16 February 2016).

[13] Conservative Party, *The Conservative Party Manifesto 2015*, 60.

[14] Conservative Party (n 12) 8.

[15] For a broader discussion, see Katja S Ziegler, Elizabeth Wicks, and Loveday Hodson, *The UK and European Human Rights: A Strained Relationship?* (Hart Publishing 2015).

[16] Lord Sumption, 'The Limits of Law' (Kuala Lumpur, 20 November 2013) <www.supremecourt.uk/docs/speech-131120.pdf> (accessed 16 February 2016).

order to impose changes on and meddle with law in the UK is a regular trope of contemporary debate about the 'rampant abuse' of human rights law.[17] Yet, as this book shows, such a view is hardly borne out by Strasbourg case law in relation to sexual orientation discrimination. The Strasbourg organs have certainly issued a number of decisions and judgments—not least in response to complaints about the total prohibition of male homosexual acts in Northern Ireland, discrimination created by the higher 'age of consent' for male homosexual acts, and the prohibition of homosexuality in the armed forces—that have propelled fundamental changes to law in the UK. However, the Strasbourg organs have also frequently adopted a conservative interpretation of the rights and freedoms contained in the Convention and, much to the disappointment of gay men and lesbians, rejected applications concerning sexual orientation discrimination. Restraint rather than activism, as this book demonstrates, has often been a hallmark of the Strasbourg organs' approach to the issue of sexual orientation discrimination.

A key aspect of the story that this book tells, therefore, is the struggle that gay men and lesbians have had—and continue to have—in persuading the Strasbourg organs that the rights and freedoms guaranteed by the Convention are applicable to and provide protection from sexual orientation discrimination. Whilst, in 2011, Hillary Clinton, then United States Secretary of State, popularized the notion that 'gay rights are human rights, and human rights are gay rights',[18] this book shows that gay men and lesbians have been making that argument for over six decades and, moreover, that the Strasbourg organs have often been unwilling to accept it. To put it simply, when gay men and lesbians have knocked at Strasbourg's door and asked for help, they have very often had the door slammed in their faces. Therefore, whilst this book shows the important role that the Convention system has played in changing law in the UK in ways that have established equality on the grounds of sexual orientation, it also demonstrates the long and difficult process of achieving this. It shows that, in most cases, a successful application to Strasbourg about sexual orientation discrimination has been preceded by one or several similar applications that have been rejected.

Although applications to Strasbourg concerning sexual orientation discrimination have often been unsuccessful, the rate of their submission and the wide range of issues that they have addressed shows that gay men and lesbians in the UK have long viewed the Convention as a potentially fruitful means by which to challenge discrimination.[19] Although individuals in many member states of the Council of Europe have brought complaints under the Convention about sexual orientation discrimination, the Strasbourg organs have issued more decisions and judgments in

[17] James Slack, 'Britain will stay signed up to European Court of Human Rights but will not slavishly follow rulings from Strasbourg judges' *The Daily Mail* (8 November 2015) <www.dailymail.co.uk/news/article-3309280/Britain-STAY-signed-European-Court-Human-Rights-not-slavishly-follow-rulings-Strasbourg-judges.html> (accessed 29 February 2016).

[18] Hillary R Clinton, 'Remarks in Recognition of International Human Rights Day' (Geneva, 6 December 2011) < http://m.state.gov/md178368.htm > (accessed 20 February 2016).

[19] For a full list of applications against the UK concerning sexual orientation discrimination, see Appendix 3.

respect of applications against the UK about sexual orientation discrimination than in respect of any other state. A number of factors account for why the Strasbourg organs have received and dealt with a large volume of applications against the UK about sexual orientation discrimination, and many of these are discussed throughout this book. These factors include the extent of law in the UK that has, until recently, discriminated against individuals on the grounds of their sexual orientation or failed to protect them from such discrimination; the existence of a number of 'gay rights' organizations that have recognized the value of attempting to challenge sexual orientation discrimination by way of supporting or coordinating applications to Strasbourg; and the limited status of the Convention in the internal legal systems of the UK which, until the enactment of the Human Rights Act 1998, meant its provisions were not enforceable by the domestic courts, forcing individuals seeking a remedy to a breach of any right or freedom guaranteed by the Convention to petition Strasbourg directly.

At the heart of this book are oral history accounts by some of the individuals who have complained to Strasbourg about sexual orientation discrimination in the UK. Many people who have experienced State-mandated discrimination—in any country of the world and in relation to any personal characteristic—will identify with the accounts in this book, because they are the accounts of 'ordinary' people seeking a means by which to live 'normal' lives. Although making a complaint to Strasbourg is uncommon—and, in that sense, extraordinary—the accounts in this book are rooted in the circumstances of mundane, routine, and everyday discrimination that will be familiar to many. The accounts provide a sharp rebuke to those who continue to believe that individuals who take legal action to address sexual orientation discrimination do so because they are part of some militant or extreme 'homosexual lobby'. On the contrary, what they show is the commonplaceness of suffering and pain created by discrimination and the value of the existence of international human rights law as a means by which to address it.

Outline of the Book

This book is divided into three parts, each of which tells the story, from a particular point of view, of how the Convention system has been used to challenge sexual orientation discrimination in the UK.

Part 1 of the book provides a sociologically informed historical analysis of the complaints that have been brought under the Convention against the UK about discrimination on the grounds of sexual orientation. This analysis focuses on sixty-three cases against the UK that originated in individual applications lodged with the Strasbourg organs between 1972 and 2010. The purpose of the analysis is to show the socio-legal context out of which applications against the UK have arisen, the jurisprudence that the Strasbourg organs have developed in response to these applications, and the impact of this jurisprudence on UK law. The overall aim of this part of the book is to provide the fullest available account of the role of the Convention system in shaping law in the UK in relation to sexual orientation.

Part 2 of the book contains oral histories of fifteen individual applicants to Strasbourg who made complaints under the Convention about sexual orientation discrimination in the UK. It also contains four oral histories of legal professionals and political campaigners who have had significant involvement with such complaints against the UK. The purpose of this part of the book is to present first-hand accounts of the process of making complaints under international human rights law. Such accounts are rare, and, therefore, the overall aim of this part of the book is to provide a unique insight into the circumstances out of which litigation arises, as well as the effect on the individuals who originate it.

Part 3 of the book provides a thematic analysis of the oral histories. The purpose of this analysis is to illuminate and examine patterns within the accounts in order to provide an in-depth understanding of the process and experience of making a complaint to Strasbourg. The analysis in this part of the book is novel in the context of existing knowledge of the Court. Previous academic research on the Court—when it has gone beyond a study of jurisprudence—has largely focused on legal professionals who work in or appear before it. In contrast, the analysis presented here is rooted in the perspectives of applicants. The aim of this part of the book, therefore, is to make an original contribution to knowledge about human rights litigation and the Court. Such knowledge may be useful to those who, in the future, decide to pursue complaints in Strasbourg.

PART 1

LEGAL HISTORY

This part of the book provides a sociologically informed historical analysis of applications made under the European Convention on Human Rights against the UK concerning discrimination on the grounds of sexual orientation. It focuses on sixty-three cases against the UK that originated in individual applications submitted to the Strasbourg organs between 1972 and 2010, a full list of which can be found in Appendix 3. Nearly all of these cases concern complaints made by individuals about a detriment they had suffered as a result of a difference in treatment based on homosexual sexual orientation. However, also discussed are a small number of cases that, although not explicitly concerned with sexual orientation discrimination, substantially involve issues related to homosexuality. In addition, two cases are considered that, although not explicitly concerned with either sexual orientation discrimination or homosexuality, address the issue of same-sex marriage. The key aim of this part of the book is to elucidate the socio-legal context of applications against the UK about sexual orientation discrimination, the jurisprudence that the Strasbourg organs have developed as a result of these applications, and the effect of this jurisprudence on the legal landscape of the UK.

1

Sexual Orientation Discrimination and the European Convention on Human Rights

A Socio-Legal Analysis of Applications against the UK

Setting the Context: Homosexuality, the UK, and the Strasbourg Organs

When the UK signed the Statute of the Council of Europe in 1949, it committed itself to 'the maintenance and further realisation of human rights and fundamental freedoms'.[1] The primary instrument to ensure the effectiveness of that commitment, the Convention for the Protection of Human Rights and Fundamental Freedoms (more commonly referred to as the European Convention on Human Rights), was signed by the UK and other member states of the Council of Europe in 1950.[2] By signing the Convention, the member states were '[r]eaffirming their profound belief in those fundamental freedoms which are the foundation of justice and peace in the world' and taking 'the first steps for the collective enforcement of certain of the rights stated in the Universal Declaration [of Human Rights]'.[3] During the process by which the Convention was created, Sir David Maxwell Fyfe told the Consultative (now Parliamentary) Assembly of the Council of Europe that the aim of the Convention was to 'delimit the conditions in which alone the dignity of the human spirit will stand free, firm and unassailed'.[4] Maxwell Fyfe appealed to 'those nations who belong to and revere the great family of Western Europe and Christian civilisation' to commit themselves to the human rights and fundamental freedoms contained in the Convention and to a machinery for enforcing them.[5]

On its entry into force in 1953,[6] the Convention established a tripartite structure to carry out the collective enforcement of the rights and freedoms to which

[1] Statute of the Council of Europe (5 May 1949) ETS No 001, art 1(b).

[2] Convention for the Protection of Human Rights and Fundamental Freedoms (4 November 1950) ETS No 005. Hereinafter referenced as 'ECHR'.

[3] ECHR, preamble.

[4] Council of Europe, First Session of the Consultative Assembly, Eighth Sitting (19 August 1949) *Collected Edition of the 'Travaux Préparatoires' of the European Convention on Human Rights*, vol 1 (Martinus Nijhoff 1975) 124.

[5] ibid.

[6] The ECHR entered into force on 3 September 1953 following the ten ratifications required by ex-art 66(2).

Going to Strasbourg: An Oral History of Sexual Orientation Discrimination and the European Convention on Human Rights. First Edition. Paul Johnson. © Paul Johnson 2016. Published 2016 by Oxford University Press.

the Contracting States had committed themselves. This structure consisted of the European Commission of Human Rights (set up in 1954),[7] the European Court of Human Rights (set up in 1959),[8] and the Committee of Ministers of the Council of Europe. The purpose of the Commission was to consider the admissibility of applications submitted to it alleging violations of provisions contained in the Convention and, in those cases when it deemed an application admissible, to establish the facts and promote a friendly settlement between the parties concerned.[9] If a friendly settlement could not be reached, the Commission was required to produce a report stating its opinion as to whether the facts of the case disclosed a breach by the State concerned of any of its obligations under the Convention.[10] The Commission was then empowered to bring a case before the Court—individual applicants were unable to petition the Court directly—and it was for the Court to give a final and binding judgment.[11] The Committee of Ministers, empowered to supervise the execution of the Court's judgments,[12] could also give a final and binding decision on complaints that were not referred to the Court.[13]

When the Convention entered into force, the UK enforced a total prohibition of male same-sex sexual acts. A man convicted of committing the 'abominable crime of buggery'[14] (or, in Scotland, sodomy[15]) with another man could be sentenced to imprisonment for life.[16] A conviction for attempting to commit buggery carried a maximum punishment of ten years' imprisonment,[17] and in Scotland, the maximum penalty for attempting to commit sodomy was imprisonment for life. In addition, the maximum sentence imposable on a man convicted of committing any act of gross indecency with another man was two years' imprisonment (with the same maximum penalty applicable to a man convicted of being a party to the commission of any act of gross indecency with another man, or for procuring or attempting to procure the commission by any man of any act of gross indecency with another man).[18] These offences provided a comprehensive framework for regulating a wide range of sexual acts committed between men—including acts that did not involve any physical contact[19]—and consent by the parties involved provided no basis for a defence against prosecution.

[7] The Committee of Ministers of the Council of Europe elected the first members of the Commission on 18 May 1954.

[8] The Consultative (now Parliamentary) Assembly of the Council of Europe elected the first judges of the Court on 21 January 1959—in accordance with the terms of ex-arts 46 and 56 ECHR—and it held its first session the following month.

[9] ECHR, ex-arts 27 and 28.

[10] ECHR, ex-art 31.

[11] ECHR, ex-art 48. Under the terms of this art, a State could also bring a case before the Court.

[12] ECHR, ex-art 54.

[13] ECHR, ex-art 32.

[14] Offences Against the Person Act 1861, s 61.

[15] Sodomy was a common law offence in Scotland.

[16] In England and Wales and Northern Ireland, the offence of buggery, when committed between human beings, consisted of sexual intercourse *per anum* between a man and another man or between a man and woman. In Scotland, the offence of sodomy applied to the same acts committed between males only.

[17] Offences Against the Person Act 1861, s 62.

[18] Criminal Law Amendment Act 1885, s 11.

[19] See *R v Hunt and Another* [1950] 2 All ER 291 which concerned the conviction of 'two grown men' who 'were found in a shed in positions which can only be described as constituting filthy exhibitions by the one to the other'.

Complaints to the Commission by those affected by the total prohibition of male homosexual acts in the UK—or any other aspect of discrimination based on sexual orientation—were not possible at the point that it began to receive applications from individuals in 1955.[20] An application to the Commission by an individual (or non-governmental organization or group of individuals) was only possible if the State complained about had made a declaration recognizing the competence of the Commission to receive such applications.[21] The UK did not make this declaration until January 1966 and, as a consequence, no individual applications could be lodged with Strasbourg before this date.[22] However, even if the UK had recognized the right of individual petition earlier, complaints to the Commission about the criminalization of male homosexual acts would have certainly failed. Since 1955, the Commission had robustly rejected a steady stream of applications lodged by men living in two States, Austria and the Federal Republic of Germany,[23] that both recognized the competence of the Commission to receive individual applications and enforced a total prohibition of male (and, in the case of Austria, female) homosexual acts.

The first such application was lodged with the Commission in October 1955 by an adult male serving a fifteen-month term of imprisonment in Germany for 'two cases of homosexuality' contrary to Paragraphs 175 and 175a of the German Criminal Code.[24] These provisions of the Criminal Code were in force in the form enacted by the National Socialist German Workers' (Nazi) Party in 1935[25] and criminalized sexual acts between men.[26] The applicant, who complained about both his conviction and the legislation under which it was secured, invoked a wide range of Articles of the Convention,[27] but the Commission focused on the complaints made under Articles 8 (right to respect for private and family life) and 14 (prohibition of discrimination). Under Article 8, the applicant complained that Paragraphs 175 and 175a infringed the 'right to privacy';[28] under Article 8 taken in conjunction with Article 14, he complained that, to the extent that Paragraphs 175 and 175a were limited to men, this infringed 'the principle of

[20] On 5 July 1955, six States had made the declarations required by ex-art 25(4) ECHR, which enabled the Commission to exercise the power to receive petitions from any individual (in respect of those six States) who claimed to be a victim of a violation of the rights contained in the ECHR.

[21] ECHR, ex-art 25(1).

[22] *Declarations recognising the competence of the European Commission of Human rights to receive individual petitions and recognising as compulsory the jurisdiction of the European Court of Human Rights* (Cmnd 2894, 1966).

[23] The Federal Republic of Germany granted the right of individual petition to the Commission on 5 July 1955, and Austria granted the same right on 3 September 1958.

[24] *W.B. v Federal Republic of Germany* (1955) Documents and Decisions 1955–1956–1957, 228. The applicant is referred to as 'X.' in Documents and Decisions but the copy of the Commission's decision in the Court's archives shows his initials as 'W.B.'. The decision is published only in French, and the text quoted is from my own translation.

[25] Gesetz zur Änderung des Strafgesetzbuchs vom 28 Juni 1935, art 6 (Reichsgesetzblatt Teil I 1935 Nummer 70 vom 5 Juli 1935, 839, 841).

[26] For a discussion of Paragraph 175 see: Günter Grau, *Hidden Holocaust? Gay and Lesbian Persecution in Germany 1933–45* (Cassell 1995).

[27] The applicant invoked arts 2, 8, 14, 17, and 18 ECHR.

[28] *W.B.* (n 24) 229.

sexual non-discrimination'.[29] In respect of Article 8, the Commission briefly stated that 'the Convention permits a High Contracting Party to legislate to make homosexuality a punishable offence' because 'private and family life may be the subject of interference' by the laws 'dealing with the protection of health or morals'.[30] In respect of Article 14, the Commission stated that the Convention 'does not exclude the possibility of a High Contracting Party differentiating between the sexes in the measures it takes with regard to homosexuality for the protection of health or morals'.[31] On this basis, the Commission declared the application, and a series of subsequent similar applications against Germany, inadmissible.[32] Further, the Commission used this case law as a basis for declaring inadmissible a series of complaints about the criminal law in Austria that enforced a blanket prohibition of homosexual acts.[33]

The Commission's consistent rejection of applications from individuals in Austria and Germany who had been convicted of 'homosexual offences' demonstrates that it did not regard the regulation of homosexual sexual acts, even in the form of a total prohibition of acts committed in private between two consenting adults, to be incompatible with the provisions of the Convention. Although Paragraphs 175 and 175a of the German Criminal Code enforced a legal framework implemented by the Nazi regime, the Commission did not regard this to be in conflict with the rights enshrined in the Convention by those 'countries which are like-minded and have a common heritage of political traditions, ideals, freedom and the rule of law'.[34] This is striking because, when the Commission received the first application relating to a conviction for homosexual offences in 1955, less than one third of those States that had signed the Convention in 1950 enforced a total prohibition of homosexual acts.[35] However, although the number of states that enforced such a prohibition always remained in the minority during the 1950s and 1960s as the number of states contracted to the Convention expanded, the Commission did not regard the criminalization of same-sex sexual acts to be antithetical to the 'traditions, ideals, freedom and the rule of law' of the majority of European states. By the time that homosexual acts were partially decriminalized in Germany and Austria, in 1969 and 1971 respectively, the Commission had never changed its opinion that complaints under the Convention about a total prohibition of homosexual acts between consenting adults were inadmissible. In short, the Commission did not regard the criminalization of homosexual sex to be an issue worthy of consideration in respect of human rights.

[29] ibid. [30] ibid. [31] ibid.

[32] For a discussion of this case law, see Paul Johnson, *Homosexuality and the European Court of Human Rights* (Routledge 2013).

[33] Strafgesetzes 1852 (Austria), paras 129 and 130. For a discussion of this case law, see Johnson (n 32).

[34] ECHR, preamble.

[35] Of the fifteen States that signed the Convention in 1950, four enforced a total prohibition of male homosexual acts in 1955: the Federal Republic of Germany, Ireland, Norway, and the UK (this discounts the Saar, which subsequently became an integral part of the Federal Republic of Germany in 1957).

In 1967, one year after the UK granted individuals the right to petition the Commission, homosexual acts—buggery and gross indecency[36]—committed in private between consenting males over the age of twenty-one years were decriminalized in England and Wales.[37] This partial decriminalization, the result of the UK Parliament enacting recommendations made in the 'Wolfenden Report',[38] was fiercely opposed by one of the chief architects of the Convention system, Sir David Maxwell Fyfe, who, sitting as Lord Kilmuir in the House of Lords, argued that law should not tolerate 'actions which the vast majority of people think wrong, unnatural and degrading'.[39] The decriminalization of male homosexual acts in England and Wales did not extend to the armed forces[40] or to members of crew on merchant ships.[41] The 'age of consent' for male homosexual acts was five years higher than for heterosexual acts (other than buggery[42]) or female homosexual acts. Male homosexual acts that involved more than two persons taking part or being present were classified as not having been done 'in private' and, consequently, remained criminalized.[43] The volume of male homosexual offences in England and Wales recorded by the police remained stable,[44] and those who published 'advertisements for the purpose of sexual practices taking place between male persons' could be convicted of conspiracy to corrupt public morals and conspiracy to outrage public decency.[45] The blanket prohibition of male homosexual acts remained in force in Northern Ireland and Scotland.

It is within this socio-legal context—in which male homosexual acts had been decriminalized in limited terms, and there existed no legal protection against discrimination on the grounds of sexual orientation—that individuals in the UK began to look to the Convention as a means of challenging the State's regulation of homosexuality. In the late 1960s and early 1970s, the Convention system offered individuals a novel and potentially powerful legal resource because, as Judge Sir Gerald Fitzmaurice described it, the Convention had:

> broken entirely new ground internationally, making heavy inroads on some of the most cherished preserves of governments in the sphere of their domestic jurisdiction or domaine

[36] In English law, the offences of buggery and indecency between men were consolidated as 'unnatural offences' by Sexual Offences Act 1956, ss 12 and 13.

[37] Sexual Offences Act 1967, s 1.

[38] Home Office, *Report of the Committee on Homosexual Offences and Prostitution* (Cmnd 247, 1957).

[39] HL Debate 24 May 1965, vol 266, col 659.

[40] Sexual Offences Act 1967, s 1(5).

[41] Sexual Offences Act 1967, s 2.

[42] The total prohibition of buggery between a man and woman endured until such acts were partially decriminalized in England and Wales in 1994 (Criminal Justice and Public Order Act 1994, s 143) and in Northern Ireland in 2003 (Criminal Justice (Northern Ireland) Order 2003, art 19).

[43] Sexual Offences Act 1967, s 1(2).

[44] In the ten-year period following the enactment of the Sexual Offences Act 1967, there was no significant change in the volume of offences recorded by the police in England and Wales for buggery (an offence not limited to sexual acts between men) and gross indecency between men. See Home Office, *Recorded crime statistics for England and Wales 1898–2001/02* <www.gov.uk/government/statistics/historical-crime-data> accessed 8 February 2016.

[45] *R v Knuller (Publishing, Printing and Promotions) Ltd. and Others* [1972] 2 QB 179, 184. Affirmed in part by the House of Lords in *Knuller (Publishing, Printing and Promotions) Ltd. and Others v Director of Public Prosecutions* [1972] 56 Cr App R 633, which quashed convictions for conspiracy to outrage public decency.

réservé. Most especially, and most strikingly, is this the case as regards what is often known as the 'right of individual petition', whereby private persons or entities are enabled to (in effect) sue their own governments before an international commission or tribunal,—something that, even as recently as thirty years ago, would have been regarded as internationally inconceivable.[46]

The remainder of this part of the book provides a critical analysis of those cases in which 'private persons' have exercised the right of individual petition to 'sue' the UK government in respect of issues relating to discrimination on the grounds of homosexual sexual orientation. These applications by individuals to Strasbourg have often (but not always) been supported or encouraged by political groups or non-governmental organizations and, as Loveday Hodson has argued, such entities 'play a central role in activating the Court's machinery and shaping its litigation'.[47] The focus of the analysis here is on the legal arguments deployed by applicants in complaints against the UK about sexual orientation discrimination and the response of the Strasbourg organs to them.

Laying the Foundations of 'Gay Rights' in the 1970s

Between 1972 and 1976, three applications were lodged with the Commission that concerned issues relating to homosexuality.[48] The first of these applications, *Handyside v the United Kingdom*, contained a complaint about the legal regulation of a publication deemed 'obscene' and did not directly raise the issue of discrimination on the grounds of sexual orientation. The second application, *X. v the United Kingdom*, contained a complaint about the male applicant's prosecution and conviction for sexual offences committed in private with other males. The third application, *Dudgeon v the United Kingdom*, contained a complaint about the total prohibition of male homosexual acts in Northern Ireland. The second

[46] *Golder v the United Kingdom* (1975) Series A no 18, separate opinion of Judge Sir Gerald Fitzmaurice, para 38.

[47] Loveday Hodson, *NGOs and the Struggle for Human Rights in Europe* (Hart Publishing 2011) 35.

[48] I do not discuss a fourth application lodged during this period relating to the seizure of pornographic magazines depicting homosexual acts because it appears from the Commission's decision that the material in question contained indecent images of children (*X. v the United Kingdom* (1978) 16 DR 32). The Commission stated that '[t]he magazines depict [inter alia] adult persons engaged in homosexual acts with adolescents and invite the readers to send their own photographs of similar character. The magazines therefore are not only obscene by whatever standard might be applied, but approve of, and even actively propagate acts which are criminal offences in English Law under the Sexual Offences Act 1956 and the Indecency with Child (sic) Act 1960' (ibid, 35). That the Commission regarded the magazines to 'actively propagate acts' that would have been an offence under the Indecency with Children Act 1960—which criminalized 'gross indecency with or towards a child under the age of fourteen'—suggests that it was convinced that the material in question contained images of 'adolescents' under the minimum age for any sexual act. Although the Commission paid particular attention to the homosexual nature of the acts depicted in the magazines, there is no reason to suggest that it would have reached a different conclusion had the magazines contained corresponding heterosexual acts.

and third applications both directly addressed the issue of discrimination on the grounds of sexual orientation. These three cases, although arising from very different circumstances and raising distinct questions, share the common feature of challenging the idea that the suppression of homosexuality is necessary in a democratic society for the protection of morals or for the protection of the rights and freedoms of others. Specifically, all three applicants contested the notion that children and young people require protection from exposure to the 'dangers' of male homosexuality.

Homosexuality and obscenity

In April 1972, the Commission received and registered a complaint by Richard Handyside, a publisher, about his prosecution and conviction for two offences of possessing for publication for gain copies of an obscene book contrary to the Obscene Publications Acts 1959 and 1964. The original decision to prosecute Mr Handyside had followed representations made to the Director of Public Prosecutions—most notably by Mary Whitehouse[49]—demanding that action should be taken against the publication of the book.[50] Mr Handyside had been convicted in a Magistrates' Court—which had fined him and ordered the destruction of over a thousand copies of the book that had been seized—and the Inner London Quarter Sessions subsequently rejected an appeal. The book in question, *The Little Red Schoolbook*, was an English language edition of a book first published in Denmark in 1969 and subsequently in several European and non-European countries. Its introduction stated that it was a 'reference book'[51] and, according to Mr Handyside, it was 'intended for teenagers between the ages of 12–18, but its appeal would be to the older ones'.[52]

The *Schoolbook* contained, inter alia, a chapter on 'pupils' that included a section on 'sex' and, within it, a subsection on 'homosexuality'.[53] It was primarily the contents of the section on 'sex' that the prosecution argued made the book obscene within the terms of the Obscene Publications Acts 1959 and 1964.[54] The Quarter Sessions had concluded that the book 'looked at as a whole does tend to deprave and corrupt a significant number, significant proportion, of the children likely to read it',[55] and that Mr Handyside could not avail himself of the statutory

[49] Mrs Whitehouse was Honorary General Secretary of the National Viewers' and Listeners' Association. For a discussion of her involvement in the case against Richard Handyside, see Michael Tracey and David Morrison, *Whitehouse* (Macmillan 1979).

[50] *Handyside v the United Kingdom* App No 5493/72 (Commission report, 30 September 1975) para 22.

[51] ibid, para 20. [52] ibid, para 52. [53] ibid, para 20.

[54] Obscene Publications Act 1959, s 1(1) states that 'an article shall be deemed to be obscene if its effect or (where the article comprises two or more distinct items) the effect of any one of its items is, if taken as a whole, such as to tend to deprave and corrupt persons who are likely, having regard to all relevant circumstances, to read, see or hear the matter contained or embodied in it'.

[55] *Handyside* (n 50) para 38.

defence[56] because, although 'there were many features about the book which, taken by themselves, were good', these were 'intermixed with things that were bad and detracted from it'.[57] As an example, the Quarter Sessions pointed out that:

> the treatment of the subject of homosexuality ... was a factual, very compassionate, understanding and valuable statement. But again, no matter how good one assessed the value of this section, it was hopelessly damning by its setting and context, and the fact that it, only, contained any suggestion of a stable relationship in relation to sex and that marriage received no such treatment at all. Moreover, there was a very real danger that this passage would create in the minds of children a conclusion that that kind of relationship was something permanent.[58]

In this respect, the Quarter Sessions had been particularly concerned with the fact that there was '[n]o mention ... that boys who have [homosexual] experiences grow out of it and have normal sexual relations including marriage'.[59]

In April 1974, the Commission declared most of Mr Handyside's complaints inadmissible[60] but declared admissible his complaints under Article 10 (freedom of expression) and Article 1 of Protocol No. 1 (protection of property) of the Convention.[61] In respect of Article 10—which was the principal focus of the case—the Commission unanimously agreed that the treatment of Mr Handyside interfered with his rights protected by that Article[62] but acknowledged 'the necessity of certain restrictions on obscene publications for the protection of the morals of ... society, particularly the morals of young people and children'.[63] In approaching the question of whether the action taken against Mr Handyside was necessary for the protection of morals, the Commission stated that, since Article 10 gave the State a certain discretion in determining the necessary limitations on freedom of expression, the 'moral standards prevailing in the country in question must be considered in order to determine whether the action taken was necessary to protect the said standards'.[64] In order to carry out this review, the Commission examined the decision of the Quarter Sessions and its assessment of the *Schoolbook*. In doing so, the Commission concluded that '[t]he United Kingdom authorities acted reasonably and in good faith and within the discretion afforded to member States in Art.10(2) for the protection of morals'.[65] Accordingly, the Commission's opinion

[56] Obscene Publications Act 1959, s 4(1) provides that '[a] person shall not be convicted of an offence ... if it is proved that publication of the article in question is justified as being for the public good on the ground that it is in the interests of science, literature, art or learning, or of other objects of general concern'.

[57] *Handyside* (n 50) para 39.

[58] *Handyside v the United Kingdom* (1976) Series A no 24, para 34.

[59] *Handyside* (n 50) dissenting opinion of Mr Ermacora. A second, revised edition of *The Little Red Schoolbook* included the following statement: '[m]any people go through a temporary homosexual phase at some stage in their life usually when they are young'.

[60] *Handyside v the United Kingdom* App No 5493/72 (Commission decision, 4 April 1974). Complaints under arts 1, 7, 9, 13, and 14 ECHR declared inadmissible.

[61] The Commission also decided to consider *ex officio* any issue that might arise under arts 17 and 18 ECHR.

[62] *Handyside* (n 50) para 139.

[63] ibid, para 149.

[64] ibid, para 154.

[65] ibid, para 157.

was, by a majority of eight votes to five (with one abstention), that the interference complained of was necessary in a democratic society for the protection of morals of young persons and, therefore, did not amount to a violation of Article 10.[66]

Three dissenting members of the Commission criticized the majority's reliance on the decision of the Quarter Sessions, which, they argued, was only one indication of the moral climate prevailing in the UK at the material time.[67] In this respect, they noted that in the UK 'there was a considerable quantity of, so-called "hard core" pornographic material, such as obscene films, sexshops, strip clubs, pornographic objects and literature, easily available' and that, moreover, '[c]hildren are also exposed to such material'.[68] They concluded that in comparison with these forms of allegedly obscene material the *Schoolbook* was, even when taking into account that its target readership was teenagers, 'tame' and that the interference complained of by Mr Handyside was not necessary in a democratic society for the protection of morals.[69] Two other dissenting members of the Commission advanced a similar argument, stating that 'the book cannot be fairly described as pornographic as that term is generally understood'.[70] They went on to argue that:

> as is obvious to any United Kingdom resident, there is, for various reasons, a measure of tolerance in the United Kingdom of publicity for sex, including homosexual activities, even when it is pornographic. It is then impossible to maintain that it is *necessary* under Art. 10(2) to prosecute a book, which is not pornographic and is a serious, even if, in the minds of some, misguided, attempt to inform, when there is a public display of publications and films that remain free from prosecution though they are manifest commercialisation of sex.[71]

When the Court considered the case it rejected this line of argument, stating that the 'publications and entertainment' cited by the minority in the Commission were not analogous to the *Schoolbook* since they were not 'aimed, to the same extent ..., at children and adolescents having ready access thereto'.[72] Although members of the Commission had candidly stated that 'as parents who have had children in school over a long period ... , we believe that the section on sex [which included the subsection on homosexuality] could hopefully be of some help rather than damaging',[73] the Court made no such pronouncement. Adopting a similar line of reasoning to the majority of the Commission, the Court concluded by a majority of thirteen to one that the treatment of Mr Handyside did not amount to a violation of Article 10.[74]

[66] ibid. [67] ibid, dissenting opinion of MM. Kellberg, Nørgaard, and Trechsel.
[68] ibid. [69] ibid.
[70] ibid, dissenting opinion of MM. Fawcett and Triantafyllides, para 11. [71] ibid.
[72] *Handyside* (n 58) para 56.
[73] *Handyside* (n 50) dissenting opinion of MM. Fawcett and Triantafyllides, para 4.
[74] The Court also unanimously held that there had been no violation of either art 1 of Prot No 1 or arts 14 and 18 ECHR. Although the Commission had declared the art 14 complaint inadmissible, the Court 'was of the opinion that it should also have regard to Article 14' because 'some of Mr Handyside's complaints ... raise the question of an arbitrary difference in treatment'. However, the Court stated that 'the data before the Court do not show that he suffered discrimination in the enjoyment of his freedom of expression and his property rights'. *Handyside* (n 58) para 66.

The implications of the Commission's opinion and the Court's judgment in *Handyside*—insofar as they relate to the content in the *Schoolbook* on homosexuality—can be considered in respect of the concerted campaign which began in the UK in the mid-1980s to prohibit 'a local authority from giving financial or other assistance to any person for the purpose of publishing or promoting homosexuality as an acceptable family relationship or for the purpose of teaching such acceptability in any maintained school'.[75] A key focus of this campaign to prevent the 'promotion of homosexuality' was the ambition to restrict children's access to published materials that, like the *Schoolbook*, contained 'positive images' of homosexuality.[76] When the UK Parliament eventually enacted what became widely known as 'Section 28' in 1988, which prohibited local authorities from promoting 'the teaching in any maintained school of the acceptability of homosexuality as a pretended family relationship',[77] it did so in the context of Strasbourg jurisprudence that had established that legal measures aimed at restricting children's access to purely factual discussions of homosexuality were not in violation of the right to freedom of expression guaranteed by Article 10. During the fifteen-year lifetime of Section 28,[78] no complaint was brought against it in Strasbourg under Article 10 or any other provision of the Convention.

The 'age of consent'

In August 1975, the Commission received an application from a man in his late twenties who was imprisoned.[79] The applicant complained that, because of a 'private and reciprocal homosexual relationship lasting nine months with an 18-year-old male adult'[80] when he was twenty-six years old, he had been investigated by the police, charged, and found guilty of the offence of buggery in respect of acts committed with two eighteen-year-old men, and been sentenced to two-and-a-half years' imprisonment. An appeal against the sentence had been rejected by the Court of Appeal on the grounds that the relationship between the applicant and one of his partners involved elements of coercion and (sado-masochistic) violence and 'the fact that the applicant is orientated towards the late teenagers and the younger men of the next generation does make him a person who ... is a danger to the public'.[81] The applicant's principal complaint to the Commission was that 'the age of consent for private acts between homosexuals is 21 years of age while a heterosexual relationship is permitted at the age of 16, a difference of 5 years'.[82] He

[75] Earl of Halsbury, HL Debate 18 December 1986, vol 483, col 311.

[76] Lord Campbell of Alloway, HL Debate 18 December 1986, vol 483, cols 312–13.

[77] Local Government Act 1988, s 28 created Local Government Act 1986, s 2A, which stated that '[a] local authority shall not—(a) intentionally promote homosexuality or publish material with the intention of promoting homosexuality; (b) promote the teaching in any maintained school of the acceptability of homosexuality as a pretended family relationship'.

[78] Local Government Act 1986, s 2A was repealed by Ethical Standards in Public Life etc. (Scotland) Act 2000, s 34 and Local Government Act 2003, s 122 and sch 8.

[79] *X. v the United Kingdom* (1977) 11 DR 36. [80] ibid, 37. [81] ibid, 38.

[82] ibid, 37.

also pointed out that the age of majority in the UK was eighteen years and, unlike at the time when the minimum age for homosexual acts was set, not twenty-one years.[83] The applicant claimed that 'homosexuals are discriminated against' and that he had 'been victimised, hauled through the courts and imprisoned because he is a homosexual'.[84]

The applicant in *X. v the United Kingdom* may have expected the Commission to declare his application inadmissible given its long-standing practice of rejecting complaints relating to the criminalization of homosexual acts. Indeed, only three days before the Commission registered his application in October 1975, it had declared inadmissible an application by a German adult male regarding his conviction for homosexual acts committed with persons under the age of consent (which at the time of the offences was twenty-one years, in contrast to the minimum age for heterosexual acts which was fourteen years).[85] In response to that applicant's complaint that enforcing a higher age of consent for male homosexual acts amounted to a violation of his right to respect for his private life guaranteed by Article 8 the Commission, although conceding that '[a] person's sexual life is undoubtedly part of his private life of which it constitutes an important aspect', stated that the 'German legislature was clearly inspired by the need to protect the rights of children and adolescents' and that the legal regulation of the applicant complied with Article 8 as being 'necessary in a democratic society for the protection of the rights of others'.[86] The Commission rejected the applicant's complaint under Article 14—that he was the victim of discrimination founded on sex because only male homosexual acts constituted a criminal offence—because it accepted that the 'need for social protection' provided an objective and reasonable justification for the difference in treatment.[87]

However, the Commission declared *X. v the United Kingdom* partially admissible and, in doing so, made it the first complaint about sexual orientation discrimination to pass this stage of review. In declaring admissible the applicant's complaint under Article 8 about the interference with his right to respect for his private life, the Commission stated that 'it should examine the issues ... taking into account the development of moral opinion in recent years concerning State interference with the private, consensual sexual lives of adults'.[88] The Commission further declared the applicant's complaint under Article 14 admissible as well as his complaint under Article 10 'that as a consequence of imprisonment he was denied the right to express his feelings of love to other men'.[89] The Commission justified its departure from its decision in the previous case against Germany on the basis that 'in that case the applicant had been convicted for indecent assault of minors under the age of

[83] The age of majority was reduced from twenty-one to eighteen years by the Family Law Reform Act 1969, Age of Majority (Scotland) Act 1969, and Age of Majority Act (Northern Ireland) 1969.

[84] *X.* (n 79) 37–8.

[85] *X. v Federal Republic of Germany* (1975) 3 DR 46.

[86] ibid, 54–5.

[87] ibid, 55–6.

[88] *X.* (n 79) 43.

[89] ibid, 45. The Commission declared inadmissible the applicant's complaint under art 10 ECHR that 'as a consequence of imprisonment he was denied ... his right to express his views'.

sixteen', whereas 'one of the fundamental issues in the present case is whether eighteen year olds ought to be considered as "young people" in need of protection'.[90]

As a consequence of declaring *X. v the United Kingdom* admissible, the Commission carried out its first extensive consideration of discrimination on the grounds of sexual orientation—which involved an assessment of written submissions by the parties, as well as of oral pleadings made at a hearing attended by the applicant in Strasbourg—and set out its opinion on the merits in a report adopted in October 1978.[91] A striking feature of the Commission's opinion is the extent to which it was influenced by the view of the English Court of Appeal that the relationship between the applicant and one of his partners was characterized by coercion. The applicant had contested this characterization by, inter alia, producing a statement by the partner in question—with whom he had resumed a relationship after his release from prison— which testified that their relationship was consensual.[92] However, the Commission accepted that 'there was an element of force involved in the relationship' and, on this basis, unanimously concluded that the prosecution and imprisonment of the applicant was necessary in a democratic society for the protection of the rights and freedoms of others and, therefore, did not amount to a violation of Article 8.[93] The Commission was more divided on the issue of the age of consent but held, by eight votes to four, that fixing the minimum age for male homosexual acts at twenty-one years was justified as being necessary in a democratic society for the protection of the rights of others—namely young men between eighteen and twenty-one years—and did not amount to a violation of Article 8.[94] The Commission dealt with the Article 14 points succinctly, concluding by nine votes to two (with one abstention) that the difference in the age of consent for homosexual and heterosexual acts did not constitute discrimination in violation of the Convention—because it had the objective and reasonable justification of 'social protection'—and, by eleven votes (with one abstention), that differences between the legal regulation of male and female homosexual acts did not amount to a form of discrimination because they were justified by the need to address the 'specific social danger [...] of masculine homosexuality'.[95] The Commission unanimously rejected the applicant's Article 10 complaint on the basis that the concept of 'expression' contained in that Article did not 'encompass any notion of the physical expression of feelings'.[96] The broader implication of this was that the right to

[90] ibid, 43.

[91] *X. v the United Kingdom* App No 7215/75 (Commission Report, 12 October 1978).

[92] ibid, para 132.

[93] ibid, paras 135–8.

[94] ibid, para 158. The Commission took into consideration the decisive rejection by the UK Parliament of the Sexual Offences (Amendment) Bill 1977 that proposed a reduction in the age of consent in England and Wales for male homosexual acts from twenty-one to eighteen years. An amendment to decline the Bill a Second Reading was agreed 146–25 (HL Debate 14 June 1977, vol 384, col 74). The Commission also noted that the age of consent was being examined by the Policy Advisory Committee on Sexual Offences which, in its *Report on the Age of Consent in relation to Sexual Offences* (Cmnd 8216, 1981)—published subsequent to the Commission's report in *X.*—recommended that the minimum age for homosexual acts between males be reduced from twenty-one to eighteen years.

[95] *X.* (n 91) paras 159–70, relying on *X.* (n 85).

[96] *X.* (n 91) para 173.

freedom of expression could not be used to challenge the legal regulation of non-verbal embodied expressions of same-sex intimacy.

The Commission's opinion in *X. v the United Kingdom*, which was validated by the Committee of Ministers,[97] demonstrates a significant reluctance to 'interfere' with the UK's capacity to determine the minimum age for male homosexual acts. The Commission explicitly rejected the applicant's argument that, because the majority of European States had an age of consent for male homosexual acts that was fixed at eighteen years or below, the minimum age of twenty-one years in England and Wales was not necessary in a democratic society.[98] Although the Commission conceded that 'the age limit of twenty-one may be regarded as high in the present era, especially when contrasted with the current position in other member States',[99] it asserted that 'what is important is not the balance struck in other European countries but the reasonable and objective nature of the arguments adduced in favour of the actual age limit chosen'.[100] This unwillingness to use an assessment of 'European consensus' in order to determine whether the UK was acting contrary to the human rights standards of other Contracting States can be seen to flow from the Commission adopting 'a cautious and conservative interpretation' of the Convention.[101] However, it must also be seen as an expression of the Commission's entrenched and institutionalized acceptance that male homosexuality represented a social danger that justified suppression through legal regulation. Mr Opsahl, in a separate opinion, characterized the interference with the private life of a man aged over twenty-one years created by setting the minimum age for male homosexual acts at twenty-one years as 'a minor one … justified by the need for the protection of others'.[102]

The breakthrough: 'Homosexual practices … amount to fundamental human rights'

In May 1976, the Commission received and registered an application from a thirty-year-old shipping clerk resident in Belfast. The applicant, Jeffrey Dudgeon, stated that he 'had been consciously homosexual from the age of 14 years' and, from the 'onset of homosexual consciousness', had 'experienced fear [which] had increased through adulthood and was directly caused by the existence of offences against homosexual behaviour in the criminal law'.[103] Mr Dudgeon complained about the blanket prohibition of male homosexual acts in Northern Ireland enforced through law regulating buggery[104] and gross indecency between males.[105] He further

[97] *X. v the United Kingdom* App No 7215/75 (Committee of Ministers decision, 12 June 1979).
[98] *X.* (n 91) para 147. [99] ibid, para 152. [100] ibid, para 147.
[101] *Golder* (n 46) separate opinion of Judge Sir Gerald Fitzmaurice, para 39.
[102] *X.* (n 91) separate opinion by Mr Opsahl.
[103] *Dudgeon v the United Kingdom* (1978) 11 DR 117, 118. The published decision refers to the applicant as 'X.' because, at this stage, he was anonymous.
[104] Offences Against the Person Act 1861, ss 61 and 62.
[105] Criminal Law Amendment Act 1885, s 11.

complained about the common law offences, insofar as they related to homosexuality, of conspiracy to corrupt public morals and conspiracy to outrage public decency. Mr Dudgeon had not been arrested, charged, or convicted of an offence, but, in January 1976, he had been questioned about his 'homosexual status, attitudes and behaviour' by the police who had also taken and retained diaries and papers from his home.[106] Further, between January and June 1976, twenty members of the Gay Liberation Society, of which Mr Dudgeon was a member, had been questioned concerning homosexual offences. Mr Dudgeon stated that he had 'suffered anxiety about prosecution' until February 1977 when he was informed that a decision had been taken not to prosecute and property taken from him by the police was returned.[107] Mr Dudgeon submitted that he was a 'victim' within the meaning of the Convention[108] because, inter alia, the law prohibiting male homosexual acts had a 'chilling or restraining effect on the free expression of his sexuality'.[109] He complained that the existence of such law violated his right to respect for his private life under Article 8 of the Convention and, furthermore, constituted a difference in treatment 'on sexual grounds' (because male homosexual acts were subject to greater restrictions than female homosexual and heterosexuals acts were) and on grounds of his residence or presence in Northern Ireland (because male homosexual acts were partially decriminalized elsewhere in the UK), which amounted to discrimination in violation of Article 14 taken in conjunction with Article 8.[110]

Whilst Mr Dudgeon's application to the Commission was pending a decision on its admissibility, the Northern Ireland Standing Advisory Commission on Human Rights had recommended that male homosexual acts be partially decriminalized in Northern Ireland in line with the law in England and Wales.[111] The UK government indicated to the Commission that it hoped to publish draft legislation designed to give effect to this recommendation in late 1977.[112] Mr Dudgeon, however, declined to withdraw his application on the grounds that '[r]ecent official pronouncements suggested that the undertaking to change the law might be abandoned or unduly delayed'.[113] This proved to be a shrewd decision given that a year after the publication of a proposal for a draft Homosexual Offences (Northern Ireland) Order 1978 the UK government announced that it would take no further action because 'it is clear that a substantial body of opinion [in Northern Ireland]—embracing a wide range of religious as well as political opinion—is opposed to the proposed change'.[114] The Commission declared inadmissible Mr Dudgeon's complaint that the existence of the common law offences of conspiracy to corrupt public morals and conspiracy to outrage public decency made advocacy of homosexual law reform and associations formed by homosexuals potentially criminal. Although

[106] *Dudgeon* (n 103) 119. [107] ibid, 124. [108] ECHR ex-art 25.

[109] *Dudgeon* (n 103) 120. [110] ibid, 128–9.

[111] Standing Advisory Commission on Human Rights, *Third Report of the Standing Advisory Commission on Human Rights: Annual Report for 1976–77* (HC 199, 1978).

[112] *Dudgeon* (n 103) 122. [113] ibid, 121.

[114] Humphrey Atkins MP, HC Debate 2 July 1979, vol 969, col 466W.

Mr Dudgeon had brought this complaint under Article 8, the Commission additionally considered it under Article 10 and Article 11 (freedom of assembly and association) but concluded that the scope of the common law offences restricted neither Mr Dudgeon's right to freedom of expression or association—which indicated that the Commission did not regard the questioning of members of the Gay Liberation Society to merit further consideration. However, the Commission declared admissible the complaints concerning the laws in force in Northern Ireland prohibiting homosexual acts between men.

A key question raised by Mr Dudgeon's complaint was whether the mere existence of the criminal law prohibiting male homosexual acts made him a 'victim' within the terms of the Convention. In support of Mr Dudgeon's claim that the mere existence of the law made him the victim of an interference with his right to respect for his private life—because 'it criminalised behaviour he might indulge in within the sphere of his private life'[115]—was the Court's then recent conclusion that 'a law may by itself violate the rights of an individual if the individual is directly affected by the law in the absence of any specific measure of implementation'.[116] In light of this, the Commission recognized that Mr Dudgeon was 'one of a particular class of persons whose conduct is ... legally restricted' and that he could claim to be made a victim under the Convention by laws prohibiting male homosexual acts.[117] Furthermore, the Commission unanimously held that such law, even if the risk that it will be enforced is not great, interfered with Mr Dudgeon's right to respect for his private life under Article 8.[118] The chief question facing the Commission, therefore, was whether such an interference was justified as necessary in a democratic society for the protection of morals or for the protection of the rights and freedoms of others—a justification it had accepted for the previous twenty-five years.

In approaching the question of whether the total prohibition of male homosexual acts in Northern Ireland was necessary in a democratic society, the Commission returned to the Court's judgment in *Handyside*. The Commission noted that the adjective 'necessary' contained in Article 8(2) implied the existence of a 'pressing social need'[119] and that, in a democratic society characterized by pluralism, tolerance and broadmindedness, any interference with the right to respect for private life must be 'proportionate to the legitimate aim pursued'.[120] In this respect, the Commission reiterated its established opinion on the issue of the 'age of consent' and stated that, insofar as the law prohibited Mr Dudgeon from engaging in male homosexual acts with persons under twenty-one years of age, this was justified as necessary in a democratic society for the protection of the rights of others.[121] However, in respect of the prohibition of male homosexual acts involving those

[115] *Dudgeon v the United Kingdom* App No 7525/76 (Commission report, 13 March 1980) para 45.

[116] *Klass and Others v Germany* (1978) Series A no 28, para 33.

[117] *Dudgeon* (n 115) para 86.

[118] ibid, paras 95–7.

[119] ibid, para 102, citing *Handyside* (n 58).

[120] ibid.

[121] *Dudgeon* (n 115) paras 105 and 116. The Commission found by eight votes to two that the total prohibition of male homosexual acts involving persons under twenty-one years did not amount to a violation of art 8 ECHR.

over twenty-one years of age, the Commission broke with its previous case law and, by nine votes to one, stated that this amounted to a violation of Article 8.[122] The Commission justified this change in opinion by stating that whilst it recognized that the legitimate aim of the prohibition of male homosexual acts was the 'protection of morals'—a term it interpreted to mean 'the protection of the moral ethos of society'—it also recognized that Article 8 'preserves to the individual an area of strictly private morality in which the State may not interfere'.[123] This approach—similar to that found in the Wolfenden Report[124] and in Hart's advocacy of personal liberty in the sphere of private sexual conduct[125]—provided the basis for the Commission's conclusion that it did:

> not consider it established that there exists any 'pressing social need' related to the protection of morality in Northern Ireland which requires the maintenance in force of the legal prohibition on private consensual male homosexual acts involving persons over 21 years of age. It has not been shown to make any contribution to the moral climate of society which could, within a reasonable relationship of proportionality, justify or counter-balance the inevitable negative effects which it has on the private lives of homosexuals, and the present applicant in particular. It cannot therefore be justified as 'necessary' under Art. 8(2).[126]

In respect of Mr Dudgeon's complaints about discrimination under Article 14, the Commission rejected the complaint regarding the prohibition of homosexual acts involving men under twenty-one years and, in respect of the prohibition of homosexual acts involving men over twenty-one years, relied on the Court's jurisprudence in *Airey v Ireland*—that it is not generally necessary to examine a case under Article 14, where a separate violation of an Article invoked both on its own and in conjunction with Article 14 has been found unless 'a clear inequality of treatment in the enjoyment of the right in question is a fundamental aspect of the case'[127]—to reach the conclusion that it was unnecessary to examine the applicant's complaints under Article 14. Mr Polak dissented from this view and, in a separate opinion, argued that:

> [t]he prohibition [of male homosexual acts], with its possibility of very heavy sanctions in case of contravention, stigmatizes homosexuality between consenting adults in private as a very severe crime. By doing so the State, which has the duty to secure to everyone within its jurisdiction the rights and freedoms defined in the Convention, supports and intensifies old and deep-seated sentiments of aversion and fear which have been proved to be unjustifiable and without factual ground. It strengthens the prejudices against homosexuals, it perpetuates their fear of prosecution and punishment, it compels them to keep secret or suppress their sexual inclinations and wishes, and it increases the danger of blackmail. By maintaining these provisions the State discriminates strongly against this group of the population in comparison with heterosexual adults who are free to have any kind of sexual contact in private. This difference amounts to a clear inequality of treatment in the enjoyment of the right in question, which is a fundamental aspect of this case ... [T]his inequality of treatment, which

[122] ibid, para 116. [123] ibid, para 108. [124] Home Office (n 38).
[125] HLA Hart, *The Concept of Law* (Oxford University Press 1961).
[126] *Dudgeon* (n 115) para 115. [127] *Airey v Ireland* (1979) Series A no 32, para 30.

constituted an integral part of the present application, has to be considered as a separate violation of the Convention, namely as a breach of Art. 14 in conjunction with Art. 8.[128]

Ignoring the fact that 'heterosexual adults' were not 'free' to engage in buggery in private—a point consistently overlooked in Strasbourg case law—Mr Polak powerfully articulates why the Commission's refusal to recognize 'a clear inequality of treatment' in Mr Dudgeon's case was problematic.

As a result of the Commission's opinion, Mr Dudgeon became the first person to reach the Court with a complaint about sexual orientation discrimination. In considering the complaint, the Court followed, in large part, the approach adopted by the Commission. It differed from the Commission insofar as, when considering whether the prohibition of male homosexual acts was necessary in a democratic society, it regarded all of the aims of the law as stated by the UK government to fall within the 'protection of morals'. The UK government had inferred from the judgment in *Handyside* that it had a wide margin of appreciation in respect of the protection of morals because of the Court's view that:

it is not possible to find in the domestic law of the various Contracting States a uniform European conception of morals. The view taken by their respective laws of the requirements of morals varies from time to time and from place to place, especially in our era which is characterised by a rapid and far-reaching evolution of opinions on the subject. By reason of their direct and continuous contact with the vital forces of their countries, State authorities are in principle in a better position than the international judge to give an opinion on the exact content of these requirements as well as on the 'necessity' of a 'restriction' or 'penalty' intended to meet them.[129]

However, the Court stated that the scope of the margin of appreciation was determined not only by the nature of the aim of the restriction but also by the nature of the activities involved and, since Mr Dudgeon's case concerned 'a most intimate aspect of private life', 'particularly serious reasons' must exist before an interference with the right to respect for private life can be 'legitimate'.[130] It further elaborated that the intimate aspect of private life in question—homosexual sexual activities—constituted 'an essentially private manifestation of the human personality'.[131] The Commission had previously recognized that Article 8 guaranteed the right to 'establish and to develop relationships with other human beings, especially in the emotional field for the development and fulfilment of one's own personality',[132] and the Court's interpretation of this conception of 'personality' to include homosexual sexual acts was significant.[133]

In approaching the question of whether the interference complained of by Mr Dudgeon was necessary in a democratic society—and, in this respect, whether it was proportionate to the legitimate aim pursued—the Court examined whether

[128] *Dudgeon* (n 115) separate opinion of Mr Polak.
[129] *Handyside* (n 58) para 48.
[130] *Dudgeon v the United Kingdom* (1981) Series A no 45, para 52.
[131] ibid, para 60.
[132] *X. v Iceland* (1976) 5 DR 86, 87.
[133] For a discussion of the relationship between art 8 ECHR and the concept of 'personality', see Loukis G Loucaides, *Essays on the Developing Law of Human Rights* (Martinus Nijhoff Publishers 1995).

the reasons given by the UK government to justify the interference were 'relevant and sufficient'.[134] The Court accepted that the reasons provided by the UK government— which hinged on the fact that 'a substantial body of opinion in Northern Ireland was opposed to a change in the law'[135]—were relevant. In considering whether the reasons given were sufficient, the Court relied on its then recently established doctrine that the Convention is 'a living instrument which … must be interpreted in the light of present-day conditions'[136] to state that:

> As compared with the era when [the impugned] legislation was enacted, there is now a better understanding, and in consequence an increased tolerance, of homosexual behaviour to the extent that in the great majority of the member States of the Council of Europe it is no longer considered to be necessary or appropriate to treat homosexual practices of the kind now in question as in themselves a matter to which the sanctions of the criminal law should be applied; the Court cannot overlook the marked changes which have occurred in this regard in the domestic law of the member States.[137]

The Court also stated that in Northern Ireland, the authorities had refrained in recent years from enforcing the law in respect of homosexual acts between consenting males over twenty-one years and that there was no evidence to suggest that this had been injurious to moral standards. [138] This combination of data on 'European consensus' and domestic practice provided the basis for the Court to conclude that:

> It cannot be maintained in these circumstances that there is a 'pressing social need' to make such acts criminal offences, there being no sufficient justification provided by the risk of harm to vulnerable sections of society requiring protection or by the effects on the public. On the issue of proportionality, the Court considers that such justifications as there are for retaining the law in force unamended are outweighed by the detrimental effects which the very existence of the legislative provisions in question can have on the life of a person of homosexual orientation like the applicant. Although members of the public who regard homosexuality as immoral may be shocked, offended or disturbed by the commission by others of private homosexual acts, this cannot on its own warrant the application of penal sanctions when it is consenting adults alone who are involved.[139]

On this basis, the Court held, by fifteen votes to four, that the existence of law prohibiting male homosexual acts was a violation of Article 8. At the same time, like the Commission, it reaffirmed the UK's margin of appreciation to determine the age 'under which young people should have the protection of the criminal law'.[140] In this respect, it acknowledged 'the legitimate necessity in a democratic society for some degree of control over homosexual conduct notably in order to provide safeguards against the exploitation and corruption of those who are specially vulnerable by reason, for example, of their youth'.[141]

In respect of Mr Dudgeon's claim that he had suffered discrimination, the Court followed the Commission and, by fourteen votes to five, held that it was

[134] *Dudgeon* (n 130) para 54. [135] ibid, para 59.
[136] *Tyrer v the United Kingdom* (1978) Series A no 26, para 31.
[137] *Dudgeon* (n 130) para 60. [138] ibid. [139] ibid. [140] ibid, para 62.
[141] ibid.

not necessary to conduct an examination under Article 14 taken in conjunction with Article 8 because, following *Airey*, 'a clear inequality of treatment' was not 'a fundamental aspect of the case'.[142] On this point, Judges Evrigenis and Garcia De Enterria dissented:

> Even accepting the restrictive formula enunciated by the Court in the Airey judgment and applied in the judgment in the present case (... 'a clear inequality of treatment' being 'a fundamental aspect of the case'), it would be difficult to assert that these conditions were not plainly satisfied in the circumstances. In any event, to interpret Article 14 ... in the restrictive manner heralded in the Airey judgment deprives this fundamental provision in great part of its substance and function in the system of substantive rules established under the Convention.[143]

Judge Matscher, who did not regard the facts of the case to disclose a violation of Article 14, was also critical of the majority for 'employing formulas that are liable to limit excessively the scope of Article 14 ... to the point of depriving it of all practical value'.[144] The Court's refusal to examine Mr Dudgeon's complaints under Article 14 cannot be seen solely as an outcome of its application of the restrictive doctrine established in *Airey*. Rather, the Court's unwillingness to recognize that the difference in treatment that Mr Dudgeon complained of amounted to 'discrimination' should be seen as an expression of its reluctance to establish the more general principle that inequality based on sexual orientation was per se repugnant to the Convention.[145]

The Court's judgment in *Dudgeon* had an extensive impact: it necessitated the partial decriminalization of male homosexual acts in Northern Ireland,[146] compelled similar law reform in jurisdictions outside the UK to which the UK had extended the Convention,[147] underpinned further judgments by the Court against Contracting States that enforced a total prohibition of male homosexual acts,[148] and shaped jurisprudence outside of Europe.[149] Although the Court had been careful to state that it was 'not concerned with making any value-judgment as to the morality of homosexual relations between adult males'[150] and that those who concluded that decriminalization of such relations implied an approval of them were 'misguided',[151] Judge Walsh astutely recognized (and bemoaned) the wider implications of the judgment:

[142] ibid, para 69.

[143] ibid, dissenting opinion of Judges Evrigenis and Garcia De Enterria.

[144] ibid, dissenting opinion of Judge Matscher.

[145] For a discussion, see Robert Wintemute, *Sexual Orientation and Human Rights: The United States Constitution, the European Convention, and the Canadian Charter* (Clarendon Press 1995).

[146] Homosexual Offences (Northern Ireland) Order 1982.

[147] Male homosexual acts were partially decriminalized in the Crown Dependencies by the Sexual Offences (Bailiwick of Guernsey) Law 1983, Sexual Offences (Jersey) Law 1990, and Sexual Offences Act 1992 (Isle of Man). For discussion beyond the Crown Dependencies, see Wintemute (n 145).

[148] *Norris v Ireland* (1988) Series A no 142; *Modinos v Cyprus* (1993) Series A no 259.

[149] For example, *Lawrence v Texas* 539 US 558 (2003).

[150] *Dudgeon* (n 130) para 54.

[151] ibid, para 61.

The judgment of the Court does not constitute a declaration to the effect that the particular homosexual practices which are subject to penalty by the legislation in question virtually amount to fundamental human rights. However, that will not prevent it being hailed as such by those who seek to blur the essential difference between homosexual and heterosexual activities.[152]

Judge Walsh was correct that, by establishing the principle that a 'homosexual person'[153] suffering a legal detriment because of their sexual orientation could successfully utilize the Convention to challenge their own government,[154] the Court had legitimized the campaign for the 'human rights of gay people'.[155]

By the time the Court had concluded with Mr Dudgeon's application, the UK Parliament had partially decriminalized male homosexual acts in Scotland. That process of law reform had begun in Parliament in 1976 with the failed attempt to omit the offence of gross indecency between males from a Bill consolidating sexual offences.[156] Bespoke Bills introduced into the House of Lords[157] and the House of Commons[158] in 1977 designed to partially decriminalize male homosexual acts had also failed. It has been claimed that, as a result of frustration with Parliament's refusal to extend partial decriminalization to Scotland, members of the Scottish Homosexual Rights Group prepared an application to Strasbourg in 1979—making almost exactly the same complaints as those raised in *Dudgeon*—and that 'it was this appeal to the European Court that finally persuaded the … government to concede homosexual law reform for Scotland'.[159] Davidson and Davis argue that this claim is debatable because the UK government's response to a proposed amendment to the Criminal Justice (Scotland) Bill 1980—the adoption of which[160] resulted in the partial decriminalization of male homosexual acts in Scotland within similar parameters as those established in England and Wales thirteen years earlier[161]—'does not suggest that any deal had been struck prior to the debate' in Parliament in July 1980.[162]

Pioneering Complaints and Outright Rejections in the 1980s

Three weeks before the Court promulgated its judgment in *Dudgeon*, the Parliamentary Assembly of the Council of Europe had debated a report on

[152] ibid, partially dissenting opinion of Judge Walsh, para 20.
[153] *Dudgeon* (n 103) 118.
[154] *Golder* (n 46) separate opinion of Judge Sir Gerald Fitzmaurice, para 38.
[155] Jeffrey Dudgeon, 'Homosexual law reform' *The Irish Times* (Dublin, 25 May 1979).
[156] The House of Commons voted in favour of retaining the offence of gross indecency between males in the Sexual Offences (Scotland) Bill 1976 by 37–27 (HC Debate 3 November 1976, vol 918, Division No 373). The offence was enacted as Sexual Offences (Scotland) Act 1976, s 7.
[157] Sexual Offences (Scotland) Bill 1977, HL Debate 8 March 1977, vol 380, col 915.
[158] Sexual Offences (Scotland) Bill 1977, HC Debate, 9 December 1977, vol 940, col 1856.
[159] Roger Davidson and Gayle Davis, 'Sexuality and the State: the Campaign for Scottish Homosexual Law Reform, 1967–80' (2006) 20 Contemporary British History 533, 547.
[160] HC Debate 22 July 1980, vol 989, Division No 421.
[161] Criminal Justice (Scotland) Act 1980, s 80.
[162] Davidson and Davis (n 159) 548.

'discrimination against homosexuals', presented by its Committee on Social and Health Questions, which contained drafts of a Recommendation and Resolution.[163] The draft Recommendation recommended that the Committee of Ministers 'urge those member states where homosexual acts, even between consenting adults, are liable to criminal prosecution, to abolish those laws and practices' and call on the governments of the Member States to address aspects of discrimination against homosexuals by, for example, ensuring 'equality of treatment, no more no less, for homosexuals with regard to employment, pay and job security, particularly in the public sector'.[164] By far the most radical aspect of the draft Recommendation was its proposal that the Committee of Ministers should 'modify Article 14 of the European Convention on Human Rights by adding to it the notion of "sexual preference" '.[165] The rapporteur of the Committee on Social and Health Questions, Mr Voogd, advocated this change to Article 14 as one aspect of a package of measures designed to establish that 'homosexuals ... should be treated with the same respect and given the same rights as their fellow citizens'.[166]

Although the Parliamentary Assembly adopted the Recommendation[167] and Resolution[168] in modified forms—which included an amendment to the Recommendation that called on the Committee of Ministers to 'urge member states to apply the same minimum age of consent for homosexual and heterosexual acts'[169] —it would not accept the proposal to recommend the modification of Article 14. Mr Berrier, rapporteur of the Legal Affairs Committee, stated, 'changing Article 14 of the Convention would be a lengthy, burdensome and far from certain process', that 'the word "sex" in Article 14 ... has a much wider significance than merely making a distinction between men and women, and may well cover notions such as "sexual orientation" or "sexual preference" ' and that, therefore, 'it would be better to wait for a ruling ... of the Commission because there would always be time to return to the question if its opinion were unfavourable'.[170] Several other members of the Parliamentary Assembly were against amending Article 14 to include 'sexual preference' because, for example, it would 'recognise that everyone has the right to have an unnatural sexual preference'[171] and 'would make the Council of Europe appear absurd'.[172] However, one member of the Legal Affairs Committee, Mr Stoffelen, strongly advocated an amendment to Article 14 of the Convention on the grounds that it was 'not very likely' that the Commission or the Court would interpret Article 14 to include 'sexual preference'.[173] Mr Stoffelen argued, '[i]f we want to ban discrimination on the ground of sexual preference, we have to make that absolutely clear; and better be sure than sorry'.[174] The Chairman of the

163 Council of Europe, *Report on discrimination against homosexuals* (Doc 4755, 1981).

164 Council of Europe, Second Part of the Thirty-Third Ordinary Session of the Parliamentary Assembly, Tenth Sitting (1 Oct 1981) in *Official Report of Debates, Vol II, Sittings 8 to 19* (Council of Europe 1982) 276.

165 ibid. 166 ibid, 259.

167 Council of Europe, Parliamentary Assembly, Recommendation 924 (1981).

168 Council of Europe, Parliamentary Assembly, Resolution 756 (1981).

169 Council of Europe (n 164) 277–8. 170 ibid, 260.

171 Mr Margue, ibid, 267. 172 Mr Page, ibid, 270. 173 ibid, 262.

174 ibid.

Legal Affairs Committee, Mr Grieve, reiterated that such a change was unnecessary because distinctions based on sexual orientation that fell within the scope of the jurisprudence already established by the Court[175] would be regarded as discrimination in violation of Article 14.[176] Therefore, the principal reason that the Parliamentary Assembly deleted the proposal that 'sexual preference' be added to Article 14 from the Recommendation was that it was 'much wiser to wait for case law on the matter to be established by the Court'.[177]

Whether adding 'sexual preference' to Article 14 would have significantly affected the jurisprudence of the Commission or the Court in respect of complaints about sexual orientation discrimination is debatable. The text of Article 14, with its use of the words 'on any ground such as ...' and '... or other status', was already formulated in such a way that allowed the Strasbourg organs to interpret it to include 'sexual preference' (or an equivalent formulation). However, in light of the long-standing reluctance of the Commission to deem complaints about sexual orientation discrimination admissible under Article 14, a modification of Article 14 to explicitly include a reference to sexual preference may have been an effective means by which to 'kick start' an evolution in the Commission's approach to the human rights of sexual minorities. On the other hand, including sexual preference in Article 14 would not have guaranteed that the Commission and the Court would have become more amenable to recognizing that differences in treatment based on sexual orientation amounted to discrimination in violation of the Convention. In *Dudgeon*, the Court found it unnecessary to examine the complaints about discrimination under Article 14 not because of the absence of an explicit reference to sexual orientation in Article 14 but, rather, because it did not recognize that a 'clear inequality of treatment' was 'a fundamental aspect of the case'.[178] It is questionable, therefore, whether an explicit reference to 'sexual preference' in Article 14 would have resulted in the Court considering the merits of Mr Dudgeon's Article 14 complaints.

What is clear from an examination of Strasbourg jurisprudence in the decade following *Dudgeon* is that neither the Commission nor the Court had any intention of recognizing that a difference in treatment based on sexual orientation amounted to discrimination in violation of Article 14. Only one complaint about a difference in treatment based on sexual orientation was upheld during this period and the applicant himself did not invoke Article 14.[179] When applicants did make complaints under Article 14 about differences in treatment based on sexual orientation they were declared inadmissible. Despite this, applications to the Commission relating to sexual orientation discrimination, particularly against the UK, burgeoned

[175] That art 14 is violated if a difference in treatment (in respect of any of the rights and freedoms contained in the ECHR) has no objective and reasonable justification and there is no reasonable relationship of proportionality between the means employed and the aim sought to be realized. See *Case 'relating to certain aspects of the laws on the use of languages in education in Belgium'* (1968) Series A no 6, section 'Interpretation adopted by the Court' para 10.

[176] Council of Europe (n 164) 274.

[177] Mr Berrier, ibid, 278.

[178] *Dudgeon* (n 130) para 69.

[179] *Norris* (n 148).

during this period. Whereas the period between 1955 and 1980 had been almost exclusively dominated by complaints about the criminalization of male homosexual acts, the 1980s witnessed, along with further complaints of this type, a range of applications relating to issues such as discrimination in housing and immigration law. In addition, for the first time, a female applicant lodged a complaint about discrimination on the grounds of sexual orientation.[180] The response of the Strasbourg organs to these complaints in the 1980s was characterized by a stubborn refusal to move beyond *Dudgeon* and recognize that the wide range of detriments suffered by individuals because of their sexual orientations amounted to discrimination contrary to the Convention.

Challenging the partial decriminalization of male homosexual acts

Between 1981 and 1983, three applications were lodged with the Commission that challenged aspects of English law that continued to make male homosexual acts committed in private between consenting adults an offence. This group of complaints can be seen as a concerted effort to confront and dismantle the legal settlement reached in England and Wales in 1967[181]—and subsequently in Northern Ireland[182] and Scotland[183]—whereby male homosexual acts were legalized only in limited circumstances.

In *B. v the United Kingdom*, the applicant, a male non-commissioned officer who had served in the British army for eight years, complained about his conviction for consensual homosexual acts committed in private on separate occasions with a gunner in his regiment and a civilian.[184] The gunner was aged twenty years and six months at the time the sexual acts for which the applicant was charged took place, and the applicant was twenty-seven years old at the time of his conviction. A consensual homosexual act committed in private by a member of the armed forces could constitute an offence under service law in force at the time.[185] The applicant, who had an exemplary military record, was convicted after admitting to three charges under provisions in the Army Act 1955 relating to 'disgraceful conduct of a cruel, indecent or unnatural kind'[186] and was sentenced to a reduction in rank and to nine months' imprisonment with corrective military training, followed by dishonourable discharge. Although the custodial sentence was subsequently cancelled, the applicant was dishonourably discharged and, in his complaint to

[180] *Simpson v the United Kingdom* App No 11716/85 (Commission decision, 14 May 1986).

[181] Sexual Offences Act 1967.

[182] Homosexual Offences (Northern Ireland) Order 1982.

[183] Criminal Justice (Scotland) Act 1980.

[184] *B. v the United Kingdom* (1983) 34 DR 68.

[185] Sexual Offences Act 1967, s 1(5) stated that, insofar as homosexual acts committed in private between two consenting males over twenty-one years had been decriminalized, this did 'not prevent an act from being an offence (other than a civil offence) under any provision of the Army Act 1955, the Air Force Act 1955 or the Naval Discipline Act 1957'.

[186] Army Act 1955, s 66.

the Commission, he argued that his conviction was a violation of his rights under Article 8 and Article 14 taken in conjunction with Article 8 of the Convention.

In its consideration of the applicant's complaint under the private life limb of Article 8, the Commission invoked the Court's conclusion in *Dudgeon* that some regulation of male homosexual conduct could be considered necessary in a democratic society for the protection of morals and, moreover, this regulation may extend to consensual acts committed in private when there is need to provide sufficient safeguards against exploitation and corruption of young people.[187] In this respect, the Commission noted that one of the charges for which the applicant had been convicted involved 'a soldier junior in rank to him and under 21 years of age' (a fact relevant because the minimum age for male homosexual acts under 'civilian' law was twenty-one years).[188] Furthermore, the Commission stated that the blanket prohibition of homosexual acts involving service personnel could be considered necessary in a democratic society for the prevention of disorder because of the need to 'maintain stricter rules over homosexual conduct in the military sphere than would be justifiable in the civilian sphere'.[189] The Commission reached this conclusion by uncritically accepting the then view of the UK Ministry of Defence that a prohibition of homosexuality in the armed forces was 'essential'.[190] Therefore, the Commission rejected the applicant's Article 8 complaint on the basis that his 'court-marital and dismissal from the service can be considered "necessary in a democratic society" for the "protection of morals" and also "for the prevention of disorder" in the context of military service'.[191] The Commission provided the briefest reason for rejecting the applicant's complaint under Article 14 taken in conjunction with Article 8, stating that his treatment pursued a legitimate aim, was not disproportionate and, being objectively and reasonably justified, could not be considered discriminatory. The baldness of the Commission's reasoning is particularly striking given that the applicant had been convicted of offences that, in part, involved private and consensual sexual acts committed with a civilian (who was over twenty-one years) that were, other than under service law, legal.

In 1982, the Commission received an application from a seventeen-year-old man who stated that his 'sexual orientation is directed towards members of his own sex' and that 'consensual homosexual acts for which he could be prosecuted are legal when engaged in by his heterosexual and lesbian contemporaries'.[192] The applicant, Richard Desmond, complained that fixing the age of consent for male homosexual acts at twenty-one years—compared with sixteen years for heterosexual acts (other than buggery) and female homosexual acts—constituted an unjustified interference with, and discrimination in the enjoyment of, his right to respect for his private life.[193] This was the first time that an applicant who was younger

[187] *Dudgeon* (n 130) paras 49 and 62. [188] *B.* (n 184) 72. [189] ibid.

[190] Armed Forces Bill Select Committee, *Special Report from the Select Committee on the Armed Forces Bill 1980/81* (HC 253, 1981) 32.

[191] *B.* (n 184) 72.

[192] *R.D. v the United Kingdom* App No 9721/82 (Commission decision, 7 May 1984) section 'The Facts'.

[193] ibid, section 'Complaints and Submissions'.

than the minimum age prescribed for male homosexual acts had complained to the Commission and, as such, it required the Commission to address the question—which had been acknowledged, but left unanswered, by Mr Opsahl in *X. v the United Kingdom*[194]—of whether denying men under twenty-one years the legal ability to engage in same-sex sexual acts was necessary in a democratic society.

Mr Desmond argued under Article 8 that the interference with his right to respect for his private life created by maintaining the minimum age for male homosexual acts at twenty-one years had no justification because it did not address a 'pressing social need'.[195] As evidence for this, Mr Desmond cited, inter alia, the report of the Policy Advisory Committee on Sexual Offences that, ten months before he lodged his complaint, had recommended a reduction of the minimum age for male homosexual acts to eighteen years.[196] In addition, he noted that the Royal College of Psychiatrists supported a reduction in the age of consent for male homosexual acts to sixteen years, and the British Medical Association recommended a reduction to eighteen years. It is clear from the evidence presented by Mr Desmond that a fundamental aim of his application was to challenge the Commission's previously accepted view that engaging in male homosexual acts was harmful to young men aged between sixteen and twenty-one years, and this justified maintaining a higher legal minimum age. In this respect, Mr Desmond testified that the fear of being prosecuted 'has inhibiting effects on the development of his personality both in regard to his pursuit of happiness and his honesty and integrity'.[197] In other words, Mr Desmond asserted that the criminal law was causing him, rather than protecting him from, harm.

The Commission, in its review of Mr Desmond's Article 8 complaint, stated that it did not 'attach any significance to the fact that the present application is brought by a young man under 21' because the 'criterion of social protection or the protection of the moral interests and welfare of young people' still remained the basis on which the State could justify an interference with the right to respect for private life.[198] The Commission reiterated that it 'falls to the national authorities to fix the age under which young people should have the protection of the criminal law' and, clearly unwilling to engage in an area it regarded as 'difficult and sensitive', defaulted to the notion that the UK was 'entitled to assert its power of appreciation'.[199] In respect of Mr Desmond's complaint under Article 14 taken in conjunction with Article 8 the Commission, although acknowledging 'the changing and developing views on this issue' of the age of consent, briefly stated that it saw no reason to depart from its previous decisions.[200] As such, the Commission would not consider the merits of Mr Desmond's claim that the existence of law that placed men aged between sixteen and twenty-one years under the threat of the sanction of a term of imprisonment if they were prosecuted for engaging in

[194] *X.* (n 91) separate opinion by Mr Opsahl.
[195] *R.D.* (n 192) section 'The Law' para 5.
[196] Policy Advisory Committee on Sexual Offences (n 94).
[197] *R.D.* (n 192) section 'The Facts'. [198] ibid, section 'The Law' para 11.
[199] ibid. [200] ibid, para 15.

a same-sex sexual relationship—a sanction that did not exist in respect of heterosexual or female homosexual acts—amounted to discrimination. Significantly, the Commission paid no heed to the Parliamentary Assembly's view that Member States of the Council of Europe should 'apply the same minimum age of consent for homosexual and heterosexual acts'.[201]

The Commission's inclination to barricade itself against attempts to develop human rights for gay men and lesbians is epitomized by a series of obstructive arguments it advanced in 1986 in its decision in *Johnson v the United Kingdom*.[202] The applicant, Martin Johnson, complained that, in the course of holding a party in his home to which he had invited approximately forty people, the police had entered his flat where, it was claimed, they found '[g]roups of men ... in all the rooms, talking, holding hands and cuddling' and in the bedroom 'six men, naked or only partly clothed, two of whom were getting up from one of the mattresses lying on the floor'.[203] Mr Johnson alleged that the police removed various items from his bedroom, arrested him and thirty-seven others, and took them to the police station. He stated that the police accused him of 'permitting homosexual acts to take place at the party', questioned him about his sexual orientation, and detained him for several hours.[204] Mr Johnson stated that he did not invite anyone under the age of twenty-one years to his home but had subsequently learned that one of the invited guests had brought along a man who was under that age. Mr Johnson was not prosecuted, but he and his guests were upset and frightened, and publicity in the press caused them further distress. In addition, Mr Johnson believed that the publicity resulted in him losing an offer of permanent employment.

The parties disputed the reasons for the raid on Mr Johnson's home and for his arrest. The government submitted that the police entered Mr Johnson's home because of a suspicion that men younger than the minimum age for male homosexual acts (twenty-one years) were involved in homosexual acts and that Mr Johnson had been arrested on suspicion of procuring such acts. English law made it an offence for a man to procure other men to commit a homosexual act—for example, by procuring 'another man to commit with a third man an act of buggery'—regardless of whether the sexual act itself was an offence.[205] Mr Johnson contested the claim that the reason the police raided his party was because they suspected him of an offence of procurement. The principal focus of his complaint to the Commission concerned the existence of law that made it an offence to commit male homosexual acts in circumstances 'when more than two persons take part or are present'.[206] No such restriction existed in respect of heterosexual or female homosexual acts committed between consenting adults in private, and, by the time of Mr Johnson's complaint, the UK Criminal Law Revision Committee had tentatively recommended the repeal of the restriction in respect of male homosexual

[201] Council of Europe, Parliamentary Assembly, Recommendation 924 (1981) para 7.2.

[202] *Johnson v the United Kingdom* App No 10389/83 (Commission decision, 17 July 1986).

[203] ibid, section 'Observations of the Parties'.

[204] ibid, section 'The Facts'.

[205] Sexual Offences Act 1967, ss 4(1) and 4(3).

[206] Sexual Offences Act 1967, s 1(2)(a).

acts—on the grounds that it was an 'unjustified interference with the privacy of homosexuals in their own homes'—providing that the law continued to allow 'control over homosexual acts in clubs and other places of common resort'.[207]

Mr Johnson complained under Article 8 that the police entry into his home was an interference with his right to respect for his private life and his home and, furthermore, that the legislation under which this was done put him at risk of interference with his private life. The Commission would not consider the complaint about the police entry into Mr Johnson's home because they stated it was introduced out of time. In respect of the complaint about the existence of the law prohibiting homosexual acts 'when more than two persons take part or are present', the Commission accepted the government's argument that this had not been the basis on which the police had entered Mr Johnson's home. Moreover, the Commission stated that Mr Johnson had 'not alleged that he is disposed to the commission of homosexual acts when more than two persons take part or are present', and there was no 'evidence that such acts took place in [his] home'.[208] On this basis, the Commission concluded that the law did not 'continuously and directly'[209] affect Mr Johnson's private life or his home and, consequently, could not be seen to constitute an interference with these aspects of his rights under Article 8. This conclusion is problematic because it suggests that, in order to establish that the law created an interference with his rights under Article 8, Mr Johnson needed to declare that he had participated in criminal acts and intended to do so again in the future—a declaration that would have put him at risk of prosecution. This is contrary to *Dudgeon* in which the Commission accepted that, because the applicant was 'a male homosexual and the laws prohibit homosexual acts between males',[210] the existence of the law created a 'degree of fear or restraint' amounting to an interference with the right to respect for private life.[211]

In respect of Mr Johnson's complaint under Article 14 taken in conjunction with Article 8, the Commission reiterated its established view that, insofar as Mr Johnson was subject to arrest on the basis of suspicion of a criminal offence relating to a male committing a homosexual act with another male under the age of twenty-one years, there was an objective and reasonable justification for treating him differently to heterosexuals and female homosexuals. Furthermore, the Commission stated that enforcing a prohibition of sexual acts when more than two persons take part or are present only in respect of male homosexual acts had an objective and reasonable justification because 'heterosexuality and lesbianism do not give rise to comparable social problems'.[212] The Commission's decision implicitly legitimatized the belief that consensual homosexual acts committed in private by

[207] Criminal Law Revision Committee, *Fifteenth Report: Sexual Offences* (Cmnd 9213, 1984) para 10.16.

[208] *Johnson* (n 202) section 'The Law'.

[209] ibid. The test of whether legislation 'continuously and directly' affects private life was adopted from *Dudgeon* (n 130) para 41.

[210] *Dudgeon* (n 115) para 86.

[211] ibid, para 94.

[212] *Johnson* (n 202) section 'The Law'.

men in circumstances where more than two people take part or are present was 'dangerous'—a view encouraged in the 1980s by the argument that the existence of AIDS required that 'promiscuous homosexual acts should remain discouraged by the criminal law'[213]—and that the regulation of such acts was necessary for, as Judge Walsh described it in *Dudgeon*, the 'prevention of corruption' and 'the preservation of the moral ethos of ... society'.[214]

Same-sex couples and 'family life'

Several applications against the UK that were lodged with the Commission in the 1980s raised, for the first time, complaints about sexual orientation discrimination in the area of family life. The first of these applications, *X. and Y. v the United Kingdom*, concerned a complaint by a same-sex couple about the refusal by immigration authorities to allow the first applicant, a Malaysian citizen, to remain in the UK with the second applicant, a British citizen.[215] The UK made no provision in its immigrations rules to enable the settlement of a foreign national with a same-sex British partner.[216] The Commission considered whether the applicants' relationship fell within the scope of the right to respect for private and family life guaranteed by Article 8 of the Convention. Although the Commission noted the 'modern evolution of attitudes towards homosexuality', it stated that the applicants' relationship did not fall within the scope of the right to respect for family life—a heteronormative view of the family that endured in Strasbourg until 2010[217]—but was a matter of their private life.[218] The Commission declared the complaint inadmissible on the grounds that 'the applicants are professionally mobile' and could 'live together elsewhere', thereby endorsing the idea that it was the responsibility of bi-national same-sex couples to find 'friendly' nations to reside in.[219]

In *Simpson v the United Kingdom* the Commission developed a more robust framework for rejecting complaints about alleged discrimination against same-sex couples in respect of their family life.[220] The applicant, Mary Simpson, complained to the Commission after domestic courts refused to recognize her asserted right to succeed to the secure tenancy of her deceased same-sex partner. At the material time of the complaint, the Housing Act 1980 made provision for a person to succeed to a secure tenancy if that person 'occupied the dwelling-house as his only or principal home at the time of the tenant's death' and was either 'the tenant's spouse' or 'another member of the tenant's family and has resided with the tenant throughout the period of twelve months ending with the tenant's death'.[221] Ms Simpson,

[213] ibid, section 'Observations of the Parties'.

[214] *Dudgeon* (n 130) partially dissenting opinion of Judge Walsh, para 14.

[215] *X. and Y. v the United Kingdom* (1983) 32 DR 220.

[216] For a challenge to this, see *R v Immigration Appeal Tribunal Ex p. Wirdestedt* [1982] Imm AR 186; *R v Immigration Appeal Tribunal Ex p. Wirdestedt* [1984] The Times, 12 December 1984.

[217] *Schalk and Kopf v Austria* ECHR 2010-IV, paras 93–4.

[218] *X. and Y.* (n 215) 221.

[219] ibid, 222.

[220] *Simpson* (n 180).

[221] Housing Act 1980, s 30.

who had lived with the secure tenant (her partner) for two and a half years until the tenant's death and therefore satisfied the criteria relating to residence, claimed that she was a member of the tenant's family within the terms of the Housing Act 1980, which defined 'family' as including those who 'live together as husband and wife'.[222] Ms Simpson had argued in the Court of Appeal that the existence of the word 'as' in the phrase 'live together as husband and wife' made it applicable to 'unions which gave the appearance of two people living together in a kind of matrimonial state'[223] and—in light of the fact that '[n]owadays nobody blanches at the fact that two women who are lesbians live together'[224]—that it must be taken to include same-sex unions. This claim, which sought to establish that cohabiting same-sex couples (who were not legally permitted to marry) were analogous to unmarried opposite-sex couples who 'live together as husband and wife', can be seen as one of the earliest attempts to establish that rights and benefits associated with marriage should extend to partners of the same sex.[225] Watkins LJ had dismissed Ms Simpson's claim on the basis that:

> if Parliament had wished homosexual relationships to be brought into the realm of the lawfully recognised state of a living together of man and wife for the purpose of the relevant legislation, it would plainly have so stated in that legislation, and it has not done so ... I am also firmly of the view that it would be surprising in the extreme to learn that public opinion is such today that it would recognise a homosexual union as being akin to a state of living as husband and wife. The ordinary man and woman ... would in my opinion not think even remotely of there being a true resemblance between those two very different states of affairs.[226]

The Commission declared inadmissible Ms Simpson's complaints that, inter alia, she had been denied respect for her private and family life, as well as for her home, and that she had been discriminated against. In doing so, the Commission reiterated that a same-sex relationship fell outside of the scope of the family life limb of Article 8, would not consider the complaint under the private life limb of Article 8, and circumvented the complaint under the home limb of Article 8 by advancing the obtuse argument that:

> the applicant was occupying the house, of which her partner had been the tenant [and] on the death of the partner, under the ordinary law, the applicant was no longer entitled to remain in the house, and the local authority [that owned the property] was entitled to possession so that the house could no longer be regarded as 'home'.[227]

[222] Housing Act 1980, s 50(3).

[223] *Harrogate Borough Council v Simpson* [1985] 17 HLR 205, 209.

[224] ibid.

[225] The rights and benefits in question can be seen to be associated with marriage insofar as it had been determined that, at least in the field of social security benefits, '[a] man and woman who live together as husband and wife though not married, are ... treated as though they were married'. Supplementary Benefits Commission, *Supplementary Benefits Commission Annual Report 1979* (Cmnd 8033, 1980) para 10.2.

[226] *Harrogate Borough Council* (n 223) 210.

[227] *Simpson* (n 180) section 'The Law'.

The Commission went on to state that even if Ms Simpson's right to respect for her home under Article 8 was engaged, the interference with it was necessary 'for the protection of the contractual rights of the landlord'.[228]

It was, however, the Commission's response to Ms Simpson's claim that she had suffered discrimination that revealed the extent of its unwillingness to extend the protection of the Convention to the family life of same-sex couples. The Commission, which considered the complaint under Article 14 in conjunction with the home limb of Article 8, recognized that 'the treatment accorded to the applicant was different from the treatment she would have received if the partners had been of different sexes'.[229] However, it stated that this difference in treatment was the result of legislation designed to 'protect the family' and that, because the family (which included both married opposite-sex couples and unmarried opposite-sex couples living together as husband and wife) merited 'special protection in society', it was objectively and reasonably justified.[230] In terms of proportionality, the Commission noted that the concept required that any measure be reasonably related to its objective and, because Ms Simpson's complaint was that relevant provisions of the Housing Act 1980 did not apply to her, the issue of proportionality did not arise. This approach can be seen as a deliberate strategy designed to avoid addressing the question of whether providing same-sex couples in these circumstances with no protection was proportionate to the aim of protecting the family life of opposite-sex couples. Discrimination against same-sex couples in respect of the right of succession was eventually successfully challenged in the UK in 2002[231] and in Strasbourg in 2003.[232]

In *W.J. and D.P. v the United Kingdom*, the applicants, a same-sex couple who were in circumstances similar to those in *X. and Y.*, complained about the refusal of domestic authorities to allow the first applicant, a New Zealand citizen, to remain in the UK with the second applicant, a UK citizen.[233] The applicants argued, inter alia, that the absence of consideration of same-sex relationships in the immigration rules and the refusal to recognize their relationship violated their right to respect for private life under Article 8. The Commission stated that exceptional circumstances must exist to regard the refusal to allow a person to remain in a country where they have been living and working for several years to be an interference with the right to respect for private life under Article 8. In light of this, the Commission stated that the absence of provision in UK immigration rules to enable the settlement of a foreign national on the basis of a relationship other than a family relationship (which did not include same-sex partners) did not disclose any appearance of a violation of Article 8. In respect of the factual circumstances of the applicants, it is noteworthy that the Commission stated that they had not 'provided any substantiation of their claim that it would be impossible to live together in New Zealand or elsewhere',

228 ibid. 229 ibid. 230 ibid.

231 *Antonio Mendoza v Ahmad Raja Ghaidan* [2002] EWCA Civ 1533. See also *Ghaidan v Godin-Mendoza* [2004] UKHL 30.

232 *Karner v Austria* ECHR 2003-IX.

233 *W.J. and D.P. v the United Kingdom* App No 12513/86 (Commission decision, 13 July 1987).

which reiterated the notion that it was incumbent upon same-sex couples themselves to find residence in jurisdictions 'hospitable' to them.[234] In declaring the Article 8 complaint inadmissible, the Commission made clear that the deportation of the same-sex partner of a citizen of a Contracting State was not sufficiently 'exceptional' to constitute an interference with the right to respect for private life.

The applicants in *W.J. and D.P.* further complained under Article 8 taken in conjunction with Article 14 that they had been discriminated against, because same-sex relationships did not receive the same protection as opposite-sex relationships under relevant UK immigration rules (which made no provision for the reunification of same-sex couples but did permit foreign spouses and fiancés to join their opposite-sex partners). The Commission conceded that this distinction was 'true' but, relying on its decision in *Simpson*, concluded that the aim of the immigration rules was to 'protect the family' (married and unmarried opposite-sex couples) and that the difference in treatment had an objective and reasonable justification.[235] The Commission further stated that no issue of proportionality arose between the aims of the immigration rules and their application to the applicants because the 'family life provisions of the Rules did not apply in this case'.[236] This obtuse approach can be seen as a further example of the Commission deliberately avoiding answering the question of whether excluding same-sex couples from rights and benefits available to opposite-sex couples was proportionate to the aim of protecting the right to respect for family life of opposite-sex couples.

The Commission adopted a similar approach to complaints raised under Articles 8 and 14 in *C. and L.M. v the United Kingdom*.[237] The applicants, a mother and daughter who were both Australian citizens, complained about the refusal by domestic authorities to allow the first applicant, the mother, to remain in the UK on the basis of her relationship with her partner, a British woman. The applicants argued that the relationship between the first applicant and her partner could only be pursued in the UK and stressed that, together with the second applicant, they formed a de facto family unit. The complaints advanced in *C. and L.M.* were novel for a number of reasons, not least because one of the applicants was a child who claimed that the 'destruction of the family unit' caused by deportation constituted discrimination on the grounds of the 'sexual preference' of her mother.[238] However, the most significant aspect of the case was that the applicants invoked Article 12 of the Convention (right to marry), making it the first use of this provision in an application concerning the relationship of a same-sex couple. The applicants asserted that their deportation from the UK interfered with the Article 12 right of the first applicant and her partner to 'found a family' and that, furthermore,

[234] ibid, section 'The Law'. [235] ibid.

[236] ibid. The Commission additionally stated that the first applicant had primarily been refused leave to remain in the UK 'not because he was a homosexual' but because he was not in approved employment and, therefore, that it 'considers that the principle of proportionality between the means employed and the aim sought to be realised, i.e. the economic well-being of the country, was respected'.

[237] *C. and L.M. v the United Kingdom* App No 14753/89 (Commission decision, 9 October 1989).

[238] ibid, section 'Complaints'.

the exercise of such a right was not 'dependent on the right to marry which they are unable to do under national law'.[239] This argument is significant because of its attempt to decouple the right to 'found a family' from the right 'to marry' and, moreover, extend the scope of its applicability beyond a heteronormative understanding of the phrase '[m]en and women of marriageable age' that is contained in Article 12.[240]

The Commission paid little attention to the applicants' argument and, relying on the Court's judgment in *Rees v the United Kingdom*—which established that 'the right to marry guaranteed by Article 12 … refers to the traditional marriage between persons of opposite biological sex'[241]—concluded that 'the first applicant's relationship with her lesbian cohabitee does not give rise to a right to marry and found a family within the meaning of Article 12'.[242] One member of the Commission who decided *C. and L.M.*, Mr Schermers, had previously advanced the argument that:

> the right to marry and to found a family … cannot be set aside in the public interest … The right to live in a family and—when of marriageable age—to found a family is of paramount importance for the individual. Denial of this right means condemnation to solitude and loneliness. There must be strong arguments to justify such a condemnation. In my opinion the fundamental human right underlying Article 12 should … be granted to homosexual and lesbian couples. They should not be denied the right to found a family without good reasons.[243]

This view—atypical in Strasbourg jurisprudence, which is characterized by the consistent rejection of complaints relating to same-sex relationships brought under Article 12[244]—did not prevail in *C. and L.M.*, and the Commission declared the complaint inadmissible.

The Commission's refusal to recognize that deporting a person from a Contracting State who is engaged in a same-sex relationship with a national of that State amounted to a violation of the Convention was given further, forceful expression in *Z.B. v the United Kingdom*.[245] The Commission, which hastily issued its decision nine days after the application was registered, declared inadmissible a complaint by a Cypriot national about the refusal of domestic authorities to allow him to remain in the UK with his same-sex partner (a UK national) who he had lived with continuously for approximately five years. A key aspect of the applicant's complaint to the Commission was his claim that if deported to Cyprus, a jurisdiction that operated a total prohibition of male homosexual acts,[246]

[239] ibid.

[240] For a historical account of the drafting and interpretation of the wording in art 12 ECHR, see Paul Johnson, '"The Choice of Wording Must Be Regarded as Deliberate": Same-Sex Marriage and Article12 of the European Convention on Human Rights' (2015) 40 EL Rev 207.

[241] *Rees v the United Kingdom* (1986) Series A no 106, para 49.

[242] *C. and L.M.* (n 237) section 'The Law'.

[243] *W. v the United Kingdom* App No 11095/84 (Commission report, 7 March 1989) partially dissenting opinion of Mr Schermers.

[244] *Schalk and Kopf* (n 217); *Hämäläinen v Finland* [GC] App No 37359/09 (ECtHR, 16 July 2014); *Oliari and Others v Italy* App Nos 18766/11 and 36030/11 (ECtHR, 21 July 2015).

[245] *Z.B. v the United Kingdom* App No 16106/90 (Commission decision, 10 February 1990).

[246] Criminal Code of Cyprus, ss 171–3.

he would be at risk of prosecution and imprisonment. He also claimed that, should he be deported, his partner could not join him in Cyprus because their relationship would likely lead to prosecution and imprisonment. In reviewing the applicant's complaint under the private life limb of Article 8, the Commission stated that the evidence available to it indicated that, although the applicant might at some stage be subject to the risk of prosecution in Cyprus for homosexual acts, the risk was not high and, moreover, in the Turkish Republic of Northern Cyprus—which was where the applicant would be returned—homosexuals were not 'persecuted by the authorities'.[247] The evidence that underpinned the Commission's view was primarily taken from the judicial review proceedings instigated by the applicant in the High Court, during which it had been argued by the domestic authorities that, if the applicant was returned to the Turkish Republic of Northern Cyprus, 'the risk of prosecution would be avoided by self restraint'.[248]

The Commission declared the Article 8 complaint inadmissible on the basis that the applicant's deportation from the UK, as a legitimate measure of immigration control, could be justified as being necessary in a democratic society for the prevention of disorder. In this respect, it noted that 'the possibility that the applicant will be subjected to hostility and social ostracism because of his homosexuality [does] not outweigh valid considerations relating to the proper enforcement of immigration controls'.[249] In line with its established case law, the Commission also declared inadmissible the complaint that the difference in treatment between same-sex and opposite-sex couples created by immigration rules amounted to discrimination in violation of Article 14. The decision in *Z.B.* clearly shows the steadfast unwillingness of the Commission to evolve its interpretation of the Convention in order to provide same-sex couples with any protection. Instead, confronted by a petition from one partner of a same-sex couple who was to be deported to a jurisdiction that criminalized homosexual sexual acts, the Commission implicitly endorsed the idea that the applicant should exercise 'restraint' over giving expression to his sexual orientation in order to avoid prosecution.

Homosexuality and blasphemy

In 1982, the Commission issued its decision in respect of the first of two applications concerning blasphemy laws that involved issues related to homosexuality. The first application, lodged by the publishers of *Gay News* and its editor, Denis Lemon, concerned their conviction for the offence of blasphemous libel.[250] The conviction was the result of a private prosecution brought by Mary Whitehouse in respect of a poem published by *Gay News* in 1976 entitled 'The Love that Dares to Speak Its Name', which was accompanied by a drawing illustrating its subject matter. Lemon

[247] *Z.B.* (n 245) section 'The Law'. [248] ibid, section 'The Facts'.

[249] ibid, section 'The Law'.

[250] *X. Ltd. and Y. v the United Kingdom* (1982) 28 DR 77. The offence of blasphemous libel under the common law of England and Wales was abolished by Criminal Justice and Immigration Act 2008, s 79.

and the publishers were convicted in 1977 of the offence of having 'unlawfully and wickedly published or caused to be published … a blasphemous libel concerning the Christian religion namely an obscene poem and illustration vilifying Christ in His life and in His crucifixion'.[251] Both the Court of Appeal and the House of Lords dismissed appeals against the convictions. Lord Diplock, in the House of Lords, described the poem in the following terms:

> [It] purports to describe in explicit detail acts of sodomy and fellatio with the body of Christ immediately after His death and to ascribe to Him during His lifetime promiscuous homosexual practices with the Apostles and with other men.[252]

The case, if not the poem, is well known and has been much discussed and documented because of both the issues involved and the circumstances of the prosecution.[253] Unlike in the Handyside case, the Director of Public Prosecutions would not undertake to prosecute Mr Lemon and the publishers and, consequently, Mrs Whitehouse pursued a private prosecution.

Mr Lemon and the publishers complained to the Commission that their conviction for the offence of blasphemous libel amounted to an unjustified interference with their right to, inter alia, freedom of thought and religion guaranteed by Article 9 (freedom of thought, conscience and religion) and freedom of expression guaranteed by Article 10. They further complained that they had suffered discrimination contrary to Article 14 taken in conjunction with Articles 9 and 10. The Commission focused primarily on the applicants' right to freedom of expression and acknowledged that, particularly in respect of their freedom to impart ideas, this had been subject to interference. The UK government defended this interference on the grounds that it was aimed at the prevention of disorder, the protection of morals, and the protection of the rights of others.[254] The Commission rejected the first two aims on the basis that, since the public authorities themselves had not considered it necessary to institute criminal proceedings against the applicants, it could not be said that the restriction of the applicants' freedom of expression was based on the public interest of preventing disorder or protecting morals. However, the Commission did accept that the interference pursued the legitimate aim of the protection of the rights of others because the main purpose of the offence of blasphemous libel was to protect the right of citizens not to have their religious feelings offended by publications. The Commission concluded that the interference with the applicants' freedom of expression on this ground could be regarded as necessary in a democratic society because:

> If it is accepted that the religious feelings of the citizen may deserve protection against indecent attacks on the matters held sacred by him, then it can also be considered as

[251] *Whitehouse v Lemon, Whitehouse v Gay News Ltd.* [1979] AC 617, 620.

[252] ibid, 632.

[253] See: Ben Thompson (ed), *Ban this Filth: Letters from the Mary Whitehouse Archive* (Faber and Faber 2012); Leslie J Moran, 'Dangerous Words and Dead Letters: Encounters with Law and *The Love that Dares to Speak its Name*' (2001) 23 Liverpool Law Review 153.

[254] *X. Ltd. and Y.* (n 250) 82.

necessary in a democratic society to stipulate that such attacks, if they attain a certain level of severity, shall constitute a criminal offence triable at the request of the offended person … The issue of the applicants' journal containing the incriminated poem was on sale to the general public, it happened to get known in some way or other to the private prosecutor who was so deeply offended that she decided to take proceedings against the publication of this poem, and the outcome of these proceedings showed that not only the private prosecutor herself, but also the judicial authorities of all degrees were convinced of its blasphemous nature.[255]

This decision shows that the Commission uncritically accepted that the poem in question constituted an 'indecent attack' on 'religious feelings'. As such, the Commission gave no credence to the notion that the publication of the poem was itself the exercise of a religious or other belief and, as such, was protectable by Article 9. Nor did it consider that the restriction on freedom of expression imposed on the applicants as a result of one citizen claiming to be 'deeply offended' was disproportionate. The Commission's decision suggests that it regarded the opinion of the domestic judicial authorities to be a proxy for wider public sentiment and, on this basis, reached the conclusion that the restriction placed on the applicants was necessary in a democratic society to protect the rights of Mrs Whitehouse and others. The Commission can therefore be seen to endorse implicitly Lord Scarman's view that the purpose of the criminal offence of blasphemous libel, in protecting religious belief from 'scurrility, vilification, ridicule and contempt', was to 'safeguard the internal tranquillity of the kingdom'.[256] On this basis, the Commission would not entertain the applicants' claim that they had suffered discrimination contrary to Article 14 because they had been singled out for prosecution on grounds related to homosexuality and concluded that the poem was restricted only because of its blasphemous character. This can be regarded as an obdurate interpretation of the facts of the case given Mrs Whitehouse's fervent and widely publicized homophobia.[257]

In the case of *Wingrove v the United Kingdom*, which concerned a complaint about the refusal of the British Board of Film Classification (BBFC) in 1989 to issue a classification certificate for the film 'Visions of Ecstasy' on the grounds that it considered its content to infringe the criminal law of blasphemy,[258] the Commission evolved its approach. The film in question purported to portray St. Teresa of Avila 'having an erotic fantasy involving the crucified figure of Christ, and also a Lesbian erotic fantasy'.[259] It is debatable whether the decision of the BBFC was influenced by the homoerotic content of the film. The BBFC had originally stated that it would not grant the film an '18' certificate because the 'sexual imagery is focused on the figure of the crucified Christ [and] [i]f the male figure were not Christ, the

[255] ibid, 83. [256] *Whitehouse v Lemon* (n 251) 658.

[257] See Thompson (n 253); Geoffrey Robertson, *The Justice Game* (Vintage Books 1999).

[258] The offence has since been abolished by Criminal Justice and Immigration Act 2008, s 79.

[259] *Wingrove v the United Kingdom* App No 17419/90 (Commission report, 10 January 1995) para 26.

problem would not arise'.[260] However, subsequent statements by the BBFC to the Video Appeals Committee, as well as that Committee's own published findings, show importance attached to the lesbian nature of the imagery.[261] Mr Wingrove relied solely on Article 10 to complain that the BBFC's decision amounted to an interference with his right to freedom of expression, including the right to receive and impart information and ideas. The Commission declared the complaint admissible[262] and subsequently reached the opinion that the refusal to certify the film did amount to a violation of Article 10 because the film would not be on display to the general public and the:

> fact that certain Christians, who had heard of the existence of the video, might be outraged by the thought that such a film was on public sale and available to those who wished to see it, cannot … amount to a sufficiently compelling reason to prohibit its lawful supply.[263]

However, the Court accepted that the restriction placed on Mr Wingrove's freedom of expression was intended to protect the right of citizens not to be insulted in their religious feelings—an aim which 'undoubtedly corresponds to that of the protection of "the rights of others" within the meaning of paragraph 2 of Article 10'[264]—and that the domestic authorities had not overstepped the margin of appreciation available to them to determine what restrictions were necessary to ensure such protection. Consequently, the Court held by a majority of seven to two that a complete ban on the film's distribution did not amount to a violation of Article 10. A key aspect of the Court's reasoning was that:

> it is in the nature of video works that once they become available on the market they can, in practice, be copied, lent, rented, sold and viewed in different homes, thereby easily escaping any form of control by the authorities. In these circumstances, it was not unreasonable for the national authorities, bearing in mind the development of the video industry in the United Kingdom … , to consider that the film could have reached a public to whom it would have caused offence. The use of a box including a warning as to the film's content … would have had only limited efficiency given the varied forms of transmission of video works mentioned above.[265]

The Court's deference to the UK's margin of appreciation is problematic because, as Judge Lohmus noted, the interference with Mr Wingrove's freedom of expression was based on the BBFC's opinion about the feelings that they claimed to be protecting and, in the absence of any robust assessment of the actual opinion of Christian believers, it was not possible to conclude that the interference corresponded to a pressing social need.[266]

260 ibid, para 24. 261 ibid, paras 26–30.
262 *Wingrove v the United Kingdom* App No 17419/90 (Commission decision, 8 March 1994).
263 *Wingrove* (n 259) para 68.
264 *Wingrove v the United Kingdom* Reports of Judgments and Decisions 1996-V, para 48.
265 ibid, para 63. 266 ibid, dissenting opinion of Judge Lohmus.

Evolving 'Gay Rights' in the 1990s

In 1990, when surveying the outcome of complaints made by UK applicants to Strasbourg in the 1980s about sexual orientation discrimination, Peter Ashman concluded that 'the Commission is resolutely opposed to interpreting the Convention in such a way as to give equal enjoyment and protection of the Convention rights to homosexuals'.[267] In the early 1990s, gay men and lesbians in the UK who aspired to challenge and eradicate sexual orientation discrimination would have been forgiven for concluding that complaining to the Strasbourg organs was a lost cause. The Court's case law demonstrated that it was only prepared to uphold complaints about sexual orientation discrimination when applicants complained about a total prohibition of homosexual sexual acts. Anyone who examined Strasbourg case law in the early 1990s would have found little to suggest that those charged with interpreting the Convention were prepared to recognize that any other aspect of the endemic discrimination against gay men and lesbians amounted to a violation of any provision of the Convention. Although Ed Bates has argued that the Court's judgment in *Dudgeon* is an exemplar of the 'impressive growth in the breadth and depth of the Convention jurisprudence' in the 1980s—a decade in which Strasbourg jurisprudence 'was flourishing and there was a "qualitative evolution" in the case law'[268]—such a characterization does not adequately encapsulate the systematic and routine rejection of the vast majority of complaints about sexual orientation discrimination by the Commission during this period.

The other organs of the Council of Europe showed a similar indifference towards addressing sexual orientation discrimination. This is clearly demonstrated by the response of the Committee on Legal Affairs and Human Rights of the Parliamentary Assembly to a 'Motion for a recommendation on the elimination of discrimination based on sexual orientation' that had been referred to it in early 1991 by the Bureau of the Assembly.[269] The Motion recommended that the Committee of Ministers 'elaborate an additional protocol to the European Convention ... concerning the elimination of discrimination based on sexual orientation'.[270] The Motion was accompanied by a draft of the protocol and an explanatory memorandum, which stated that the purpose of the protocol was to ensure that the Convention 'applies equally to lesbians and gays' and to 'overrule decisions of the ... Commission ... which have had the effect of allowing member States to discriminate against homosexuals'.[271] The text of the proposed protocol prohibited discrimination on the

[267] Peter Ashman, 'A summary of recent lesbian/gay cases taken under the Convention', information provided to participants at the 'Study-conference on the possibilities of expanding the European Convention on Human Rights to eliminate discrimination based on sexual orientation' held in Copenhagen on 26–27 May 1990. Personal copy provided by Nigel Warner.

[268] Ed Bates, *The Evolution of the European Convention on Human Rights: From its Inception to the Creation of a Permanent Court of Human Rights* (Oxford University Press 2010) 18–19.

[269] Council of Europe, Bureau of the Assembly, 'Progress Report' (AS/Bur(42)41, 28 January 1991).

[270] Council of Europe, Parliamentary Assembly, 'Motion for a recommendation on the elimination of discrimination based on sexual orientation' (Doc 6348, 7 December 1990).

[271] ibid, explanatory memorandum.

grounds of sexual orientation 'in the content or application of the law'.[272] The response of the Committee on Legal Affairs and Human Rights, in providing advice on whether the Motion justified an official reference to an Assembly Committee, was that Article 14, in prohibiting discrimination on 'any ground', did not exclude sexual orientation and '[t]here is therefore no reason to modify Article 14 to include "sexual orientation" as one may assume that it does so already'.[273] The Committee made no substantive comment on the proposed protocol but stated that it would be desirable to include a consideration of sexual orientation in a future study to be made on Article 14. In short, the Committee showed no interest in taking forward a proposal that sought to challenge the Commission's failure to apply Article 14 to sexual orientation discrimination.

Given the state of Strasbourg case law in the early 1990s, it would be reasonable to assume that the number of applications to the Commission concerning sexual orientation discrimination would have begun to decline. However, the number of such applications increased during the 1990s, and a significant number of them were from individuals in the UK. This increase in applications must be understood within the context of an overall increase in the number of individual applications submitted to the Commission: the Commission had registered 404 applications in 1981, and this had increased to 2,037 applications in 1993.[274] As a consequence of this rise in individual applications, more cases were being referred to the Court and to the Committee of Ministers.[275] Several factors account for the increase in the volume of applications,[276] but the growing status and authority of both the Convention and the Court must be seen as a key stimulus. By 1995, both the Commission and the Court had declared that the Convention was a 'constitutional instrument of European public order'[277]—lending credence to the idea that the Convention was a European 'constitutional bill of rights'[278]—and the Court was 'increasingly taking on a role akin to that of a constitutional court'.[279] It was the growing perception of the Court as the 'Supreme Court of Europe' in the field of human rights[280] that encouraged individuals and non-governmental organizations to submit increasing numbers of applications.[281] The restructuring of the Strasbourg organs in the late 1990s, which resulted in the abolition of the Commission and the

[272] ibid, art 3.

[273] Council of Europe, Parliamentary Assembly, Committee on Legal Affairs and Human Rights, 'Elimination of discrimination based on sexual orientation' (AS/Jur(43)42, 23 March 1992), para 3(ii).

[274] Council of Europe, 'Explanatory Report to Protocol No. 11 to the Convention for the Protection of Human Rights and Fundamental Freedoms, restructuring the control machinery established thereby' (Strasbourg, 11 May 1994) para 20.

[275] ibid, para 21.

[276] For a discussion, see Bates (n 268).

[277] *Chrysostomos, Papachrysostomou and Loizidou v Turkey* App Nos 15299/89, 15300/89 and 15318/89 (Commission decision, 4 March 1991) section 'The Law' para 22; *Loizidou v Turkey* (preliminary objections) (1995) Series A no 310, para 75.

[278] David Harris, Michael O'Boyle, Ed Bates, and Carla Buckley, *Law of the European Convention on Human Rights* (2nd edn, Oxford University Press 2009) 6.

[279] Hodson (n 47) 33.

[280] Michael D Goldhaber, *A People's History of the European Court of Human Rights* (Rutgers University Press 2007) 1.

[281] See Hodson (n 47) for an extensive discussion of the growth in litigation undertaken by NGOs.

establishment of a full-time and permanent Court to which individual applicants had direct access,[282] further encouraged the idea that the Court was the 'conscience of Europe'[283] to which gay men and lesbians suffering discrimination could turn.

The battle over the 'age of consent' resumes

In April 1993, the Commission received an application from three men, represented by the then director of Stonewall, Angela Mason, which contained a complaint about the minimum age for male homosexual acts.[284] The three applicants, who advanced arguments similar to those made by Mr Desmond eleven years earlier, complained that enforcing a higher minimum age for male homosexual acts than that set for other acts constituted a disproportionate interference with their private lives amounting to a violation of Articles 8 and 14 of the Convention. The law in England and Wales in respect of the minimum age for male homosexual acts had not changed since 1967, and acts of buggery and gross indecency between males remained prohibited except when committed in private between two males aged twenty-one years or over. The three applicants, Ralph Wilde, Hugo Greenhalgh, and William Parry, argued that 'attitudes have changed fundamentally' since the Commission had last considered the issue of the age of consent and pointed out that the UK 'now has the highest homosexual age of consent in Europe'.[285]

The complaint made in *Wilde, Greenhalgh and Parry v the United Kingdom* was novel in presenting the wide range of problems created by the higher minimum age for male homosexual acts. Mr Wilde, who was nineteen years old at the time that the application was lodged, complained that two years earlier, he had suffered a homophobic attack and that 'the higher age of consent for male homosexuals which is meant to protect young men … actually made him more vulnerable to physical attack and inhibited him from cooperating with the police'.[286] Mr Greenhalgh and Mr Parry, who were nineteen and twenty-four years old respectively, had similarly suffered a homophobic attack and argued that 'the criminalisation of homosexual activity for people of their age creates a climate of hostility to homosexual men'.[287] They also stated that, following a reference to their sexual relationship by Mr Greenhalgh on a radio programme, the police had interviewed them. The overall thrust of the complaint, therefore, was that enforcing a higher minimum age for male homosexual acts did not protect young men from the 'dangers' of homosexuality but, on the contrary, encouraged and exposed them to a climate

[282] Protocol No. 11 to the Convention for the Protection of Human Rights and Fundamental Freedoms, restructuring the control machinery established thereby (11 May 1994) ETS No 155. Entered into force 1 November 1998. As a result of Prot No 11, the Committee of Ministers was no longer empowered to deal with the merits of applications but retained its role of supervising the execution of the Court's judgments.

[283] John Coleman (ed) *The Conscience of Europe* (Council of Europe 1999).

[284] *Wilde, Greenhalgh and Parry v the United Kingdom* App No 22382/93 (Commission decision, 19 January 1995).

[285] ibid, section 'Complaints'. [286] ibid, section 'The Facts'. [287] ibid.

of violence and subjected them to intrusive investigations into their private and intimate relationships.

The application to the Commission, although only one aspect of a much wider political campaign by Stonewall,[288] can be seen to have played an important role in motivating a proposed amendment to the Criminal Justice and Public Order Bill 1993/94 that sought to lower the minimum age for male homosexual acts to sixteen years.[289] In moving that amendment in the House of Commons, Edwina Currie MP stated that the issue of the age of consent for gay men was a 'human rights' issue and argued that:

> [t]he United Kingdom is likely to have to change its law before much longer, for a case has been brought before the European Court of Human Rights on equality grounds, with an excellent chance of success. The Government have already been told that they have a case to answer, and they must give their response before the end of March. The European Court of Human Rights, which we helped to set up in 1953, is likely to rule in favour of equality, as it has done in similar cases in respect of other countries, which have complied. Surely it is better for us to change our law in the House of Commons, on a free vote, than to be forced to conform, possibly in an election year.[290]

Mrs Currie's rendering of *Wilde, Greenhalgh and Parry*—as is often the case when litigation in Strasbourg is discussed in the UK Parliament[291]—can be seen to exaggerate both the status of the application and its likelihood of success. The claim that the UK government had been informed that it had 'a case to answer' is an overstatement because, although the Commission had communicated the case to the government and requested their observations on the admissibility and merits of the application, this occurred before a decision on the admissibility of the application. To an observer at that time, the Commission's existing case law would have supported the view, contrary to Mrs Currie's, that it was highly likely that the Commission would have declared the application inadmissible. Mrs Currie's claim that the Court was 'likely to rule in favour of equality, as it has done in similar cases in respect of other countries', is factually inaccurate because the Court had never upheld a complaint about a difference in the minimum age for homosexual and heterosexual acts. Nevertheless, some MPs accepted Mrs Currie's argument and stated that 'it is appropriate that we should decide tonight to bring the law into line with the convention rather than wait to be forced to do so in two or three years' time'.[292] Mrs Currie's amendment was defeated,[293] but the House of Commons did agree an amendment that, upon enactment in the Criminal Justice and Public

[288] See Will Parry's film 'Age of Dissent' (1994).

[289] HC Debate 21 February 1994, vol 238, col 74. On introduction, the amendment related only to Great Britain.

[290] ibid, col 75.

[291] Paul Johnson, 'Beliefs about the European Court of Human Rights in the United Kingdom Parliament', in Anthony Amatrudo and Regina Rauxloh (eds) *Law in Popular Belief: Myth and Reality* (Manchester University Press, in press).

[292] Mike Watson MP, HC Debate 21 February 1994, vol 238, col 104.

[293] Negatived 307–280, HC Debate 21 February 1994, vol 238, Division No 136.

Order Act 1994, reduced the minimum age for male homosexual acts to eighteen years.[294]

The Criminal Justice and Public Order Act 1994 retained a range of legal inequalities between male homosexual and heterosexual sexual acts across the UK. Although heterosexual buggery was partially decriminalized in England and Wales[295]—the minimum age of eighteen years was set for both heterosexual and homosexual acts in private—buggery between men remained subject to stricter privacy requirements.[296] Moreover, other genital sexual acts between men remained subject to a higher minimum age of eighteen years, in contrast to the minimum ages set across the UK for heterosexual acts. Nevertheless, in light of the reduction in the minimum age for male homosexual acts, the UK government invited the Commission to strike *Wilde, Greenhalgh and Parry* out of its list of cases on the grounds that the applicants were not victims of any alleged violations of the Convention. The applicants argued that in respect of the material time of their complaint, when the minimum age for male homosexual acts was twenty-one years, they remained victims of violations under Articles 8 and 14. In such circumstances, although the matter complained of had effectively been resolved, the Commission was empowered to 'continue the examination of a petition if respect for human rights as defined in [the] Convention so requires'.[297] The Commission chose not to continue with its examination of the application and, as a consequence, did not consider the merits of the complaint. However, the Commission did state that '[q]uestions concerning a minimum age of 16 for engaging in homosexual acts' were not affected by its decision, thereby indicating that it was prepared to consider a future complaint about maintaining a higher age of eighteen years for male homosexual acts.[298]

When the Commission issued its decision in *Wilde, Greenhalgh and Parry*, it was already in receipt of an application lodged by seventeen-year-old Euan Sutherland, who complained that 'he, as a homosexual male, has the only sexual orientation under which he is precluded from any lawful possibility of expressing an important and intimate aspect of his personality'.[299] What is striking about Mr Sutherland's application is that it contains the candid disclosure that he 'had his first homosexual encounter when he was 16, with another person of his own age who was

[294] Agreed 427–162, HC Debate 21 February 1994, vol 238, Division No 137. The House of Lords subsequently voted 176–113 in favour of a reduction in the minimum age for male homosexual acts from twenty-one to eighteen years. HL Debate 20 June 1994, vol 556, Division No 2.

[295] Criminal Justice and Public Order Act 1994, s 143. Heterosexual sodomy had never been criminalized in Scotland (there was an unsuccessful attempt to partially criminalize it in 2000: HL Debate 13 November 2000, vol 619, col 65). Heterosexual buggery remained illegal in Northern Ireland until its partial decriminalization in 2003 (see n 42).

[296] Criminal Justice and Public Order Act 1994, s 143(3) (amending Sexual Offences Act 1956, s 12) provided that all acts of buggery remained criminalized unless they took place 'in private', but in respect of an act of buggery by one man with another it reiterated the requirement of the Sexual Offences Act 1967, s 1(2) that no act would be deemed to be 'in private' if done when more than two persons take part or are present, or in a public lavatory.

[297] ECHR, ex-art 30.

[298] *Wilde, Greenhalgh and Parry* (n 284) section 'Reasons for the Decision'.

[299] *Sutherland v the United Kingdom* App No 25186/94 (Commission decision, 21 May 1996) section 'Complaints'.

also homosexual' and that, although they 'had sexual relations', they 'both worried about the law'.[300] The admission that he had engaged in criminal acts was vital to Mr Sutherland's complaint about the imposition of criminal liability and sanctions on those younger than the minimum age for male homosexual acts. The application had been lodged less than four months after the House of Commons had rejected the proposal to reduce the minimum age for male homosexual acts to sixteen years and advanced similar arguments, under Articles 8 and 14, to those in *Wilde, Greenhalgh and Parry*. The Commission took the significant step of holding an oral hearing before making a decision on the admissibility of the application. The government relied on the Commission's established case law to claim that a prohibition of consensual homosexual acts involving persons of or over sixteen years but under eighteen years—the aim of which was to 'protect young men from conduct by which they will set themselves apart [from] the rest of society and which they may well regret when they reach greater maturity'—was within the margin of appreciation available to it.[301] The Commission, by a majority, declared the complaint admissible, making it the first complaint by a person younger than the minimum age set for male homosexual acts to pass this stage of review.

In its consideration of the merits of Mr Sutherland's application, the Commission stated that it regarded it appropriate to examine the complaint under Article 8 taken in conjunction with Article 14. This approach, which brought the issue of discrimination to the foreground, required the Commission to clarify the scope of Article 14 in respect of sexual orientation:

> The different minimum ages for lawful sexual relations between homosexuals and heterosexuals are a difference based on sexual orientation. In terms of Article 14 ... of the Convention, it is not clear whether this difference is a difference based on 'sex' or on 'other status' ... The Commission for its part considers that it is not required to determine whether a difference based on sexual orientation is a matter which is properly to be considered as a difference on grounds of 'sex' or of 'other status'. In either event, it is a difference in respect of which the Commission is entitled to seek justification.[302]

This statement—considered in the context of earlier debates in the Council of Europe about the extent to which sexual preference or orientation was covered by Article 14—was extremely significant because it established that sexual orientation fell within the scope of the non-discrimination grounds contained in Article 14 (two years later, the Court definitively established that sexual orientation is 'a concept which is undoubtedly covered by Article 14').[303] The Commission also made the significant statement that it considered it opportune to consider its earlier case law in the light of developments that included, inter alia, the fact that 'equality of treatment in respect of the age of consent is now recognised by the great majority of Member States of the Council of Europe'.[304]

300 ibid, section 'The Facts'. 301 ibid, section 'The Law'.

302 *Sutherland v the United Kingdom* App No 25186/94 (Commission report, 1 July 1997) paras 50–1.

303 *Salgueiro da Silva Mouta v Portugal* ECHR 1999-IX, para 28.

304 *Sutherland* (n 302) para 59.

In response to the two principal arguments advanced by the UK government to justify the higher age of consent for male homosexual acts—that 'young men between the ages of 16 and 18 do not have a settled sexual orientation and that the aim of the law is to protect such vulnerable young men' and that 'society is entitled to indicate its disapproval of homosexual conduct and its preference that children follow a heterosexual way of life'[305]—the Commission stated that neither offered a reasonable and objective justification for maintaining a different age of consent for homosexual and heterosexual acts and that it did not consider maintaining such a difference was proportionate to any legitimate aim. The Commission legitimized this radical departure from its previous case law by stating that it accepted that 'sexual orientation is fixed in both sexes by the age of 16 and that men aged 16–21 are not in need of special protection because of the risk of their being "recruited" into homosexuality'.[306] Furthermore, the Commission stated that it would no longer accept 'that it is a proportionate response to the need for protection to expose to criminal sanctions not only the older man who engages in homosexual acts with a person under the age of 18 but the young man himself who is claimed to be in need of such protection'.[307] The Commission added that it would not accept that 'society's claimed entitlement to indicate disapproval of homosexual conduct and its preference for a heterosexual lifestyle' was a justification for an inequality of treatment under the criminal law.[308]

The Commission concluded that Mr Sutherland's application disclosed discriminatory treatment in the exercise of his right to respect for his private life and was of the opinion, by fourteen votes to four, that he had suffered a violation of Article 8 taken in conjunction with Article 14. Two of the dissenting members of the Commission critiqued the majority's argument regarding the existence of a European consensus on equal treatment in respect of the age of consent:

> While, as we believe, all States parties to the Convention share the view expressed by the Court that the Convention is a living instrument which must be interpreted in the light of present-day conditions … , it is also true that when interpreting its provisions, the developments and commonly accepted standards in the policy of the Member States of the Council of Europe in the relevant field will have to be taken into account … In the field of the minimum age of consent for sexual relationships there does, however, not seem to exist a common standard. A number of States parties to the Convention still maintain different minimum ages for homosexual and heterosexual relations, sometimes as far as four years apart. According to the majority of the Commission 'equality of treatment in respect of age for consent is now recognised by the great majority of Member States of the Council of Europe' … Does that statement really reflect the present situation?[309]

The Commission's opinion in *Sutherland* represented a watershed in Strasbourg jurisprudence relating to sexual orientation discrimination. It encouraged the UK Parliament to 'equalize' the minimum age for same-sex and opposite-sex sexual acts[310]

[305] ibid, para 63. [306] ibid, para 64. [307] ibid. [308] ibid, para 65.

[309] ibid, dissenting opinion of MM. K Herndl and I Békés.

[310] As a result of Sexual Offences (Amendment) Act 2000, s 1 in England and Wales, the minimum age for homosexual and heterosexual acts of buggery was reduced to sixteen years, and the minimum age for male homosexual acts of gross indecency was also reduced to sixteen years. In Scotland the

in order to avoid an adverse judgment of the Court[311]—a contentious legislative process that required the use of the Parliament Acts 1911 and 1949.[312] It also established the principle that a difference in treatment based on sexual orientation, 'given that it impinges on a most intimate aspect of affected individuals' private lives', required that 'the margin of appreciation must be relatively narrow'.[313] This principle, which effectively reduced the scope of the discretion afforded to Contracting States to maintain legal differences between individuals on the basis of their sexual orientation, was adopted by the Court in a range of subsequent cases relating to the minimum age for homosexual acts.[314] In light of this, acknowledging that Strasbourg jurisprudence made 'law reform absolutely necessary',[315] and in order to avoid an adverse judgment of the Court,[316] Jersey, as well as the other Crown Dependencies, equalized the minimum age for homosexual and heterosexual acts.[317]

'Not every aspect of private life automatically qualifies for protection under the Convention'

Sutherland demonstrated that the Strasbourg organs were prepared to evolve their interpretation of the Convention in order to apply the prohibition of discrimination contained in Article 14 to the sexual lives of young gay men. However, the

minimum age for male homosexual acts was reduced to sixteen years. In Northern Ireland the minimum age for male homosexual acts was reduced to seventeen years—however, because heterosexual acts of buggery remained criminalized until 2003, this did not create equality in the minimum age for buggery (see n 42)—and this was subsequently further reduced to sixteen years for all heterosexual and homosexual acts by the Sexual Offences (Northern Ireland) Order 2008.

[311] Following the Commission's opinion, the UK government pledged to make legislative provision to reduce the minimum age for homosexual acts and the parties agreed that, once the legislation had been passed, they would apply to the Court inviting it to approve a friendly settlement. On this basis the Court subsequently struck Mr Sutherland's application from its list: *Sutherland v the United Kingdom* (striking out) [GC] App No 25186/94 (ECtHR, 27 March 2001). The Court took the same action in respect of the almost identical application lodged by Christopher Morris: *Morris v the United Kingdom* (dec.) App No 31701/96 (ECtHR, 27 November 2001).

[312] For a discussion of this legislative process, see Paul Johnson and Robert M Vanderbeck, *Law, Religion and Homosexuality* (Routledge 2014).

[313] *Sutherland* (n 302) para 57.

[314] In respect of a successful complaint against the UK see *B.B. v the United Kingdom* App No 53760/00 (ECtHR, 10 February 2004). For an example of an unsuccessful complaint about the existence of a difference in the minimum age for homosexual and heterosexual acts, in the context of a prisoner convicted for murder released on life licence, see *Waite v the United Kingdom* App No 53236/99 (ECtHR, 10 December 2002).

[315] Senator W Kinnard, States of Jersey, Official Report 17 January 2006, section 10.2.

[316] *Small v the United Kingdom* (dec.) App No 7330/06 (ECtHR, 2 June 2009).

[317] Sexual Offences (Jersey) Law 2007, art 12 amended the law relating to 'sodomie' to make the minimum age sixteen years for both same-sex and opposite-sex acts. Equalization of the minimum age for homosexual and heterosexual acts was achieved in the Isle of Man by the Sexual Offences (Amendment) Act 2006 and in Guernsey by the Sexual Offences (Bailiwick of Guernsey) (Amendment) Law 2011. Not all territories for whose international relations the UK is responsible and to which the ECHR applies have equalized the minimum age for homosexual and heterosexual acts. In Bermuda, for example, the Criminal Code Act 1907, ss 177 and 179 maintains a higher minimum age (eighteen years) for acts of buggery and gross indecency between male persons compared with the minimum age (sixteen years) for other heterosexual or female homosexual acts.

outcome of two applications that were submitted in the 1990s—*V. W. X. Y. and Z. v the United Kingdom* and *Laskey, Jaggard and Brown v the United Kingdom*—demonstrated that the Strasbourg organs were not prepared to extend the protection of the Convention to all consensual and private sexual practices. The applications related to the judgment given in 1993 by the House of Lords in *R v Brown*[318] which dismissed an appeal by a group of men who had been convicted of assaults occasioning actual bodily harm[319] and, in some cases, unlawful wounding[320] as a result of their involvement with each other in consensual sado-masochistic homosexual acts. Their Lordships held by a majority that a person could be convicted for these offences as a result of committing sado-masochistic acts which inflicted injuries that were neither transient nor trifling notwithstanding that the person on whom the injuries were inflicted consented to the acts. In reaching this conclusion, their Lordships rejected arguments made by the appellants in respect of Article 8 of the Convention and, in doing so, Lord Templeman stated:

> It is not clear to me that the activities of the appellants were exercises of rights in respect of private and family life. But assuming that the appellants are claiming to exercise those rights I do not consider that art 8 invalidates a law which forbids violence which is intentionally harmful to body and mind. Society is entitled and bound to protect itself against a cult of violence. Pleasure derived from the infliction of pain is an evil thing. Cruelty is uncivilised.[321]

In response to the judgment in *R v Brown*, five applicants—a gay man, a heterosexual man, a lesbian woman, and a heterosexual couple—who participated in sado-masochistic sexual practices complained to the Commission that the judgment rendered their sexual activities liable to criminal sanction and that this amounted to an unjustified interference with their right to respect for their private lives guaranteed by Article 8.[322] In addition, they argued that they suffered discrimination contrary to Article 14 taken in conjunction with Article 8 because other activities that involved the infliction of actual bodily harm—such as ritual circumcision, boxing, tattooing, and body piercing—were treated differently in law. In respect of the complaint under Article 8, the Commission recalled its established principle that where an applicant claims to be made a victim of a violation of a Convention right by the existence of law, he or she must establish that the law in question continuously and directly affects his or her private life. In this respect, the Commission noted that the applicants had not been prosecuted, threatened with prosecution, or investigated by the police. The Commission further noted that the 'conduct of the defendants in the Brown case was of a nature and degree significantly different to the conduct to which the applicants make reference'.[323] This conclusion is perplexing given that the applicants had candidly stated that, like the appellants in

[318] *R v Brown* [1993] 2 All ER 75.
[319] Offences Against the Person Act 1861, s 47.
[320] Offences Against the Person Act 1861, s 20.
[321] *R v Brown* (n 318) 84.
[322] *V. W. X. Y. and Z. v the United Kingdom* App No 22170/93 (Commission decision, 18 January 1995).
[323] ibid, section 'The Law'.

R v Brown, they engaged in acts that, inter alia, caused 'minor cuts, bruising or otherwise leave marks' and resulted in 'cuts or breaks in the skin'.[324] The Commission declared the Article 8 complaint inadmissible and, as a consequence, concluded that Article 14 was not engaged.

The Commission also received an application from three of the appellants in *R v Brown* and declared it partly admissible.[325] In its opinion on the merits of the application, the Commission concluded by a majority of eleven votes to seven that the conviction of the applicants did not amount to a violation of Article 8. Although the majority recognized that the conduct for which the applicants had been convicted fell within the scope of Article 8, they concluded that the interference caused to the applicants' right to respect for their private lives by their convictions could be considered as necessary in a democratic society for the aim of protecting health. The majority stated that the conviction of the applicants was not disproportionate—because the 'conduct in question … was, on any view, of an extreme nature'[326]—and fell within the margin of appreciation available to the UK government to impose measures designed to protect its citizens from physical injury. The dissenters, by contrast, stated that such a conclusion 'inevitably [opens] the way to Governments to intrude into persons' bedrooms to investigate allegations, for example, that spouses engage in sado-masochistic activities'.[327] The Court not only adopted the majority view of the Commission but went on to question whether the sexual activities fell within the ambit of Article 8:

> [A] considerable number of people were involved in the activities in question which included, inter alia, the recruitment of new 'members', the provision of several specially equipped 'chambers', and the shooting of many videotapes which were distributed among the 'members' … [and it] may thus be open to question whether the sexual activities of the applicants fell entirely within the notion of 'private life'.[328]

Whilst the Court ultimately accepted that the activities did fall within the scope of Article 8, it unanimously held that the applicants' convictions did not amount to a violation of the Convention. The Court rejected the applicants' argument that 'their case should be viewed as one involving matters of sexual expression, rather than violence'[329] in favour of the government's argument that it was entitled to punish acts of violence—some of which it compared with 'genital torture'[330]—and prohibit activities because of their potential danger. The Court accepted that the government's arguments were relevant and sufficient to justify the interference

[324] ibid, section 'The Facts'.

[325] *Laskey, Jaggard and Brown v the United Kingdom* App Nos 21627/93, 21826/93 and 21974/93 (Commission decision, 18 January 1995).

[326] *Laskey, Jaggard and Brown v the United Kingdom* App Nos 21627/93, 21826/93 and 21974/93 (Commission report, 26 October 1995) para 62.

[327] ibid, dissenting opinion of Mr L Loucaides joined by MM. S Trechsel, HG Schermers, CL Rozakis, J-C Geus, J Mucha, and E Konstantinov.

[328] *Laskey, Jaggard and Brown v the United Kingdom* Reports of Judgments and Decisions 1997-I, para 36.

[329] ibid, para 39.

[330] ibid, para 40.

complained of. Moreover, the Court did not regard the interference to be disproportionate given, inter alia, 'the degree of organisation involved in the offences'.[331] In his concurring opinion, Judge Pettiti argued that the 'concept of private life cannot be stretched indefinitely', that not 'every aspect of private life automatically qualifies for protection under the Convention', and that the 'fact that the behaviour concerned takes place on private premises does not suffice to ensure complete immunity and impunity'.[332] He went on to state that the 'protection of private life means the protection of a person's intimacy and dignity, not the protection of his baseness or the promotion of criminal immoralism'.[333]

Leslie Moran has argued that the Court's judgment in *Laskey, Jaggard and Brown* illustrates the limitations of human rights law in protecting particular kinds of sexual acts and those who engage in them:

> [H]uman rights are not necessarily about inclusion and recognition of difference. Human rights may also be about the violence of exclusion and the denial of human rights. In that process human rights is about ontological categorisation: is the humanity of those who derive pleasure from the consensual giving and receiving of pain worthy of recognition? In this instance the Court has denied the humanity of those who so act.[334]

In this respect it is important to recognize that, by the time the Court considered the complaint in *Laskey, Jaggard and Brown*, the English Court of Appeal had held that the actions of a man who branded his initials on his wife's buttocks with a hot knife at her instigation should not constitute an offence of assault occasioning actual bodily harm and, in reaching this conclusion, had stated that 'consensual activity between husband and wife, in the privacy of the matrimonial home, is not, in our judgment, normally a proper matter for criminal investigation, let alone criminal prosecution'.[335] The applicants in *Laskey, Jaggard and Brown* had cited this as evidence of how they had been singled out by the domestic authorities because of a bias against homosexuals.[336] The applicants were unable to pursue a complaint about discrimination under Article 14 in the Court because the Commission had declared this part of their application inadmissible.[337] However, the Court rejected the applicants' claim of discrimination on the basis that the circumstances in the case of the heterosexual married couple were not 'comparable in seriousness'.[338] Some may agree with Moran that this demonstrates the violence of gay men's exclusion from and denial of access to human rights. It is certainly the case that the Court did not regard the suppression of consensual sado-masochistic sexual acts committed between men to violate 'respect for human dignity and human freedom'[339]—the essence of the Convention—and this is significant given that human dignity and human freedom 'imply that a man should be free to shape himself and his fate in

[331] ibid, para 49. [332] ibid, concurring opinion of Judge Pettiti. [333] ibid.

[334] Leslie J Moran, 'Laskey v the United Kingdom: Learning the Limits of Privacy' (1998) 61 MLR 77, 83.

[335] *R v Wilson* [1997] QB 47, 50. [336] *Laskey, Jaggard and Brown* (n 328) para 47.

[337] *Laskey, Jaggard and Brown* (n 325). [338] *Laskey, Jaggard and Brown* (n 328) para 47.

[339] *C.R. v the United Kingdom* (1995) Series A no 335-C, para 42.

the way that he deems best fits his personality'.[340] The Court would not accept that this particular expression of 'sexual personality'[341] should be regarded as a form of 'personal autonomy'[342] worthy of protection by the Convention from interference by the State.

It is tempting to conclude that the Court's judgment in *Laskey, Jaggard and Brown* is 'paternalistic'.[343] That conclusion can be most easily reached by way of accepting the applicants' argument that consensual sado-masochistic sexual practices fall within the sphere of 'private morality',[344] which, as the Wolfenden Report put it, is 'not the law's business'.[345] However, it was in respect of the protection of health, rather than morals, that the Court considered that the prosecution and conviction of the applicants could be considered necessary in a democratic society.[346] Only the strictest observance of Mill's 'harm principle'[347] would have led the Court to deprive the UK of its margin of appreciation to determine whether 'public health considerations' about sado-masochistic acts—which involved the maltreatment of genitalia and the infliction of injuries leading to the flow of blood and scarring—necessitated the 'general deterrent effect of the criminal law'.[348] Given that the Convention is not a 'libertarian bill of rights',[349] and that the Court is exercising 'European supervision',[350] it is difficult to imagine that the Court would have adopted such an approach.

Private life and 'group sex'

A lingering suspicion created by the judgment in *Laskey, Jaggard and Brown* is that it demonstrates the Court's inability to recognize and address discrimination that arises from 'value assumptions about the worthiness of heterosexual marital relations in contrast to the questionable value of "homosexual" relations'.[351] However, three years after *Laskey, Jaggard and Brown* the Court issued its judgment in *A.D.T. v*

[340] *Cossey v the United Kingdom* (1990) Series A no 184, dissenting opinion of Judge Martens, para 2.7.

[341] *Laskey, Jaggard and Brown* (n 328) para 34.

[342] ibid, para 44. For a consideration of personal autonomy in this context, see Katri Lõhmus, *Caring Autonomy: European Human Rights Law and the Challenge of Individualism* (Cambridge University Press 2015).

[343] Christopher Nowlin, 'The Protection of Morals Under the European Convention for the Protection of Human Rights and Fundamental Freedoms' (2002) 24 Human Rights Quarterly 264, 284.

[344] *Laskey, Jaggard and Brown* (n 328) para 45.

[345] Home Office (n 38) para 61.

[346] The Court did state that, although it did 'not find it necessary to determine whether the interference with the applicants' right to respect for private life could also be justified on the ground of the protection of morals', this 'should not be understood as calling into question the prerogative of the State on moral grounds to seek to deter acts of the kind in question'. *Laskey, Jaggard and Brown* (n 328) para 51.

[347] John Stuart Mill, *On Liberty* (Penguin Books 1859/2003).

[348] *Laskey, Jaggard and Brown* (n 328) para 44.

[349] Virginia Mantouvalou, 'Is There a Human Right Not to be a Union Member? Labour Rights Under the European Convention on Human Rights' in Colin Fenwick and Tonia Novitz (eds) *Human Rights at Work: Perspectives on Law and Regulation* (Hart Publishing 2010) 454.

[350] *Handyside* (n 58) para 49.

[351] Moran (n 334) 84.

the United Kingdom,[352] in which it returned to the issue of the criminalization of consensual sexual acts committed between males in private 'when more than two persons take part or are present'.[353] The applicant had been charged and convicted of the offence of gross indecency—the principal evidence adduced consisted of video footage, seized by police from the applicant's home, which showed him and up to four other men engaging in acts of oral sex and mutual masturbation—and it had been established that there was 'no element of sado-masochism or physical harm involved'.[354] The applicant complained under Article 8 that both the existence of the law prohibiting male homosexual acts in private involving the presence or participation of more than two people and the criminal prosecution brought against him amounted to an unjustified interference with his right to respect for his private life. The UK government invoked the Court's judgment in *Laskey, Jaggard and Brown* to support their claim that there was no interference with the applicant's right to respect for his private life because the sexual activity in question fell outside the scope of 'private life' by virtue of the number of individuals present and the fact that the activities were recorded on videotape.

The Court stated that the applicant was made a victim of an interference with his right to respect for his private life by both the existence of the law and his conviction under it. It rejected the government's contention that 'where groups of men gather in order to engage in sexual activities, the possibility of such activities being publicised is inevitable' and, 'because of the less intimate nature of group activities, the margin of appreciation afforded to the national authorities is a significant one'.[355] Although the Court stated that it could 'agree with the Government that, at some point, sexual activities can be carried out in such a manner that State interference may be justified, either as not amounting to an interference with the right to respect for private life, or as being justified for the protection, for example, of health or morals'—which implicitly reiterated its judgment in *Laskey, Jaggard and Brown*—it went on to conclude:

> The facts of the present case, however, do not indicate any such circumstances. The applicant was involved in sexual activities with a restricted number of friends in circumstances in which it was most unlikely that others would become aware of what was going on. It is true that the activities were recorded on videotape, but the Court notes that the applicant was prosecuted for the activities themselves, and not for the recording, or for any risk of it entering the public domain. The activities were therefore genuinely 'private', and the approach of the Court must be to adopt the same narrow margin of appreciation as it found applicable in other cases involving intimate aspects of private life.[356]

The 'purely private nature of the behaviour'[357] in question was undoubtedly crucial to the Court reaching its unanimous judgment that the treatment of the applicant amounted to a violation of Article 8. As I have argued elsewhere,[358] the significance the Court accorded to the 'private' nature of the sexual acts can be seen to reiterate

[352] *A.D.T. v the United Kingdom* ECHR 2000-IX.
[353] Sexual Offences Act 1967, s 1(2)(a).
[354] *A.D.T.* (n 352) para 10.
[355] ibid, para 35.
[356] ibid, para 37.
[357] ibid, para 38.
[358] Johnson (n 32).

the long-standing and problematic idea that male homosexual acts should be free of legal regulation only when they are sufficiently shielded from public view. However, the importance of the Court's judgment, that sexual acts committed by groups of men are protectable as a human right, should not be underestimated. Although the Court would not consider the applicant's complaint about discrimination under Article 14 taken in conjunction with Article 8, its judgment impelled the repeal of discriminatory laws that made consensual sexual acts committed in private between or in the presence of more than two adults an offence only when this involved sexual acts committed between men. In England and Wales, the repeal of that legislation was part of a wholesale reform of sexual offences law that included the repeal of the offences of buggery and gross indecency and, as a consequence, the elimination of specific 'homosexual offences'.[359] The same process of reform was achieved, albeit in a more piecemeal manner, in Scotland[360] and Northern Ireland.[361] The judgment in *A.D.T.* also led to the UK government capitulating in respect of a similar complaint made in *Connell and Others v the United Kingdom*.[362]

The Armed Forces

In 1991, the House of Commons Select Committee responsible for scrutinizing the quinquennial Armed Forces Bill recommended that 'homosexual activity of a kind that is legal in civilian law should not constitute an offence under Service law'.[363] The Committee was encouraged to reach this opinion primarily because of the government's policy that 'Service law should as far as possible reflect civilian law'.[364]As a consequence of the Select Committee's recommendation, male homosexual acts were partially 'decriminalized' in the armed forces in 1994.[365] The effect of this legislative change was that a homosexual sexual act that was not an offence under criminal (civilian) law ceased to be a disciplinary offence for serving armed forces

359 Sexual Offences Act 2003, s 140 and sch 7 repealed Sexual Offences Act 1956, ss 12 ('buggery') and 13 ('gross indecency'), and provisions relating to 'homosexual acts' in Sexual Offences Act 1967.

360 Convention Rights (Compliance) (Scotland) Act 2001, s 10(a) repealed Criminal Law (Consolidation) (Scotland) Act 1995, s 13(2)(a) (provision relating to male homosexual acts 'when more than two persons take part or are present'). Subsequently, Sexual Offences (Scotland) Act 2009, s 61 and sch 6 repealed provisions relating to 'homosexual offences' in Criminal Law (Consolidation) (Scotland) Act 1995, s 13; and Sexual Offences (Scotland) Act 2009, s 52 abolished the common law offence of sodomy.

361 Sexual Offences Act 2003, s 140 and sch 7 repealed Offences Against the Person Act 1861, ss 61 and 62 ('buggery'), Criminal Law Amendment Act 1885, s 11 ('gross indecency'), and provisions relating to 'homosexual acts' in Homosexual Offences (Northern Ireland) Order 1982. Sexual Offences Act 2003, s 140 and sch 7 also repealed Criminal Justice (Northern Ireland) Order 2003, art 19(4)(a) (provision relating to acts 'when more than two persons take part or are present'). Sexual Offences (Northern Ireland) Order 2008, art 83 and sch 3 repealed Criminal Justice (Northern Ireland) Order 2003, art 19 ('buggery').

362 *Connell and Others v the United Kingdom* (dec.) App No 43495/98 (ECtHR, 8 January 2002).

363 Armed Forces Bill Select Committee, *Special Report from the Select Committee on the Armed Forces Bill 1990/91* (HC 179, 1991) para 41.

364 ibid, para 6.

365 Criminal Justice and Public Order Act 1994, ss 146 and 147. This also applied to the merchant navy.

personnel.[366] The result was, as Rubin argues, 'the removal of the most overt but increasingly irrelevant form of discrimination against homosexuals in the armed forces'.[367] It was 'increasingly irrelevant' because in the vast majority of cases in which the armed forces successfully took action against a homosexual serviceperson because of their sexual orientation, this resulted in the serviceperson being administratively discharged without any formal disciplinary charge being laid.[368] The partial 'decriminalization' of homosexual acts under service law did not affect the capacity of the armed forces to administratively discharge a serviceperson for engaging in a homosexual act—indeed, this was made explicit in legislation[369]—or because it was established that the serviceperson had a 'homosexual orientation'.[370]

In 1995, four service personnel—John Beckett, Graeme Grady, Duncan Lustig-Prean, and Jeanette Smith—who had recently been administratively discharged from the armed forces because of their sexual orientation sought to challenge the legality of such a discharge in the domestic courts. The principal ground for this challenge was that the Ministry of Defence policy of discharging homosexuals from the armed forces was irrational but, in addition, that it was also in violation of the Convention. Because the domestic litigation took place at a time when the rights and freedoms guaranteed by the Convention were not enforceable by UK courts, the argument that the policy on homosexuality in the armed forces was in violation of Articles 8 and 14 provided only a 'background' to the applicants' complaint.[371] However, when the High Court dismissed the applications for judicial review of the decisions to discharge the applicants, Simon Brown LJ, in consideration of the Convention, stated: 'I for my part strongly suspect that so far as this country's international obligations are concerned, the days of this policy are numbered.'[372] Moreover, when the Court of Appeal subsequently dismissed the applicants' appeal, Sir Thomas Bingham stated that 'it may be necessary for the applicants, if all else fails, to incur the expense and endure the delay of pursuing their claim in Strasbourg'.[373]

Mr Beckett, Mr Grady, Mr Lustig-Prean, and Ms Smith did pursue their claim in Strasbourg. The complaints made in *Lustig-Prean and Beckett v the United Kingdom*[374] and *Smith and Grady v the United Kingdom*[375] related to a series of

[366] The relevant service law at this time was contained in the Army Act 1955, the Air Force Act 1955 and the Naval Discipline Act 1957.

[367] Gerry R Rubin, 'Section 146 of the Criminal Justice and Public Order Act 1994 and the "Decriminalization" of Homosexual Acts in the Armed Forces' (1996) Crim LR 393, 402.

[368] Armed Forces Bill Select Committee (n 363) para 38.

[369] Criminal Justice and Public Order Act 1994, ss 146(4) and 147(3). Provisions relating to the armed forces in these sections were repealed by Armed Forces Act 2016, s 14. For a discussion, see Paul Johnson, 'UK Parliament Poised to Repeal Final Discriminatory Law Relating to Homosexuality and the Armed Forces' *The Huffington Post* (London, 8 January 2016) < http://www.huffingtonpost.co.uk/paul-johnson-1/armed-forces-bill_b_8937612.html> (accessed 10 February 2016).

[370] Sir Thomas Bingham MR, *R v Ministry of Defence, ex parte Smith* [1996] QB 517, 551.

[371] ibid, 558. [372] ibid, 542.

[373] ibid, 559. On 19 March 1996, the Appeal Committee of the House of Lords dismissed petitions for leave to appeal.

[374] *Lustig-Prean and Beckett v the United Kingdom* App Nos 31417/96 and 32377/96 (ECtHR, 27 September 1999).

[375] *Smith and Grady v the United Kingdom* ECHR 1999-VI.

events experienced in similar ways by the applicants. All four applicants had been reported to and investigated by the 'service police' operating in their respective branch of the armed forces in relation to their sexual orientation. Mr Beckett, for example, a substantive weapons engineering mechanic in the Royal Navy, who had spoken with a chaplain about his sexual orientation, was called for interview by the service police, cautioned that he did not have to answer questions and that any responses could be used in evidence later, and subjected to a search of his personal possessions. During the interview with the service police, to whom he 'immediately confirmed his homosexuality', Mr Beckett was asked a range of questions relating to his sexual partners and practices.[376] This included detailed questions about how he and his partner 'had sex and whether they used condoms, lubrication and other sex aids' and 'whether they ever had sex in a public place'.[377] The Court declared admissible complaints made by the four applicants under Article 8 and under Article 14 taken in conjunction with Article 8.[378] In addition, it declared admissible complaints by Mr Grady and Ms Smith brought under a range of other Articles, including Articles 3 (prohibition of torture) and 10 taken alone and in conjunction with Article 14.[379]

The focus of the Court's review in *Lustig-Prean and Beckett* and *Smith and Grady* was the applicants' complaint that the investigations into their homosexuality and their subsequent discharge from the armed forces on the sole ground that they were homosexual constituted a violation of their right to respect for their private lives guaranteed by Article 8. The UK government defended the policy of discharging homosexuals from the armed forces on the basis that, although members of the armed forces had the right to be protected by the Convention, 'different, and stricter, rules applied in this context' and, given the 'national security dimension', 'a wide margin of appreciation was properly open to the State'.[380] Moreover, the government argued that admitting homosexuals to the armed forces would have a 'significant and negative effect on the morale of armed forces' personnel and, in turn, on the fighting power and the operational effectiveness of the armed forces'.[381] To substantiate this claim, the government relied on a report published in 1996 by the Homosexuality Policy Assessment Team, which had reached the conclusion that 'any relaxation of the existing policy is likely to have a detrimental effect on operational effectiveness'.[382] In respect of the investigations into the sexual relationships and orientation of the applicants the government argued that, whilst it did not seek to defend certain questions asked by the service police, the bulk of the questioning was justified by the need to verify the applicants' homosexuality

[376] *Lustig-Prean and Beckett* (n 374) para 19. [377] ibid.

[378] *Lustig-Prean and Beckett v the United Kingdom* (dec.) App Nos 31417/96 and 32377/96 (ECtHR, 23 February 1999); *Smith and Grady v the United Kingdom* (dec.) App Nos 33985/96 and 33986/96 (ECtHR, 23 February 1999).

[379] The Court declared inadmissible complaints under art 5 alone and in conjunction with art 14 ECHR. *Smith and Grady* (n 378).

[380] *Lustig-Prean and Beckett* (n 374) para 70. [381] ibid, para 71.

[382] Nicholas Soames MP, HC Debate 4 March 1996, vol 273, col 5W.

and, therefore, did not amount to a violation of their right to respect for their private lives.

The Court stated that it regarded the interference with the applicants' right to respect for their private lives as 'especially grave'[383] for a number of reasons. First, the investigation process 'was of an exceptionally intrusive character',[384] carried out according to methods based on criminal procedures, and sometimes involving a range of individuals associated with the applicants. For example, Ms Smith's partner, Margaret Fleming, who was not a member of the armed forces, was interviewed and asked, inter alia, 'what sexual acts she and her partner performed and whether she and her partner had had sex with their foster daughter'.[385] Secondly, the discharge of the applicants had a 'profound effect on their careers and prospects'.[386] Thirdly, the policy under which the applicants were discharged was of an 'absolute and general character', which operated 'irrespective of the individual's conduct or service record'.[387]

The Court held that the UK government had not provided convincing and weighty reasons to justify the interference with the applicants' right to respect for their private lives created by the policy against homosexuals in the armed forces and, in pursuance of it, their discharge. It reached this view principally by way of stating that the perceived problems identified as a threat to the fighting power and operational effectiveness of the armed forces were founded 'solely upon the negative attitudes of heterosexual personnel towards those of homosexual orientation'[388] and:

> [t]o the extent that they represent a predisposed bias on the part of a heterosexual majority against a homosexual minority, these negative attitudes cannot, of themselves, be considered by the Court to amount to sufficient justification for the interferences with the applicants' rights ... any more than similar negative attitudes towards those of a different race, origin or colour.[389]

The Court unanimously held that there had been a violation of Article 8 and, although it went on to hold that the applicants' complaints about discrimination under Article 14 taken in conjunction with Article 8 did not give rise to any separate issue, this established the strong principle that homophobia, just like racism, could not justify an interference with the right to respect for private life. This represented a landmark in Strasbourg jurisprudence because, for the first time, the Court recognized that a difference in treatment based on homosexual 'orientation' rather than on 'acts' amounted to a violation of the Convention.

There are aspects of the Court's judgments in *Lustig-Prean and Beckett* and *Smith and Grady* that can, as I have argued elsewhere, be regarded as problematic.[390] Of particular concern is the Court's conclusion in *Smith and Grady* that it was not necessary to consider the complaint made under Article 10—that the policy on

[383] *Smith and Grady* (n 375) para 90. [384] ibid, para 91.

[385] *Fleming v the United Kingdom* App No 33987/96 (Commission decision, 20 May 1997) section 'The Facts'. Ms Fleming lodged her own complaint with the Commission, but this was declared inadmissible on the ground that it was submitted out of time.

[386] *Smith and Grady* (n 375) para 92. [387] ibid, para 93. [388] ibid, para 96.

[389] ibid, para 97. [390] Johnson (n 32).

homosexuality in the armed forces limited the applicants' right to give expression to their sexual identity—because the sole ground for the investigation and discharge of the applicants was their sexual orientation and, since sexual orientation is 'an essentially private manifestation of human personality', the issue of freedom of expression was subsidiary to their right to respect for their private lives.[391] This fails to address the ways in which the sphere of an individual's private life is significantly shaped by their freedom to express their sexual orientation publically—not least because such public expression is often imperative to contest and resist forms of discrimination in the area of private life. Also of concern is the Court's rejection of the Article 3 complaint in *Smith and Grady*—that the policy of excluding homosexuals from the armed forces and the investigation and discharge of the applicants amounted to degrading treatment—on the grounds that, although 'undoubtedly distressing and humiliating for each of the applicants', their treatment did not reach the minimum level of severity to bring it within the scope of Article 3.[392] *Smith and Grady* serves to illustrate a perpetual feature of Strasbourg case law relating to sexual orientation discrimination, which is that, even at those moments of significant jurisprudential evolution, considerable judicial restraint and conservatism is usually present.[393] It took the Court a further thirteen years to find that discrimination on the ground of sexual orientation can amount to a violation of Article 3,[394] and it has never upheld a complaint brought under Article 10 about a difference in treatment based on an applicant's sexual orientation.

As a result of the Court's judgments in *Lustig-Prean and Beckett* and *Smith and Grady*, the UK government announced in January 2000 that 'homosexuality will no longer be a bar to service in Britain's armed forces'.[395] Subsequent to this, the Court upheld complaints lodged by several other gay and lesbian service personnel who had been administratively discharged because of their sexual orientation. One such complaint was lodged by Terence Perkins who, in 1996, had sought by way of judicial review to establish that the policy on homosexuality in the armed forces was contrary to the Equal Treatment Directive (of the European Union) that prohibited discrimination in employment on the grounds of 'sex'.[396] Although a reference was made by the High Court to the European Court of Justice seeking a preliminary ruling on whether the prohibition of discrimination on the grounds of sex in the Directive extended to sexual orientation,[397] this was subsequently withdrawn in

[391] *Smith and Grady* (n 375) paras 124–8. For a critical discussion, see Johnson (n 32). See also Michael Kavey, 'The Public Faces of Privacy: Rewriting Lustig-Prean and Beckett v. United Kingdom' in Eva Brems (ed) *Diversity and European Human Rights: Rewriting Judgments of the ECHR* (Cambridge University Press 2013).

[392] *Smith and Grady* (n 375) paras 117–23. For a critical discussion, see Johnson (n 32).

[393] Mahoney would argue that this is a characteristic of all Strasbourg jurisprudence. Paul Mahoney, 'Judicial Activism and Judicial Self-Restraint in the European Court of Human Rights: Two Sides of the Same Coin' (1990) 11 Human Rights Law Journal 57.

[394] *X. v Turkey* App No 24626/09 (ECtHR, 9 October 2012).

[395] Geoffrey Hoon MP, HC Debate 12 January 2000, vol 342, col 288.

[396] Council Directive 76/207/EEC of 9 February 1976 (OJ L 39/40). Superseded by: Directive 2006/54/EC of the European Parliament and of the Council of 5 July 2006 (OJ L 204/23).

[397] *R v Secretary of State for Defence* [1997] 3 CMLR 310.

light of the European Court of Justice establishing that the prohibition of discrimination on the grounds of sex contained in the Equal Pay Directive[398] did not extend to sexual orientation.[399] In 'reluctantly' withdrawing the reference, Lightman J stated that the future of the policy on homosexuality in the armed forces, which resulted in the 'draconian response of dismissal', could be considered uncertain.[400] The Court upheld Mr Perkins' complaint, joined together with a complaint by Emma Riley, under Article 8[401] and reached the same judgment in *Beck, Copp and Bazeley v the United Kingdom*.[402] The Court struck a number of similar applications from its list of cases in light of the government reaching a friendly settlement with the applicants.[403] It also struck out a number of applications at the request of the government in circumstances where the applicants had rejected the offer of a friendly settlement.[404] The Court declared inadmissible a small number of applications that it deemed to have been introduced out of time[405] or when the applicant did not wish to continue.[406]

The judgments in *Smith and Grady* and *Lustig-Prean and Beckett* marked a sea change in the Court's conceptualization of homosexuality. They demonstrated a significant absence of the view, once hegemonic in the Commission, that homosexual men and homosexual sexual practices represented a social danger that justified their containment and suppression. Although Judge Loucaides dissented from the

[398] Council Directive 75/117/EEC of 10 February 1975 (OJ L 45/19). Superseded by OJ L 204/23 (n 396).

[399] *R v Secretary of State for Defence* [1998] 2 CMLR 1116.

[400] ibid, para 12.

[401] *Perkins and R. v the United Kingdom* App Nos 43208/98 and 44875/98 (ECtHR, 22 October 2002).

[402] *Beck, Copp and Bazeley v the United Kingdom* App Nos 48535/99, 48536/99 and 48537/99 (ECtHR, 22 October 2002).

[403] *Blakemore and 41 Others v the United Kingdom* (dec.) App No 10471/05 et al. (ECtHR, 11 December 2007); *Brown v the United Kingdom* (friendly settlement) App No 52770/99 (ECtHR, 29 July 2003); *Goddard v the United Kingdom* (dec.) App No 57821/00 (ECtHR, 15 January 2002); *Greig v the United Kingdom* (dec.) App No 10567/05 (ECtHR, 7 October 2008); *Hocking v the United Kingdom* (dec.) App No 40160/03 (ECtHR, 7 October 2008); *Hunt and Miller v the United Kingdom* (friendly settlement) App Nos 10578/05 and 10605/05 (ECtHR, 23 June 2009); *Young v the United Kingdom* (dec.) App No 56276/00 (ECtHR, 23 January 2001).

[404] *Anderson v the United Kingdom* (dec.) App No 40039/03 (ECtHR, 11 December 2007); *Boden v the United Kingdom* (dec.) App No 10476/05 (ECtHR, 11 December 2007); *Chambers v the United Kingdom* (dec.) App No 10540/05 (ECtHR, 11 December 2007); *Day v the United Kingdom* (dec.) App No 10545/05 (ECtHR, 11 December 2007); *De La Maziere v the United Kingdom* (dec.) App No 10549/05 (ECtHR, 11 December 2007); *Fitzgerald v the United Kingdom* (dec.) App No 10555/05 (ECtHR, 11 December 2007); *Garford v the United Kingdom* (dec.) App No 10561/05 (ECtHR, 11 December 2007); *Garnham v the United Kingdom* (dec.) App No 10563/05 (ECtHR, 11 December 2007); *Griggs v the United Kingdom* (dec.) App No 10569/05 (ECtHR, 11 December 2007); *MacDonald v the United Kingdom* (dec.) App No 301/04 (ECtHR, 6 February 2007); *MacDonald v the United Kingdom* (dec.) App No 10600/05 (ECtHR, 11 December 2007); *O'Keefe v the United Kingdom* (dec.) App No 10610/05 (ECtHR, 11 December 2007); *Self v the United Kingdom* (dec.) App No 10615/05 (ECtHR, 11 December 2007); *Stinton v the United Kingdom* (dec.) App No 10617/05 (ECtHR, 11 December 2007); *Walton v the United Kingdom* (dec.) App No 10621/05 (ECtHR, 11 December 2007); *Wheeler v the United Kingdom* (dec.) App No 1591/04 (ECtHR, 11 December 2007).

[405] *Love and Others v the United Kingdom* (dec.) App Nos 4103/04, 5498/04, 10617/04, 14557/04 and 27313/04 (ECtHR, 13 December 2005).

[406] *Ford v the United Kingdom* (dec.) App No 10557/05 (ECtHR, 18 September 2007); *Leathart v the United Kingdom* (dec.) App No 10590/05 (ECtHR, 13 February 2007).

view that the applicants' discharge from the armed forces amounted to a violation of Article 8—because he regarded it as justified to militate against the problems created by 'the sexual orientation of homosexuals' when they are in 'communal accommodation with heterosexuals'[407]—his view was reduced to a minority status. The judgments in *Smith and Grady* and *Lustig-Prean and Beckett*, which the Parliamentary Assembly of the Council of Europe welcomed as an expression of the Court's 'opposition to all discrimination of a sexual nature',[408] provided—with the Commission's opinion in *Sutherland*—an important foundation for subsequent complaints to the Court about sexual orientation discrimination in the UK and other Contracting States.

The Declining Significance of Strasbourg for 'Gay Rights' in the UK since 2000

In early 2000, the Parliamentary Assembly of the Council of Europe returned once again to the question of whether a reference to sexual orientation should be included in the list of grounds on which the Convention prohibits discrimination. It did so in the context of providing its opinion on a draft of Protocol No. 12 to the Convention, which broadened the scope of the Convention's prohibition of discrimination—which, by virtue of Article 14, was hitherto limited to 'the rights and freedoms set forth in this Convention'—to cover 'any right set forth by law'.[409] The list of non-discrimination grounds in the draft of Protocol No. 12 was identical to Article 14 and the Committee on Legal Affairs and Human Rights strongly recommended that sexual orientation should be added to the list.[410] The Parliamentary Assembly was, for the first time, supportive of this view and adopted the opinion that 'the enumeration of grounds in Article 14 is, without being exhaustive, meant to list forms of discrimination which it regards as being especially odious' and '[c]onsequently the ground "sexual orientation" should be added'.[411] The Parliamentary Assembly repeated this recommendation in a subsequent wide-ranging Recommendation that addressed discrimination against gay men and lesbians in a number of areas.[412] Significantly, the Parliamentary Assembly recommended that the Committee of Ministers call upon Member States to 'adopt legislation which makes provision for registered partnerships' for same-sex couples.[413] This and subsequent Recommendations and Resolutions by the Parliamentary

407 *Lustig-Prean and Beckett* (n 374) partly concurring, partly dissenting opinion of Judge Loucaides.

408 Council of Europe, Parliamentary Assembly, Recommendation 1474 (2000) para 6.

409 Protocol No. 12 to the Convention for the Protection of Human Rights and Fundamental Freedoms (4 November 2000) ETS No 177, art 1(1).

410 Council of Europe, Parliamentary Assembly, Committee on Legal Affairs and Human Rights, 'Draft Protocol No. 12 to the European Convention on Human Rights: Report' (Doc 8614, 14 January 2000) para 35.

411 Council of Europe, Parliamentary Assembly, Opinion 216 (2000) para 6.

412 Council of Europe (n 408).

413 ibid, para 11.3(i).

Assembly have demonstrated its increasing willingness to engage with the issue of sexual orientation discrimination and attempt to address it.[414]

When the text of Protocol No. 12 was adopted by the Committee of Ministers[415] sexual orientation was not included in the list of grounds on which discrimination is prohibited. The reason given for this—like the reason so often given in the past—was that it was 'unnecessary from a legal point of view since the list of non-discrimination grounds is not exhaustive'.[416] Although the refusal to include an explicit reference to sexual orientation in Protocol No. 12 is significant, its importance was diminished in light of the Court having finally established that sexual orientation was a ground covered by Article 14.[417] Moreover, a subsequent Recommendation of the Committee of Ministers in 2010 that sets out measures to combat discrimination on the grounds of sexual orientation in Member States—in areas such as asylum, freedom of association, freedom of expression, employment, education, health, housing, and sports—demonstrates the 'mainstreaming' of the commitment to gay and lesbian human rights in the organs of the Council of Europe.[418] Whilst it is possible to be critical of aspects of the Recommendation—for instance, in respect of the absence of any recommendation relating to same-sex marriage—its existence signals widespread acceptance of the need to address key aspects of discrimination based on sexual orientation in Europe.

The UK's relationship with the Strasbourg organs in the twenty-first century, at least in respect of the issue of discrimination based on sexual orientation, has changed significantly. Since 2004, following the final judgment relating to the issue of the minimum age for male homosexual acts in England and Wales,[419] the UK has been the recipient of only one adverse judgment of the Court in respect of an application relating to sexual orientation discrimination.[420] There are two principal reasons for this: first, since 2000, the UK Parliament, Scottish Parliament and Northern Ireland Assembly have enacted a wide range of legislation designed to promote equality on the grounds of sexual orientation and protect gay men and lesbians from discrimination;[421] secondly, in areas where discrimination has persisted, the existence of the Human Rights Act 1998 has enabled gay men and lesbians to litigate in respect of their Convention rights in the domestic courts rather than by application to Strasbourg.[422] However, a number of applications against the UK

[414] Council of Europe, Parliamentary Assembly, Recommendation 1470 (2000); Council of Europe, Parliamentary Assembly, Recommendation 1635 (2003); Council of Europe, Parliamentary Assembly, Resolution 1728 (2010); Council of Europe, Parliamentary Assembly, Recommendation 1915 (2010).

[415] The Committee of Ministers adopted the text of Prot No 12 ECHR on 26 June 2000.

[416] Council of Europe, 'Explanatory Report to the Protocol No. 12 to the Convention for the Protection of Human Rights and Fundamental Freedoms' (Rome, 4 November 2000) para 20.

[417] *Salgueiro da Silva Mouta v Portugal* (n 303).

[418] Council of Europe, Committee of Ministers, Recommendation CM/Rec(2010)5.

[419] *B.B.* (n 314).

[420] *J.M. v the United Kingdom* App No 37060/06 (ECtHR, 28 September 2010).

[421] For a detailed discussion of a range of legislative reforms enacted by the UK Parliament, see Johnson and Vanderbeck (n 312).

[422] For example, in relation to law in Northern Ireland that discriminated against same-sex couples in respect of the adoption of a child. *Northern Ireland Human Rights Commission, Re Judicial Review* [2012] NIQB 77.

concerning sexual orientation discrimination have been submitted and dealt with by the Court since 2000. These applications, which have largely been unsuccessful, have concerned two areas: partnership rights, and asylum and immigration.

Applications against the UK concerning alleged discrimination against same-sex couples have failed principally because of the Court's strongly established jurisprudence that distinctions based on sex or sexual orientation that are created by laws that restrict marriage and its rights and benefits to opposite-sex couples do not amount to violations of the Convention. The Court's jurisprudence on marriage remains a significant problem for gay men and lesbians in many Council of Europe states. The Court has consistently rejected complaints made under Article 12 of the Convention about national laws that reserve access to marriage for opposite-sex couples[423] and has also made clear that differences in treatment between married opposite-sex couples and unmarried same-sex couples who are prohibited from marrying—for example, in respect of the adoption of a child,[424] the registration of the birth of a child,[425] and access to pension benefits[426]—do not amount to discrimination under Article 14 taken in conjunction with Article 8. Although the Court has recently upheld complaints under Article 14 taken in conjunction with Article 8 about the exclusion of same-sex couples from certain rights and benefits—for instance, in relation to the adoption of a child[427] and the registration of a civil union[428]—it has done so only when the rights and benefits in question were available to unmarried opposite-sex couples. Where rights and benefits are restricted to married couples, and where same-sex couples have no legal right to marry, the Court has asserted that, for the purposes of Article 14, an unmarried same-sex couple is not comparable to a married opposite-sex couple.[429]

In 2015, the Court took the significant step of recognizing that Article 8 creates a positive obligation to provide same-sex couples with access to a legal framework (other than marriage) that gives recognition to and protection of their relationships.[430] However, the Court was careful to limit this finding to Italy—a limitation that may not be 'conceptually possible' and therefore sustainable[431]—in order to avoid imposing a positive obligation on all Contracting States. The extent to which this will narrow the margin of appreciation available to Contracting States to reserve certain rights and benefits for married couples, whilst denying same-sex couples access to marriage, remains to be seen. It is likely that the Court will continue to treat marriage, as Loveday Hodson argues, as an 'untouchable, almost sacred, category'.[432] It has been this reluctance to interfere with a State's margin of

[423] *Schalk and Kopf* (n 217); *Hämäläinen* (n 244); *Oliari and Others* (n 244).

[424] *Gas and Dubois v France* ECHR 2012-II.

[425] *Boeckel and Gessner-Boeckel v Germany* (dec.) App No 8017/11 (ECtHR, 7 May 2013).

[426] *Manenc v France* (dec.) App No 66686/09 (ECtHR, 21 September 2010).

[427] *X. and Others v Austria* [GC] ECHR 2013-II.

[428] *Vallianatos and Others v Greece* [GC] ECHR 2013-VI.

[429] *Gas and Dubois* (n 424) para 68.

[430] *Oliari and Others* (n 244).

[431] ibid, concurring opinion of Judge Mahoney joined by Judges Tsotsoria and Vehabović, para 10.

[432] Loveday Hodson, 'A Marriage by Any Other Name? *Schalk and Kopf v Austria*' (2011) 11 Human Rights Law Review 170, 177.

appreciation to determine which rights and benefits are attached to marriage, as well as who has access to them, that has led the Court to dismiss a number of applications against the UK concerning sexual orientation discrimination.

Partnership and marriage rights

In 2005, the Court received two applications that contained complaints about the legal framework in the UK that made provision for a transsexual person to gain legal recognition of his or her gender by way of obtaining a gender recognition certificate. Upon enactment the Gender Recognition Act 2004 provided that if a successful applicant for a gender recognition certificate was married they would be issued with an interim certificate and—because UK law did not permit marriage between persons of the same sex—were required to end their marriage in order to obtain a full certificate (the grant of an interim certificate providing a ground for a marriage being voidable or, in Scotland, a ground for divorce).[433] Having ended a marriage it was then open to a same-sex couple to enter into a civil partnership.[434] Anita and Wena Parry, a married couple living in Wales, complained about the inability of Wena Parry to obtain a full gender recognition certificate without first annulling their marriage.[435] The applicants claimed that requiring them to annul their marriage—something neither of them wished to do—violated a wide range of their Convention rights including, because of their 'strongly held religious beliefs' about marriage, their rights guaranteed by Article 9.[436] The principal focus of the Court's review was on complaints made under Articles 8 and 12. It adopted the same approach in respect of an application based on similar facts, *R. and F. v the United Kingdom*,[437] lodged by a married couple living in Scotland.

In response to the applicants' claim that making the grant of a full gender recognition certificate conditional on them ending their marriage amounted to a violation of their right to respect for private and family life guaranteed by Article 8, the Court recognized that the legislative framework 'clearly puts the applicants in a quandary' because the transsexual spouse 'must, invidiously, sacrifice her gender or their marriage'.[438] The Court acknowledged that this had a 'direct and invasive effect' on the applicants' enjoyment of their right to respect for their private and family life.[439] However, the Court also noted that the 'applicants may continue their relationship in all its current essentials and may also give it a legal status akin, if not identical to marriage, through a civil partnership which carries with it almost all the same legal rights and obligations'.[440] In light of this, the Court declared the

[433] Gender Recognition Act 2004, s 4 and sch 2. The requirement to end an existing marriage was removed in England and Wales by Marriage (Same Sex Couples) Act 2013, s 12 and sch 5 and in Scotland by Marriage and Civil Partnership (Scotland) Act 2014, pt 4 and sch 2.

[434] Civil Partnership Act 2004.

[435] *Parry v the United Kingdom* (dec.) ECHR 2006-XV.

[436] ibid, section 'Remaining Complaints'.

[437] *R. and F. v the United Kingdom* (dec.) App No 35748/05 (ECtHR, 28 November 2006).

[438] *Parry* (n 435) section 'Article 8 of the Convention'.

[439] ibid.

[440] ibid.

Article 8 complaint inadmissible on the basis that the requirement placed on the applicants to end their marriage was not disproportionate and that a fair balance had been struck between the general interest of the community and the interests of the individual. The Court's reasoning can be regarded as disingenuous because had the opportunity for the applicants to enter into a civil partnership not have existed it would have almost certainly reached the same decision. This is because, at the time of the application, the Court was unwilling to recognize that a same-sex couple had a right under the Convention to have their relationship legally recognized.

The Court also declared inadmissible the applicants' complaint that the requirement to end their marriage violated their right to marry guaranteed by Article 12, which, they asserted, must include the right to ongoing recognition of their marriage. Although the Court had previously established that any limitations placed on marriage by a Contracting State must not 'restrict or reduce the right in such a way or to such an extent that the very essence of the right is impaired',[441] it reiterated its entrenched heteronormative view that Article 12 'enshrines the traditional concept of marriage as being between a man and a woman' and concluded that 'the matter falls within the appreciation of the Contracting State as how to regulate the effects of the change of gender in the context of marriage'.[442] In this respect, the Court stated that:

> [i]t is of no consolation to the applicants ... but nonetheless of some relevance to the proportionality of the effects of the gender recognition regime that the civil partnership provisions allow such couples to achieve many of the protections and benefits of married status. The applicants have referred forcefully to the historical and social value of the institution of marriage which give it such emotional importance to them; it is however that value as currently recognised in national law which excludes them.[443]

Although there was no explicit consideration of sexual orientation in either *Parry* or *R. and F.*—the applicants remaining silent, perhaps strategically so, about whether they regarded themselves as heterosexual or homosexual—the Court's willingness to accept that the legal framework about which they complained was compatible with Article 12 can be seen as synonymous with its view that Article 12 does not impose an obligation on Contracting States to grant a 'homosexual couple' access to marriage.[444] As Damian Gonzalez-Salzberg has argued, *Parry* and *R. and F.* are examples of the Court's commitment to interpreting Article 12 in a way that sustains 'the *illusion* of heterosexual marriage' and 'an understanding of marriage as a heterosexual institution'.[445] This, as Gonzalez-Salzberg notes, is particularly ironic in the circumstances of these cases because it is an interpretation of marriage that is 'completely detached from the sexuality and genitalia of the spouses'.[446]

441 *F. v Switzerland* (1987) Series A no 128, para 32.

442 *Parry* (n 435) section 'Article 12 of the Convention'.

443 ibid.

444 *Schalk and Kopf* (n 217).

445 Damian A Gonzalez-Salzberg, 'Confirming (the Illusion of) Heterosexual Marriage: *Hämäläinen v Finland*' (2015) 2 Journal of International and Comparative Law 173, 183.

446 ibid.

The Court's reluctance to interfere with the heteronormative organization of marriage in Contracting States is exemplified by its decision in *Courten v the United Kingdom*.[447] The applicant, Andrew Courten, following the death of his same-sex partner, complained about the refusal of the UK authorities to grant him an extra-statutory tax concession equivalent to the exemption from inheritance tax available to a surviving spouse.[448] In refusing Mr Courten's request, the domestic authorities had relied on case law that established that the exemption from inheritance tax was not available to unmarried opposite-sex co-habiting couples.[449] Mr Courten informed the relevant authorities that, unlike opposite-sex couples, he and his partner had never been able to marry and, as a consequence, had been given no opportunity to access the right to the exemption. Although at the time that Mr Courten's partner died, the UK Parliament had enacted the Civil Partnership Act 2004—which provided same-sex couples with a formal mechanism by which to receive the same exemption from inheritance tax available to opposite-sex married couples—the legislation had not been commenced, and, therefore, Mr Courten and his partner had not had the opportunity to register a civil partnership. As Mr Courten rightly pointed out, he and his partner had been 'unable at the relevant time, through no choice of his own, to enter into a legally-binding arrangement akin to marriage'.[450] Mr Courten complained that denying the survivor of a same-sex couple, who were unable to marry, access to the exemption from inheritance tax available to married couples violated his rights under Article 14 taken in conjunction with Article 1 of Protocol No. 1.

A fatal aspect of Mr Courten's application, which resulted in the Court declaring it inadmissible, was that it focused upon a difference in treatment between married and unmarried couples. According to the Court's established case law, Article 14 provides protection against discrimination in circumstances when persons in relevantly similar situations are treated differently without an objective and reasonable justification and, for Mr Courten's claim to succeed, it had to be established 'that the situation of the alleged victim can be considered similar to that of persons who have been better treated'.[451] However, as I outlined above, the Court has consistently refused to accept that unmarried same-sex couples—even when they live in circumstances where they wish to marry but are prohibited by law from doing so—are in an analogous situation to opposite-sex married couples.[452] Consequently, the Court regarded Mr Courten and his partner to have lived together in a 'long term but informal relationship' and would not compare this to the relationship of a married couple.[453] For this reason, the Court did not consider whether the difference in treatment complained of had a reasonable and objective justification.

[447] *Courten v the United Kingdom* (dec.) App No 4479/06 (ECtHR, 4 November 2008).

[448] Inheritance Tax Act 1984, s 18.

[449] *Holland v IRC* [2003] STC (SCD) 43.

[450] *Courten* (n 447) section 'The Law'.

[451] *Fredin v Sweden (no 1)* (1991) Series A no 192, para 60.

[452] For further discussion see Paul Johnson, 'Marriage, Heteronormativity and the European Court of Human Rights: A Reappraisal' (2015) 29 International Journal of Law, Policy and the Family 56.

[453] *Courten* (n 447) section 'The Law'.

The Court adopted the same approach in *M. W. v the United Kingdom* and declared inadmissible a complaint about the inability of the survivor of a same-sex couple to claim a bereavement payment (a social security benefit) available to the survivor of a married couple.[454] I have argued elsewhere that refusing to compare unmarried same-sex couples with opposite-sex married couples, when no right exists for same-sex couples to contract marriage, can be regarded as perverse or obtuse.[455] Such an approach significantly restricts the opportunity of same-sex couples to advance complaints under Article 14 about the discrimination that results from excluding them from marriage and the rights and benefits attached to it. The Supreme Court of Bermuda has recently held that the Court's method is not 'a rational basis'[456] for reviewing a complaint about sexual orientation discrimination in these circumstances and called it a 'somewhat technical restrictive approach'.[457]

The Court did uphold a complaint in *J.M. v the United Kingdom*[458] about child support regulations,[459] which, when applied to calculate an 'absent' parent's financial contribution to the cost of their child's upbringing, created a difference in treatment on the grounds of sexual orientation. This arose because the regulations provided that if the absent parent had entered into a new relationship (whether married or unmarried) this would be taken into account when calculating the amount payable. Crucially, however, this applied only to opposite-sex couples.[460] Because the applicant, a divorced mother of two children who was in a cohabiting relationship with a woman, did not complain about a difference in treatment between unmarried same-sex couples and married opposite-sex couples, the Court was prepared, for the purposes of Article 14, to compare her situation with the situation of an absent parent who had formed a relationship with a person of the opposite sex. On this basis, the Court stated that the 'only point of difference' was created by sexual orientation—same-sex and opposite-sex couples 'in all other relevant respects [being] similar'—and concluded that no sufficient justification existed for maintaining such a difference in law.[461] However, had the regulations reserved specific rights for married couples, the Court would have certainly found against the applicant on the grounds that she was not in a relevantly similar

[454] *M. W. v the United Kingdom* (dec.) App No 11313/02 (ECtHR, 23 June 2009).

[455] Paul Johnson, 'Adoption, Homosexuality and the European Convention on Human Rights: *Gas and Dubois v France*' (2012) 75 MLR 1136.

[456] *A. and B. v Director of Child and Family Services and Attorney General* [2014] SC (Bda) 11 Civ, para 35.

[457] *Bermuda Bred Company v The Minister of Home Affairs and The Attorney General* [2015] SC (Bda) 82 Civ, para 87.

[458] *J.M.* (n 420).

[459] Child Support (Maintenance Assessments and Special Cases) Regulations 1992.

[460] *J.M.* (n 420) para 21.

[461] ibid, para 55. It is interesting to compare this approach with the Court's approach in *Craig v the United Kingdom* (dec.) App No 45396/99 (ECtHR, 21 March 2000). The applicant, Helen Craig, was in a same-sex relationship with a woman, Ms L., who had four children. The care and custody of the children was subject to High Court proceedings, the result of which was that Ms L.'s former husband was awarded custody of the children who would spend alternative weeks with Ms L. As part of this settlement, Ms L. agreed that she would not permit the children to come into contact with or remain in the company of Ms Craig or any other person known to Ms L. to be lesbian. Ms Craig complained to

situation to a married couple. It is probable that the Court would accept that the legalization of same-sex marriage in England and Wales[462] and Scotland[463] places opposite-sex and same-sex married couples in an analogous position, but, of course, because same-sex couples can now marry in Great Britain, they are far less likely to bring complaints under the Convention about a difference in treatment based on sexual orientation in respect of rights and benefits attached to marriage.

Immigration and asylum

Strasbourg case law relating to sexual orientation discrimination in the areas of immigration and asylum remains significantly underdeveloped. The most recent decision issued by the Court in respect of a complaint brought against the UK by a same-sex couple about immigration law was in *Cardoso and Johansen v the United Kingdom* in 2000.[464] The applicants, who had lived together in the UK for eighteen years, complained about the refusal by immigration authorities to provide Mr Cardoso (a Brazilian national) with leave to enter the UK on his return from a visit to Brazil. This refusal was in the context of Mr Cardoso having travelled using a false passport, having previously entered the UK illegally, having falsely claimed benefits and having had a marriage of convenience with a woman in an attempt to remain in the UK.[465] The domestic authorities informed Mr Cardoso that he could not benefit from available concessions for same-sex bi-national couples[466] on the basis of his relationship with Mr Johansen (a British citizen) because, although he had lived in the UK for an extended period with his partner, he was seeking leave to enter and not leave to remain. The day before removal directions were due to be issued, the Court requested that any expulsion measures be suspended pending its review of the applicants' complaints under Articles 3 and 8 of the Convention. The government subsequently informed the Court that immigration authorities had reconsidered Mr Cardoso's case and, as a consequence, he was granted leave to enter the UK. The applicants' complaint to Strasbourg can be seen to have encouraged the domestic authorities to change their decision pragmatically in order to avoid an adverse judgment in an area of policy in which the State wished to maintain maximum discretion. In 2016, the Court significantly evolved its jurisprudence by holding that immigration provisions in Croatia that enabled 'family reunification'

the Court that this requirement, inter alia, interfered with her right to respect for her private and family life and was discriminatory. The Court unanimously declared Ms Craig's application inadmissible.

[462] Marriage (Same Sex Couples) Act 2013.

[463] Marriage and Civil Partnership (Scotland) Act 2014.

[464] *Cardoso and Johansen v the United Kingdom* (dec.) App No 47061/99 (ECtHR, 5 September 2000).

[465] *R v Secretary of State for the Home Department Ex p. Cardoso* [2000] Imm AR 1.

[466] The UK had, in 1997, introduced a concession in respect of the immigration rules for the unmarried partner (including same-sex partner) of a person present and settled in the UK. 'Concession Outside the Immigration Rules for unmarried partners …' (13 October 1997) <http://www.refworld.org/docid/3ae6b5764.html> (accessed 11 February 2016).

for unmarried and married opposite-sex bi-national couples, but which excluded bi-national same-sex couples, amounted to a violation of the Convention.[467]

In *F. v the United Kingdom*, the Court considered an application from an Iranian citizen who had entered the UK illegally and subsequently claimed asylum on the basis that he feared persecution because of his sexual orientation.[468] The applicant stated that Iranian security forces had come to his house and that he and his same-sex partner were remanded in custody. He claimed that after spending over three months in prison, which involved being beaten, he was released on the payment of bribes by his family. Iran enforces a total prohibition of same-sex sexual acts, and a person convicted of committing such acts can be sentenced to death.[469] The UK domestic authorities refused the applicant's request for asylum on the grounds that, inter alia, his account of events in Iran lacked credibility and that 'it was extremely unlikely that homosexual activity conducted in private would result in ill-treatment or harassment'.[470] To reach this conclusion the domestic authorities relied on a range of evidence, including a report by the Canadian Immigration and Refugee Board that stated:

> All in all, the situation in practice in Iran is drastically different from the impression conveyed by the Shari'a inspired penal code. According to the information from usually very reliable sources, no homosexuals have been executed in Iran for the last few years. In order to risk policiary sanctions—maltreatment or a short time in custody/jail, regardless of the fact that the penalty according to the law is death or whipping—a homosexual couple must behave with great indiscretion, almost provocatively, in a public place.[471]

The essence of this is, like the argument advanced in *Z.B.*, that gay men and lesbians can militate against criminal prosecution and punishment by being 'discrete'.

The applicant in *F.* made a number of complaints, including that if he was expelled to Iran he would be at risk of extra-judicial killing contrary to Article 2 (right to life) and face a real risk of torture and ill-treatment contrary to Article 3. In this respect, the applicant pointed out that the evidence relied on by the domestic authorities demonstrated the 'possibility of under-reporting of executions and floggings' in Iran for those convicted of homosexual acts and stated that there was evidence of convicted individuals having been stoned and executed.[472] The Court reiterated its established jurisprudence that, although a right to asylum is not protected by the Convention, Article 3 implies an obligation not to expel an individual from a Contracting State if there are 'substantial grounds' for believing that he or she would face a 'real risk' of being subjected to torture or to inhuman or degrading treatment or punishment in the receiving country.[473] On this basis, the Court

[467] *Pajić v Croatia* App No 68453/13 (ECtHR, 23 February 2016).

[468] *F. v the United Kingdom* (dec.) App No 17341/03 (ECtHR, 22 June 2004).

[469] Islamic Penal Code of the Islamic Republic of Iran 2013, Bk. Two, Pt. Two, Ch. Two; previously, Islamic Penal Code of the Islamic Republic of Iran (first adopted) 1991, Bk. Two, Chs. Two and Three.

[470] *F.* (n 468) section 'The Facts'. [471] ibid. [472] ibid, section 'The Law'.

[473] *Chahal v the United Kingdom* Reports of Judgments and Decisions 1996-V, para 80.

examined together the applicant's complaints under Articles 2 and 3 and, in doing so, reached the conclusion that:

> [a]lthough it is not disputed in theory … that very draconian punishment can be imposed on homosexual acts, the Court is not persuaded that the applicant has shown that he is at a real risk of falling foul of the authorities on that ground. While he claimed that he had been arrested after a visit by the security forces to his house and held in detention, subject to beatings and under threat of execution, for some months, the Court recalls that the [domestic authorities] found that this aspect of the applicant's account was lacking in credibility and untruthful. It must give a certain weight in this respect to the findings of the domestic authorities reached on the basis of the witness evidence before them and their general experience … Although it must be acknowledged that the general situation in Iran does not foster the protection of human rights and that homosexuals may be vulnerable to abuse, the applicant has not established in his case that there are substantial grounds for believing that he will be exposed to a real risk of being subjected to treatment contrary to those Articles.[474]

In declaring the Article 2 and 3 complaints inadmissible, the Court implicitly legitimized the idea that gay men and lesbians who are 'discrete' about their sexual orientation can protect themselves from criminal sanctions.[475] As I have argued elsewhere, the failure of the Court in this and other cases to protect gay and lesbian individuals from being returned to contexts in which they risk treatment contrary to Articles 2 and 3 is a major gap in contemporary human rights law.[476] Returning gay men or lesbians to a country that operates a total legal prohibition of homosexual sexual acts and imposes a sentence of death as a punishment for engaging in such acts amounts, at the very least, to a form of degrading treatment contrary to Article 3 because it exposes them to significant risks that may induce feelings of 'fear, anguish and inferiority capable of humiliating and debasing them and possibly breaking their physical or moral resistance'.[477]

The applicant in *F.* also complained under Article 8 that his 'physical and moral integrity' would be compromised by expulsion to Iran.[478] The Court has long recognized that the concept of 'private life' in Article 8 'covers the physical and moral integrity of the person, including his or her sexual life'.[479] However, the Court stated that, although the applicant's deportation would mean that 'he would live under a ban against homosexual adult consensual relations, which would in Contracting States disclose a violation of Article 8', on a 'purely pragmatic basis, it cannot be required that an expelling Contracting State only return an alien to a country which is in full and effective enforcement of all the rights and freedoms set out in the Convention'.[480] The Court further stated that it had not been established that

[474] *F.* (n 468) section 'The Law'.

[475] The UK Supreme Court has rejected the idea that 'discretion' is an appropriate basis for assessing the risk of deporting gay men and lesbians to nation states that criminalize homosexual acts. *H.J. (Iran) & H.T. (Cameroon) v Secretary of State for the Home Department* [2010] UKSC 31.

[476] Johnson (n 32).

[477] *Smith and Grady* (n 375) para 120.

[478] *F.* (n 468) section 'The Law'.

[479] *X. and Y. v the Netherlands* (1985) Series A no 91, para 22.

[480] *F.* (n 468) section 'The Law'.

the applicant's moral integrity would be substantially affected to a degree falling within the scope of Article 8 and declared the complaint inadmissible. Implicit to the Court's decision is the principle that the UK and other Contracting States who deport gay men and lesbians to jurisdictions in which consensual same-sex intimate relationships are criminalized are acting in accordance with their obligations under Article 8.[481] The Court has, to date, never held that deporting a gay man or lesbian from a Contracting State to a country of origin, which criminalizes homosexual acts or where there is significant social hostility towards homosexuality, amounts to a violation of any aspect of the Convention.[482]

Conclusion

A socio-legal analysis of applications submitted to Strasbourg against the UK about sexual orientation discrimination brings into stark relief a number of issues. First, the analysis demonstrates the importance of the existence of the Convention system for gay men and lesbians in the UK who, since the mid-1970s, have utilized it in an attempt to address a wide range of discriminatory treatment. Secondly, it shows the ways in which the Strasbourg organs, and the wider Council of Europe, have often stubbornly refused to recognize that discrimination on the grounds of sexual orientation amounts to a violation of human rights and fundamental freedoms. Thirdly, and relatedly, the analysis shows that gay men and lesbians have been persistent and tenacious in demanding recognition of their Convention rights and freedoms. Fourthly, it demonstrates that when applications to Strasbourg against the UK by gay men and lesbians have been successful, the consequence has often been significant and beneficial change in domestic law. Finally, the analysis demonstrates that applications by gay men and lesbians against the UK have contributed to the development of a body of Strasbourg jurisprudence that has potentially positive implications for sexual minorities in other Council of Europe states. All of these issues are addressed in the oral histories that are contained in Part 2 of this book.

[481] The Court did not consider a complaint about the refusal by UK authorities of an application for asylum by a female Zimbabwean national who claimed that she could not be returned to Zimbabwe because she would be at risk 'not only from her family, but also from the wider community because of their attitude towards gays and lesbians'. *D.B.N. v the United Kingdom* (dec.) App No 26550/10 (ECtHR, 31 May 2011) section 'The Facts'. Although Zimbabwean law does not criminalize same-sex sexual acts between women, the applicant claimed she was at risk of significant ill treatment because of social discrimination against homosexuals: for a discussion of this issue, see *LZ (homosexuals) Zimbabwe* CG [2011] UKUT 00487 (IAC). However, in light of the applicant having seemingly voluntarily departed from the UK and failing to contact her representatives, the Court struck the application from its list of cases.

[482] For recent jurisprudence, see *M.E. v Sweden* App No 71398/12 (ECtHR, 26 June 2014); *M.E. v Sweden* (striking out) [GC] App No 71398/12 (ECtHR, 8 April 2015).

PART 2

ORAL HISTORY

This part of the book contains the oral histories of fifteen individuals who submitted complaints to the Strasbourg organs about sexual orientation discrimination in the UK. Chapter 2 contains the accounts of six individuals who lodged complaints between 1976 and 1994 about discrimination created by the criminal law. Chapter 3 contains five accounts by individuals who lodged complaints between 1996 and 1999 about discrimination in the armed forces. Chapter 4 contains the accounts of four individuals who lodged complaints between 1985 and 2006 about discrimination in areas related to family life. This part of the book also contains, in Chapter 5, the oral histories of four individuals who have worked closely with or provided support to people who have submitted complaints to the Strasbourg organs about sexual orientation discrimination. A discussion of how the oral histories were produced can be found in the note on method contained in Appendix 1.

PART 2

ORAL HISTORY

2
The Criminal Law

Dudgeon v the United Kingdom (1976–1983)

In 1976, Jeffrey Dudgeon complained to the European Commission of Human Rights about the existence in the law in force in Northern Ireland of certain offences relating to male homosexual acts. Unlike in England and Wales, where male homosexual acts had been partially decriminalized in 1967, the law in Northern Ireland prohibited all acts of buggery and gross indecency between males. This law provided the basis for 'police raids' on the homes of gay men who, as Mr Dudgeon's account shows, were subjected to extensive investigation and the threat of prosecution. In 1981, the European Court of Human Rights upheld Mr. Dudgeon's complaint that the existence of the law about which he complained amounted to an unjustified interference with his right to respect for his private life. The Court would not examine Mr Dudgeon's complaint that he had suffered discrimination.

Jeffrey Dudgeon MBE

I came back to Belfast in 1974 and there was a Gay Lib Society at Queen's University. I joined a small but dynamic group of about twenty people. I had some earlier experience in political life in the Northern Ireland Labour Party and other left-wing groups, so I was probably the person who pushed for parliamentary law reform as much as gay liberation. I was a bit older than the GLS people, who were a mixed bag of very serious as well as very lively individuals. We started a local campaign to try and get the Assembly to address homosexual law reform along the lines of the 1967 Act in England and Wales. It just so happened that the Assembly had come back to life after the Parliament had been prorogued two or three year earlier. We even had an Alliance Party law reform minister, Oliver Napier, so we thought we could maybe get somewhere—perhaps not very far, but we'd try it anyway—but he turned down any prospect. About a year later, in 1975, I met up with Kevin Boyle, a law lecturer and barrister in the University, who said to me that we had a good chance with a case at Strasbourg. He had done one for the Irish government against the British government on alleged torture which ultimately won, except the torture was downgraded to ill-treatment. Anyway, he had considerable experience and he said, basically, it's the cost of the postage stamp to take a case. He said he would do the legal work but we'd need a solicitor. It seemed a good idea and in 1975 at least one letter was sent to Strasbourg initiating the case.

Going to Strasbourg: An Oral History of Sexual Orientation Discrimination and the European Convention on Human Rights. First Edition. Paul Johnson. © Paul Johnson 2016. Published 2016 by Oxford University Press.

Then, in January 1976, the police raids happened. That was over a six-month period and about twenty-five people were questioned. It started with a mother's complaint. She'd discovered a love letter in her son's laundry and informed the local police. It went to a very senior rank in Belfast—Assistant Chief Constable—and the first person arrested was the boyfriend of the son. The son, a young man, had nowhere to live, so it had been arranged that he stay temporarily at my house. One evening I came home and there was a knock at the door. The police had arrived with a warrant to search for drugs. Part of the deal for putting up the young man was that some grass was going to be handed over as a gift to one of the other guys, Richard Kennedy, living in the house. The police dog went straight to the cupboard and found it. Richard was in England at the time but was arrested three days later coming off the boat, charged with possession and distribution, and convicted. To this very day he has to declare those convictions. His was the only one out of the whole thing. It transpired that the drugs were a ruse, because the main interest was the gay issue. It also turned out that the young man staying in my house was, by then, a police agent; he'd been suborned by them.

The police removed every piece of paper in the house and took me away for questioning, for about six or seven hours, at Castlereagh, which is the main interrogation centre in Belfast. The questioning was somewhat disorganized; they didn't quite know what or who was what. They were reading furiously all through my letters and diaries and they recognized that they had a few revealing letters, particularly from my then boyfriend, Doug Sobey. He was Canadian—and actually in West Africa at the time doing some research—and he had written back including various explicit, or revealing, nuggets in the letters. They put these to me and I said, 'Look, I'm not hiding the fact that I'm a homosexual but I'm not going to be admitting to any criminal act.' They weren't friendly but they weren't brutal or screaming or anything like that; just hard and sour. They were reading out bits of the letters to me and asking for my comment. They asked me to write a statement which I did, but I didn't admit to any criminal offence, and they then sent me home. I was taken back about midnight and, oddly, the police constable who drove me said something like, 'I don't know why we're pursuing this, it seems not useful.'

There's a small interesting fact relating to the Kincora Boys' Home in East Belfast where, in 1981/1982, three of the wardens were found to have been and were convicted for abusing boys. The Hughes Report, a local enquiry published in 1985, shows that the same guy that drove me home, Detective Constable Cullen, on that very same day had gone to William Meharg, the Assistant Chief Constable, to discuss misbehaviour in Kincora. The great irony is that the police didn't pursue Kincora, but they did pursue us. Meharg was put in charge of what became known as the 'RUC Gay Squad'. They treated our activities as a conspiracy, and they were right.

For a year, we were under the permanent terror of being jailed and arrested. We were angry and not cowed. Some people were treated worse than me and didn't have the courage, stamina or experience to resist. They suffered. One guy in particular—I was only told last week—became a recluse after it. We certainly knew of twenty-two people who had been brought in for questioning. The only one arrested was my boyfriend. I was in bed with him and the doorbell rang and it was the 'Saturday Morning Cops'—as we called them because they were doing it on overtime—and, when we didn't answer, they said, 'We're going to fucking break down your door and take you for questioning.' Doug said, 'I'm not going in for questioning', and they said, 'We'll arrest you', and he said, 'Okay, arrest me.' We'd learned by that time that you'd more rights if you were arrested.

Exactly a year after I'd been questioned, we were told there would be no prosecutions. Originally, I thought that the Attorney General had squashed the whole thing on the grounds that it was out of step with London and they were going to be changing the law but, no, it wasn't radical Sam Silkin, Labour Attorney General, just sweeping aside nonsense, it was very much a process of accretion and, only at the last minute, did he use his power to stop it. In fact, the Director of Public Prosecutions had signed the papers to authorize prosecution and they were in the post room out-tray to go to the RUC when London finally said no. I discovered this fact recently, after a Freedom of Information request.

We didn't think the Stormont government had the ability or power to reform the law because this was Northern Ireland and there was a war on. Homosexual law reform was deeply unpopular in the Protestant/Unionist community for religious fundamentalist reasons. There is and was a strong vein of homosexuality in the Ulster Unionist Party—that sort of vein you get in the Tory Party—but certainly not in Paisley's Democratic Unionist Party. After the Assembly was prorogued, and we had direct rule, law reform was only going to happen through Westminster. They put the issue into the Standing Advisory Commission on Human Rights and it recommended law reform. But the Ulster Unionists had a pivotal role in 1978/1979 in Westminster, in voting terms, and the Northern Ireland Office offered them no law reform to keep them happy. The Northern Ireland Office used the gay issue to unite Catholics and Protestants because it was one of the few things they found where they thought everyone was of one mind. Then in 1979/1980, Thatcher took power and when a paper on law reform was put in front of Hugh Rossi, the Northern Ireland Minister, he wrote on it something to the effect of, 'Leave it to Strasbourg to find against us.'

I'm not a lawyer, I'm a politically minded individual so, in terms of the Strasbourg application, I did the politics, as I thought best, and Kevin Boyle and the solicitor, Francis Keenan, did the legal stuff. We sensed we were on to a winner because it was absurd that you could go to jail for life in Belfast for something that was not a crime in Birmingham. They were doing Article 8, private life stuff, but, being a radical, I wanted to pursue Article 14. We thought we were going to win on Article 8, so I thought why not push for an extra step and get the issue of discrimination into play. There were so many elements of discrimination to address: differences within the United Kingdom, and between men and women. With some reluctance, the lawyers did pursue that point but it created some tension and, after we won at the Commission, I changed lawyers because they weren't willing to pursue Article 14 hard enough. We also had a bit of a fight because the lawyers were doing deals, or having conversations, with Strasbourg about what was and wasn't possible—I suppose it was normal tactics and legal guidance—and not telling me. It reached the point were they weren't even telling me developments. Letters were coming in from Strasbourg that were for me and the details weren't being passed to me. So, in the end, I switched to gay lawyers in London—a solicitor, Paul Crane, and a barrister, Terry Munyard—and a senior counsel, Lord Tony Gifford. Obviously, that was hard and it was sad in a way. I always felt a bit guilty and a bit annoyed that I'd had to do it. And poor old Kevin Boyle, who had done all the graft, never got the glory because he didn't conclude the case. But pursuing Article 14 wasn't political unreality; we were going to win on Article 8, so why not push the boat out? It would have been neglectful not to.

The case started off with me being anonymous, as X., and then it became necessary for me to become public to do the public advocacy. There was a lot of effort involved because we had to do a fund raising campaign through *Gay News* in London. There was tremendous support from up and down England, Scotland and Wales. We didn't make as much as we could of the police invasion into our correspondence and private life and, had that been today, we'd have had the world's press screaming. But we ran a very good press campaign about the whole thing and a couple of mainstream journalists from the *Irish Times* and the *New Statesman*, Fionnuala O'Connor and Mary Holland, ran occasional pieces. So we were running a social life, a political campaign, and personal lives all at the same time. There was a war going on in the city, people were being shot and killed right, left and centre. The case didn't really become problematic until I actually appeared on a BBC Northern Ireland TV programme, *Spotlight,* in 1976. I worked in the docks, in a transport company, and I remember being summonsed to the dockers' canteen and basically interrogated by a shop steward-type in front of seven or eight dockers. He was progressive and supportive, one was aggressive and hating, and it was a bit of an ordeal. We all lived a sort of life that was above the ordinary life of the world, and had the strength to do it. Anger was your diet—that kept you afloat—rage and solidarity, and all that. So we survived.

My family was largely supportive. I've since discovered that I had one aunt who wrote to my father about her anger and sorrow and rage. And another uncle, I later learned, was very hating. But others were friendly. My mother, father and sister were supportive, significantly. I sometimes think I was rather hard on them because I put them through it all and I never consulted them; I told them things after the event. I had come out to them as a teenager and, luckily, my mother was sort of progressive politically; my father was more traditional and conservative, but not hard. It must have been rougher for them than it was for me. It was a dangerous time in Northern Ireland and they also had to deal with this whole problem that parents have of an expectation dashed, of everything sharply coming to a grinding halt and realizing you're not going to have a married child and you won't be a grandparent. But we were living slightly at a distance so I didn't see them that often. I don't recall any advice or counsel or caution. I suppose I was already too much of a rebel; hopeless!

I went to Strasbourg twice. It was slightly disappointing, I suppose. The Commission, in sleek offices, was a day of legal arguments and I didn't say anything. For the Court hearing, I went over with Tony, Terry and Paul, and Richard from here. We brought a German academic, Martin Dannecker, as a witness to argue the Article 14 case and to challenge the German precedents—cases from the 1950s which were based on sociological stuff published in the 1930s that was imperial and Nazi in some respects—but the Commission in the end wouldn't allow him to be called. In the Court, I trotted up with my lawyers to their places and the Commission officials grabbed me and shunted me back into the audience, saying 'You're not part of the team, sonny.'

The British government lawyer from Northern Ireland was there to say things like Northern Ireland didn't want this sort of rubbish and was religiously and fervently against such ghastliness. He was Brian Kerr, who later became Lord Chief Justice of Northern Ireland. I recently went to a lecture when he was asked—not by me but by somebody else—what he thought about being part of the government team trying to prevent homosexual law reform and—to paraphrase—he said that he was being constantly attacked at dinner parties for his role and that his pleadings were a nonsense. The chief UK lawyer was Nicolas Bratza, who ended up President of the European Court of Human Rights. I looked at his website recently and he lists the Dudgeon case as one of his achievements, but he forgets to say that he was on the wrong side! In some societies they'd have been dragged to the guillotine. Instead they got significant honours bestowed on them and applause from the liberal establishment. It makes me feel pissed off, you know, but I suppose it's inevitable that this happens; it's just the way of the world. I've been rewarded to some degree, so I'm not complaining. I haven't been neglected; far from it.

In terms of the judgment, I was very satisfied with the vote on Article 8, which was fifteen to four—Matscher from Austria, Pinheiro Farinha from Portugal, Walsh from Ireland, and Zekia from Cyprus voted against—but I was unhappy that we didn't get anywhere on Article 14. That aspect was the one that produced separate opinions, some of which were interestingly progressive. But there was one that was actually rather dangerous because it basically said I was a criminal and referred to things that weren't adduced in evidence, so that was a bit frightening. Brian Walsh, the Irish judge, gave a well-argued, Catholic case for not wanting change. The most irritating thing of all was the costs and damages—the Article 50 judgment. It's hard to believe, but the Foreign Office put in an objection to everything—like forty pence on a stamp—with about ten words, like 'unjustified', 'unreasonable', 'ridiculous', set against every item. No damages were awarded 'just satisfaction'—the change in law was regarded as sufficient. That was okay because, if there had been money awarded, it would probably have led to more problems as people would have said it wasn't mine or had to be given to something else. The worst thing was that they actually cut the costs by one third to £3,315 because they had invented this notion that the case had been done on a contingency, no win no fee, basis. That hadn't been the case and I don't know where they got that idea. I rather think it had come from my former solicitor and it struck me that Strasbourg almost conspired to punish me because I'd changed lawyers. Actually, the structure of the group of judges that made up the Article 50 chamber was ridiculously unbalanced; three of the seven had been negative in the original judgment and one was the UK judge.

The greater problem created by the judgment was how to deal with the publicity and the spin. I was going to be on TV and that could bring issues locally. I had refused to do any TV interviews with Paisley and oppositionalists until the case concluded or until the law reform happened, on the slightly specious grounds that my dispute was with the British government and not local religious leaders. Then, when the law reform went through in October 1982, I did TV interviews with Peter Robinson and Ian Paisley. I can remember getting my make-up done in the BBC and the make-up girl saying to me, 'I did Peter Robinson's as bad as I possibly could!' I did experience a lot of trouble at home, from attacks that happened shortly after the law reform, in 1983 and 1984. There were a series of attacks on my house, with breezeblocks through the window, and injuries and all that. That is very disturbing, to say the least, and lingers for years. I am a slightly nervous person, so I'm always a bit nervous of problems; gay people have always experienced that nervousness and fear. I was both bold and fearsome.

In one sense, I won and we won and we got the law changed. But in another sense, we didn't win because nothing has changed. We still have to fight every inch of the way in Northern Ireland to get more modern reforms. Even with civil partnerships, London tried to deal with the Democratic Unionist Party and said it could be delayed if they played ball. We had to fight for the first age of consent reduction in Northern Ireland and run campaigns each time. London doesn't say, 'Oh Strasbourg says we can't treat Northern Ireland differently'; they still always treat Northern Ireland differently. One of the things that was hard work was getting the reforms in the Sexual Offences Act 2003 to extend to Northern Ireland. I drafted the amendment—I got a couple of law books, and cut and paste—and we got a Liberal Peer, Lord Beaumont of Whitley, to help us in the House Lords. There was quite a lot of opposition to Northern Ireland being included and some local gay community groups and people were saying, 'We've got a parliament here in Northern Ireland, this should be done locally.'

I know the Strasbourg judgment has meant a lot to other people, but it meant a lot to me as well. I've had twenty-five years of people interrogating me about it ever since. It took a while for people to start treating me as historic—as a stately homo—but there's been quite a lot published and, I suppose, I began to realize just how significant it was in terms of a precedent and a first. I was quite proud when Justice Kennedy quoted my case in the American Supreme Court in the Texas sodomy case. And, of course, it's quite a precedent for all the African, Asian and Middle-Eastern countries that are only heading down this path. I can be quite critical of the Court today, in some respects. I'm not sure whether I've got more conservative or it's got a bit more adventurous. Some say that a lot of the judges are not thoughtful like they used to be and they have produced a crisis of confidence, for example in the UK prisoners' voting case. There was also the very prominent Italian crucifix case where, as soon as there was squealing from Eastern Europe, they reversed their judgment almost immediately. There are big issues with Russia, Ukraine and Turkey producing torrents of cases. The Court is a victim of its own success in that respect. It's hugely important but I think it's moved away from a liberal position to maybe a radical one in some respects, which creates more difficulties in a complex Europe.

*

R.D. v the United Kingdom (1982–1984)

Male homosexual acts were partially decriminalized in England and Wales in 1967 but remained a criminal offence if they involved a person under the age of twenty-one years. This was in contrast to the 'age of consent' for most opposite-sex or female same-sex sexual acts, which was sixteen years. In 1982, Richard Desmond, who was seventeen years old and attending secondary school, complained to the European Commission of Human Rights that prohibiting males under twenty-one years from engaging in same-sex sexual acts constituted an unjustified and discriminatory interference with his right to respect for his private life. Mr Desmond's complaint, as his account shows, arose from his collaboration with Peter Ashman and Nigel Warner of the Campaign for Homosexual Equality. The Commission declared his application inadmissible in 1984.

Richard Desmond

Going back eighteen months or a year before the first contact with Peter Ashman and Nigel Warner, from the Campaign for Homosexual Equality law reform group as was, I started going to what was the London Gay Teenage Group, which was the only gay youth group in the country at the time. It started off at Grapevine in Islington and moved to Manor Gardens Centre in Holloway. It was an incredibly controversial group at the time. It seems difficult to remember it now, but the age of consent was twenty-one and people *were* being prosecuted, it *was* real. My friend was Chair, I later become Secretary, but it was run in a classic, old-fashioned committee way by the members.

We met on Sunday afternoons and Manor Gardens Centre had a glorious garden. We basically had the shed in the garden, a very large shed, but a shed nonetheless. And one Sunday afternoon, Nigel and Peter from the Campaign for Homosexual Equality came down to the Teenage Group to try and find somebody who was sixteen. I know that it was quite specific, looking for someone who was sixteen, and it was very specifically sixteen because of equality. The Teenage Group class of 1979/1980—sadly not many of us survive—was a bizarre, outrageous group, largely gay men with a few women, and these incredibly sensible, educated, smart men came in. I don't know whether they were more horrified or we were! We knew about the age of consent, we knew it was wrong, there was this sense of equality, but we weren't a politicized group, it wasn't something people had thought about. As soon as Nigel and Peter had talked to the Chair, it was put to the group: 'Who is interested?' I was sixteen, which was the relevant age at the time, and so I started the process.

I was in a very politicized family. Only a sixteen year old would ever make this connection but, at the time, my uncle was in prison in South Africa. He was an anti-apartheid Franciscan priest. Equality and anti-apartheid was part of what my family did. It was such a wrong thing to do, but I saw the age of consent in parallel with anti-apartheid and racism. It is so wrong as to be unbelievable, I would never do it now, but at the time that was the case that I made to my mum. My mum had a brain tumour removed in 1965. She loves me and I can't do any wrong, which is an advantage occasionally! Consequently, getting my mum to sign the paperwork was relatively easy. I didn't ask my dad and, to the best of my knowledge, to this day he doesn't know about it. But given that he is now seventy-odd and not well, I haven't bothered talking about it with him.

I was certainly enthusiastic about the case. You know, coming from a relatively poor family in the East End and being a working class gay man was relatively unusual even then. The gay scene always was kind of posh. Going to Nigel's house, with his lovely furniture and excellent taste, was completely different to my experience. Meeting these people who were completely outside my experience, being that bit older—because the only place I'd ever gone was the Teenage Group and the group for those under sixteen—yes, I was excited by it. But there was the sense that it was right. Equality is important and equality was what was at stake, and it was the right thing to do.

There was intense homophobia. You know, homophobia was far more socially acceptable. We had journalists come down to the Teenage Group. Now we get the *Daily Mail* being pro-gay, but at that point it would have been 'these people want to corrupt your children'. We had the police taking photographs of people coming into the group, and we took photographs of the police taking photographs of us—but we didn't have any film in the cameras because we had no money! It was that scary. The women, to some extent, made the group more socially tolerable. But this group of largely young gay men were all technically criminal because we were all having sex—not necessarily with each other, but largely. The Inner London Education Authority gave the first ever grant to a gay group to the Teenage Group and they gave grant funding because they didn't actually want to run it. It was just a little too risky for them to be involved.

What happened was that we met at the Teenage Group, had another conversation with Peter and Nigel, and then an interview at Nigel's house. That was basically about my sex life, such as it was in those days, which wasn't very much but sixteen year olds probably think about it more than they actually do it! I met them and we took my mum to the upstairs bar of the Edward VI. Again, my mum has got her issues with her brain surgery, but also the old duck—you know, now I can see—didn't really get to go out very much. She'd go out two or three times a year with my dad—my dad went out a lot, but mum never did—so she got to put a nice frock on and go out and be charmed by some nice gay men in return for a signature on a bit of paper. They gave her a few Cinzanos and lemonades and that was the important bit, that was getting mum's consent. I definitely used the 'it's as bad as racism argument' and, as ever with mother, she did as she's asked, was happy to do it, but she's forgot it five minutes later. Basically: 'You want me to do it dear, I will.' She is a lovely old duck in her own way. She signed the paperwork; I was too young.

I don't think I would have understood the nature of making the complaint. What I was completely sure of was that Peter Ashman was utterly trustworthy. You know, he stayed in touch until he died and was remarkably kind. I'd get longhand letters from him. Peter, and of course Nigel, were utterly trustworthy and I put my trust in them. They're a lot smarter than me. I had no idea at all what Strasbourg was like. I knew that this was our best chance of getting some kind of change on the age of consent. I've grown up and I've done my MA and all that kind of stuff, but at that point I was sixteen and I'd left the worst school in the East End by some margins with virtually no qualifications. By the time I was seventeen I was lying about my age and working in a gay leather bar. Yes, of course, it would be nice to theoretically know what the Convention was and all of that, but for me it was enough to trust those who were brighter than me. I understood the notion of it, I understood that Strasbourg existed, and we could go there and things might change. And, if it got to the Court, I would go to Strasbourg.

Then, you know, I left school and I was getting on with work. I moved in with my late partner and there was a whole load of stuff going on. Bob, my late partner, and I were born nine days apart in June 1964 and we were, as much as anything, like twins and we had to get on. We weren't at university, we didn't have any money. We did have a flat, on the twelfth floor, just down the road from here, and it was exciting and wonderful being young and in love. Like me, Bob was that other rare thing, another working class gay Londoner. Bob knew all about the case. The paperwork was done, it was sent off, Nigel and Peter handled it, but nothing happened until the results came in.

I was working in the Cellar Bar, which was Heaven's Leather Bar, and playing with lights during the day, and there was a lot going on. The fact that the case was bubbling along in the background was significant. I knew something would happen to it eventually. I remember it was 1984 and I think it was the autumn. I got a phone call from Peter at home and I wasn't there because I was in work. And I can remember—my memory is always visual—I can remember Bob coming into Heaven, into The Cellar, and telling me that it had failed. I phoned Nigel or Peter the next day.

The Commission's decision was a politicized one. The Commission's decision was to do with the fact that it was the governments' right to make their own laws rather than the Court. My understanding of it, and I may have got a copy of the decision but if I did it's thirty years since I read it, was that it was about the powers of the Commission being subordinate to the powers of the country to make its own decisions. I wasn't aware of anything they said. It wasn't actually about anything directly to do with me, it was about the politics of how those decisions would be made. I saw it, whether it is right or not, and certainly this is how it was explained to me at the time, as to do with governments being allowed to make their own decisions, and the Commission being political appointees. The Commission stage is abolished, so that changed. If anything, the Court is probably more political now, but at least it is more transparently political because the judges are giving reasoned judgments and at the first stage there is a reasoning to it.

The Commission's decision was disappointing. But, by that stage, I had a lot of other things going on. I was certainly disappointed, but I think everyone was. I don't think there was any kind of conversation. I think I got a letter through, but we didn't have a get together to close the process. It might have been nice to have dinner with Peter and Nigel or something, but we didn't. It was just, 'Oh well, it's failed.' You know, 'It's a footnote in that particular bit of history.' It wasn't a big deal, and I had enough else going on that it didn't particularly bother me at the time. Fundamentally, as later cases proved, it was the wrong decision. It proved the principle that it could happen. All the others were able to take their cases because of the work Peter did in my case. So it wasn't pointless. It laid a foundation. And, in the end, the reason we got equality, the reason the age of consent is sixteen, is because it went to Strasbourg. I don't think any government would have willingly changed the age of consent. But, on the foundation that Peter built, others were able to go forward later.

It's so long ago, but the context it needs to be put in is the kind of emotions that teenagers have. You know, teenagers have that heightened emotional state when they fall in love when they're sixteen and seventeen. It never happens again when you are a grown up. As I say, my late partner and I met at the Teenage Group and we were born nine days apart. The fact that we were by definition criminal in the relationship we had was just appalling beyond words. That was part of the motivation for doing the case, it was part of a lot of the things we did at the time. The Commission talks about intimate acts and sex, and whatever else. The fact of the matter is, what you are really dealing with is teenagers falling in love. And it's love that was denied. Sex is very easy to talk about, sex you can commodify, but what happens when young people get together—you know, planets spontaneously combust!—is a miraculous time in your youth. And for that to be illegal is just horrible, irrespective of the genders of the people involved. That's why I did it. It's the fact that I had the good fortune to fall in love with someone almost exactly my own age, and we were criminalized.

By the time the decision came we were just in to the first stages of the HIV epidemic. Then Section 28 came along. It was a backlash. I'm wary of saying this, but actually from that came the support that made a lot of other stuff later possible. In the same way amidst the worst years of the HIV epidemic—when it felt like living through wartime and we had a sense of community—the backlash from Section 28 politicized us and made people angry and want to work for equality. You know, we had a jolly parade at Pride on Saturday—I was with Switchboard and we had a lovely day—but there is only a tiniest margin that is political. Pride just isn't a political event anymore. At this point, we had to be political because we had to get those changes made. It was still relevant, people were still being prosecuted. I was never prosecuted, but I'm fairly sure that I was watched. The fact of the matter was two boring seventeen/eighteen year old blokes in a tower block in Bow were never going to set the world on fire. You know, we weren't exactly revolutionaries. If we were watched then it wasn't terribly interesting. I think perhaps if we had been more outrageous than we were then perhaps there may have been more scandal.

Everybody who knew about the case, which was very few people really, was supportive but it wasn't hugely significant. I'm not aware of any negative reaction. Unlike the later generation, Chris Morris, Ralph Wilde, and the others, it wasn't something that was hugely public. I think that was because of the

Campaign for Homosexual Equality Law Reform Committee doing it, and then it kind of collapsing. You have to remember how big the Campaign for Homosexual Equality was in the 1970s and early 1980s. There wasn't the kind of publicity mechanism and the kind of build that Stonewall had to push the later cases. In its various inclinations and various directors, Stonewall has always had a degree of prestige and a degree of organization that the Campaign for Homosexual Equality didn't.

Peter warned me that I risked notoriety. By going to Strasbourg there was the risk that I would be notorious. It didn't happen, so it wasn't something that was ever a real issue. It happened in the sense that it got to the Commission but it faded away because the case didn't get to go to court. It didn't really have any significant impact. I've not had any significant bother from the media and, you know, I've got on with my life and the ups and downs of the last thirty-five years. The Strasbourg case I'm proud to have done and glad it happened, but it didn't actually affect me to any huge extent. I was flattered to be nominated as a Pride Hero because of it. I didn't get to have my picture on the side of a bus, but I was flattered to be nominated. I'm glad it's there. When my obituary does finally get to be written, it will be in it. It's not something I talk about very often. It's something I mention occasionally, it's not something that's a big deal.

Had we not had the opportunity of the European Convention, I don't think that we would have got equalization on the age of consent. The other laws, and how Strasbourg has affected them, I'm not so sure about, I just don't have the knowledge. But politicians wouldn't touch the age of consent if they weren't made to. Yes it took the other applicants, but Strasbourg made them do it. Maybe another twenty years on they may have looked at it, but I don't think it would have happened without it. Because there is so much prejudice around sexuality. I spend a lot of my time on the Switchboard talking about people having sex and the idea that young people might actually be having sex and therefore able to give their consent to have sex—and it's not the sort of sex that they think we're having!—is appalling to politicians. You know, Dame Jill Knight and goodness how many others. I just don't think politicians would have touched it, unless the Court made them.

I'm glad it happened. I'm glad it is my bit in the history of what has happened. You know, Jeff Dudgeon was before me. But it wasn't me; the person who deserves the credit is Peter Ashman. He was just such a remarkable, kind and intelligent man. You know, there are still going to be other battles that will be fought, but it was part of a series of attempts to get to equality. There's the argument over whether equality is the relevant criteria; you know, do you want equality or do you want liberation? But equality was what we were aiming for and eventually it was successful. It would have been different had my case not been there. I'm sure the later cases would still have got heard, because they had all the weight of the newly formed Stonewall behind them, but at least mine was there as the precedent that it was possible at least to take it.

*

Wilde, Greenhalgh and Parry v the United Kingdom (1993–1995)

In 1993, Ralph Wilde, Hugo Greenhalgh, and William Parry complained to the European Commission of Human Rights about the higher 'age of consent' for male homosexual acts that remained—more than a decade after Richard Desmond's complaint—twenty-one years. At the time they made their complaint Mr Wilde and Mr Greenhalgh were both nineteen years old, and Mr Parry, who was Mr Greenhalgh's partner, was twenty-four years old. Following the submission of their application to the Commission, and largely as a result of a campaign by Stonewall out of which the application had arisen, in 1994 the UK Parliament reduced the minimum age for male homosexual acts to eighteen years. Although differences remained across the UK in respect of the minimum ages set for opposite-sex and same-sex sexual acts, the Commission regarded the 1994 law reform to have resolved the matter complained of and, as a consequence, decided in 1995 to strike the application out of its list of cases.

Ralph Wilde

I was born in Stockport and I grew up in the 1970s and 80s, one of 'Thatcher's Children'. Like many people of my age at that time, I didn't have any adolescence in terms of relationships. The law obviously denied that. That was the time when the age of consent for gay male sex was twenty-one. I saw my heterosexual peers having girlfriends and boyfriends and the usual experiences. I really didn't have that. Arrested development was, I suppose, what I had in common with many other LGBT people.

I would get picked on at school—the usual kind of low-level bullying and occasional mild violence—and there was a particular incident where I was identified as being gay by the local bullies and I was queer-bashed in the local town. It wasn't life threatening—it was just the usual being slapped around—and I was left with a blooded nose and went to A&E. The police were involved and I remember them saying, 'Well, why did this happen, why did they do this to you?' I had asked A&E to get the police but I then realized that I was potentially in a vulnerable situation if I told them the reason. I thought, maybe, I would end up being somehow investigated because, obviously, they might say, 'Well, are you gay?' That might—given that gay sex involving someone of my age was a criminal offence—have put me at risk of some sort of investigation. It stopped me, in that particular instance, of being able to come out and tell the police that I was gay and, therefore, get their protection. I think they probably figured out what was going on and maybe they wouldn't have done anything. But when you're seventeen and vulnerable, when you're not out, you worry. So that was really an illustration of a broader problem and a broader vulnerability that I felt I was subject to because of the existence of that law. It had a chilling effect. I was never prosecuted or anything like that; it was more the negative effect on how I lived my life. The symbolism of it makes you fear what might happen, separately from anything that does happen.

I went to London when I was nineteen to start a degree and in that first autumn term I went to the now defunct London Lesbian and Gay Centre. It had the free LGB newspapers that existed then and in *Capital Gay* there was an article saying that Stonewall were looking for somebody to bring a case to challenge the age of consent. Being an idealistic person who, in a fairly simplistic, naïve way, was politically engaged, wanting to get involved in politics and wanting to change the world, I thought the case would be a chance to do this. Then I thought, well, if I do that, I will have to come out. At that stage I wasn't out to anyone—not my family, not everyone I'd grown up with—apart from a few friends I'd told. I wasn't so naïve as not to realize that to do something like that would mean coming out in a big fashion to everyone, because it would be in the news and in the newspapers and it would mean it would be on the record going forward as well. So it would be a point of no return in terms of coming out. It was bound up in that broader coming out process.

It was like a leap in the dark. You really have to just go for it. There was a period when I decided to do it and I'd tell a few people and they would say, 'This is a mistake, it will harm your career, you're studying international politics, you might become a lawyer, you might become a politician, you're jeopardizing all of that and, when the campaign is over, you'll be left with the stigma.' At that stage, in the early 1990s, there were very few people who were out in public life. I think Chris Smith was just out at that stage and was the only out politician. In public life, in the media, in television, very few people were out. Basically, there was Ian McKellen, Michael Cashman and Jimmy Somerville. I didn't really have any role models, apart from those people, indicating that I could pull off being a public figure that wasn't negatively affected. Whereas, there were lots of negative examples, lots of examples of sex-scandals involving Tory MPs, lots of shame and scandals associated with being gay. There was no anti-discrimination legislation in employment at that time; you could be sacked for being gay or not employed in the first place. I was also directly drawing attention to the fact that I was breaking the criminal law.

All of that was very much in my mind and I was choosing to expose myself to that risk. The stuff that I was risking was what I wanted to change through the campaign. The two things were bound up together. So facing up to what I would expose myself to reinforced the injustice of the issue that I was trying to challenge. The more I saw what I was risking, the more I saw the value of what I was doing. It really showed up, in sharp focus, how wrong things were. But the funny thing is, I think I just had that sort of nerve that you have when you are young and idealistic and have a willingness to take a risk. I don't want to take credit for that. People say, 'Oh, you were so brave and courageous.' I think I was just wanting the adventure of doing something that was a step into the unknown. And, in hindsight, none of these awful things happened. But I didn't know that at the time.

In terms of the application to Strasbourg, the way it worked was that Angela Mason, who was the head of Stonewall—which was very much a shoestring operation and not the kind of slick operation it is today—enlisted the help of Peter Duffy, who was a barrister, one of the leading experts at that time in European human rights law, and Peter agreed to do the case *pro bono*. The case was prepared by Angela and Peter and they interviewed me for the purposes of the submission. I think they did the best that they could do to make the case. When I read the application, I'm quite struck by all the personal information that has to go in. In a way, the older I've got and the person I've become, I'm quite struck by how willing I was, and needed to be, to have very personal things put out there on the record like that. I mean, I don't mind it, I don't regret it for a second—quite the reverse, I feel incredibly privileged to have had that experience and to have been able to play a small part in something I believe in—but it does make you realize, looking now more dispassionately, what applicants in those cases have to do in terms of revealing personal, intimate information of a sensitive nature.

I certainly didn't know anything about Strasbourg before the campaign. I didn't know much about Strasbourg for a lot of the campaign other than that it was a court that I could go to that was supranational and was somehow at a different level to the UK legal system. I think I got the thing that it wasn't the European Union but I don't think I understood what international and European human rights law was. What was significant, politically, was the way that it was quite a powerful thing to say, 'I am suing my own government.' Rhetorically and politically, to speak at a rally as a nineteen year old and say, 'I am bringing a legal action against the United Kingdom', was a very empowering thing to declare. A lot of people were taken aback when I would say that. There's something empowering about that, for the applicant. It changes the dynamic—especially when you are trying to challenge something which is a source of humiliation and disempowerment, of shame and scandal—and has a transformatory effect. It does give you a sort of confidence and standing. It makes people pay attention.

It seems funny now, but when we started we thought nobody was going to take much notice. This was the very beginning of Stonewall's existence; it was Stonewall's first ever campaign. We thought we'll start this, but the political campaign or the legal case are unlikely to go very far. We thought it was an arguable case, but the view was taken that we would be pushing the envelope because the other cases at that stage at Strasbourg—Dudgeon and Norris—were about absolute prohibition, whereas this was about a differential in the age of consent. The nature of the complaint was not about a particular incident but about the mere existence of the law. Most people wouldn't even know that that itself is a violation that would be actionable. That was the idea that was established in the gay cases and it was still fairly early in the development of that idea, within human rights law, that the mere existence of discriminatory legislation would be sufficient to make you a victim for the purposes of bringing a case. I wouldn't have known that and I think many lawyers didn't know that.

Another aspect of the case is that it was the three of us. The legal submissions themselves addressed different aspects of the law. With me it was about how the existence of law prevented me from having relationships and prevented me from getting protection from the police at that time. Whereas with Hugo and Will, the existence of the law was about their actual relationship they were having and the effect of it on that. You could only identify those different aspects with more than one person because, by definition, you can't deal with someone who is in a relationship and someone who isn't through the same person. In some ways it reduced the pressure, because we could each deal with different aspects of the issues. That suited me personally, because I was dealing with things at a more abstract level. I was talking about what I couldn't do, whereas they were talking about it in the context of their actual relationship. I think that's an interesting aspect of collective action that is not just about a single applicant.

Doing the case actually meant being a sort of figurehead, with Hugo and Will, for a broader campaign. In many ways, the case was a marginal part of the campaign, which was doing interviews on television, in newspapers, giving speeches in various places—in Parliament and Trafalgar Square, in town halls up and down the country, in universities and public events—and the campaign for a vote in Parliament, that was led by Edwina Currie, which involved lots of meetings with Members of Parliament in the Commons and in the Lords to lobby them. That was just as significant and it was an interesting example of a full spectrum initiative to change the law, where the Strasbourg case is one element in a broader initiative. The case had its place. It wasn't everything, and it's a good example of how you can use this kind of legal strategy alongside other strategies and that they can be complementary and mutually reinforcing.

The law ultimately changed through Parliament's vote rather than because of a Strasbourg decision, because we got the vote before we got the decision. We started the case and campaign in 1992 and by the time we got to the vote, which was 1994, there'd been some kind of informal communication from the Commission to the government indicating the direction of travel, in terms of where things might go, and suggesting there was quite a strong case. So we were able to mention that in the campaign and in Parliament and, of course, the government knew that too. It would be an interesting question to ask the government whether this influenced John Major's decision to allow the time for a free vote. Certainly, on our side, we were using that argument and I think it did influence things. We were saying that we should put our own house in order domestically, rather that having the humiliation of an imposed decision from Strasbourg.

The campaign and case made me face up to all of those issues that we all have about being gay and to think about them and deal with them in a very intensive and reflective fashion, because I was talking about it the whole time. It made me deal with all those things in a particular fashion that I wouldn't have done otherwise. It was a very efficient way—a sort of therapy session—to face up to everything that you spend your teenage years having problems with and transform that into something you're not ashamed of and, moreover, are going to fight for. I think that is incredibly empowering and it gave me a sort of confidence to do other things, afterwards. It's partly a class thing—I'm from a working class family and I'm the first member of family to stay at school after the age of sixteen—and I think it helped with that too. When you do something like that and it's a risk, when you draw attention to the greatest source of shame and vulnerability in your life and it ends up not being a disaster but ends up working out really well, I think that can give you a kind of confidence that transfers over to other things. I think that has stayed with me.

It has influenced my work because I went into international law, including international human rights law, and as a scholar I'm now a lot more critical of the law and its values than I was then. I'm very much aware of its limitations and its dark side and how the law can be as much part of the problem as the solution. Of course, that was the case then, because we were using one area of law to challenge another area of law. That was the lesson of the campaign. I work with a lot of people who are very radical, critical scholars of international and human rights law, who have no time for human rights law and see it as part of the problem, not the solution. I'm always aware of my own personal experience and how useful the law was. I know what I'm talking about on this subject and—although I never play that card whenever I'm discussing things and writing about it—it is in the back of my mind. I am aware of the continued value, for better or worse, of using the language of human rights in general and human rights law in particular, and how helpful it can be for people in the real world, who are facing human rights problems, as a way of articulating their claims and needs. That is an obvious rebuttal to the absolutist critique that would do away with all international human rights law and would trash it. Whereas other scholars in my field acknowledge that on an intellectual level, I actually know on a personal level why it's significant. I continue to make the argument in my writing that we shouldn't throw the baby out with the bathwater and we should appreciate the emancipatory potential of human rights law. That is a link, genuinely, between what I write about now and my experience.

I do think that everything worked out really well but I have to say, being honest, that it was a bit of a risk to put a nineteen year old through that. I think maybe Angela Mason and Ian McKellen just thought, 'Oh gosh, he seems very confident and mature beyond his years and he'll be fine.' Maybe that was the case, but it was a bit of a risk. I'm wondering if I were in their position—and I don't want to criticize them—whether I would worry about putting someone in that position. But, of course, I was the first person to say to people older than me, 'How dare you tell me how to live my life', so I can't really have it both ways. And the campaign was all about the ways in which nineteen year olds are in a position to make decisions about their lives. But the one thing that these cases raise—because, by definition, they're all about the age of consent—is the ethics of getting young people involved in something that is going to define their lives and how you protect them. I didn't initiate the case; I didn't go to them and ask them to support me. They were looking for someone and I volunteered. So I was the sort of set-up person; set-up by them as part of their campaign. I was totally willing for that to happen, but nonetheless it's different to me having some problem that led me to want to initiate a complaint. There was no particular reason why I needed to do this. I was in no better or worse position than any other nineteen year old. I have to say, I felt very much protected by Angela Mason and Ian McKellen, by the broader Stonewall family of supporters, and by politicians. Edwina Currie was incredibly kind and supportive to me.

Hugo Greenhalgh

I lived in Edinburgh and was a student up there studying English literature. I was nineteen at that time and Will had just graduated from Edinburgh University. He'd stayed on after graduation to finish-up a couple of things and I met him at an audition for a play. Will and I were out one night at a local fairground, just walking home across the Meadows, and a couple of kids bounced out and started hitting us with inflatable plastic hammers. We thought nothing of it but then a whole bunch more kids came and joined them and started beating us up whilst screaming 'faggot' and 'fairy' and stuff like that. So it wasn't anything other than a homophobic attack. We went to the local hospital but I'm not sure we reported it to the police, which is a bit weird actually considering that we were politically minded at that stage.

I'd been involved in student activism for quite a number of years. I was the Sixth Form Gay and Lesbian Officer at my college when I was seventeen—I think one of only two in the country at that point. When I went to university I joined the local gay society and became more active. I'd seen an advert put in a paper by Stonewall who were looking for people to bring a test case on the age of consent and said to Will, this is something I deeply believe in and, considering that our relationship is not technically illegal, it is actually illegal, let's see if we can change things. So we approached Stonewall on that basis and they chose us along with Ralph Wilde. Initial conversations with Stonewall were tentative on both sides, certainly from our perspective. One thing I was quite keen to establish early on was that we weren't just going to be figureheads; we were going to be actively involved in the campaign at a grass roots level as well as popping up on tele. I was very straightforward from the outset that I wanted to be fundamentally involved in the policy elements of the campaign and also how the campaign was organized in terms of which areas and people we were targeting. I wanted to absolutely ensure that we weren't just publicity puppets to oil the machine and gain greater awareness of the issues. Publicity was important—we understood that—and was part of what we were getting into. But, certainly from my own perspective, having been a student activist, I was very keen to focus on the activism side of things and target the policies we wanted to change.

Were Stonewall receptive to us not just being figureheads, to taking an active role? Yes-ish. The relationship with Stonewall was extremely good most of the time and fraught at certain times. The last thing they wanted was to put up with a bolshie teenager, and that's absolutely understandable. You know, you're there to work on the campaign, to do what effectively became a full time job. But, at the same time, the whole point of me being part of the campaign and being involved in activism was because I was an angry teenager and I wanted to change things. So being that person, I was absolutely certain that we were going to do that within the Stonewall campaign but also through other means as well. Will and I went to a lot of Outrage! meetings during that time and took part in quite a few Outrage! demonstrations. Back in the 1990s there was quite a divide between the Outrage! form of activism and Stonewall's softly-softly parliamentary route and the two, not necessarily fought, but at times were opposed to each other in the ways and means to achieve equality. We were absolutely sure that we weren't being partisan about our particular brand of politics.

As part of the Stonewall campaign we were taking part in a publicity shoot for *Boyz* magazine, for the cover of their Pride edition, and a policeman approached us and tried to convince us to stop snogging on Parliament Green and said that if we didn't we would be arrested. That was our first brush with the law. More seriously,

I was appearing on a radio show called *Bus Stop*, and two of the other guests were Dr. Adrian Rogers—an extremely right-wing character and quite a well-known polemicist and provocateur in Exeter—and a very senior policeman from the Devon and Cornwall Constabulary. I admitted quite happily and openly that I was having a relationship with Will, that I was nineteen and he was twenty-four, that yes we were breaking the law, and Dr. Rogers leant forward and said to the policeman, 'Hugo has just admitted to a crime, will you arrest him?' The poor policeman, stuck between a strict interpretation of the law and society's determination to change that law, ummed and ahhed, sat on his hands, and basically dodged the question. Subsequent to that, Dr. Rogers tried to bring a private prosecution against us and that's when the police got officially involved.

We were called to be interviewed—I don't think it was under caution—at a police station in London. We were advised by Stonewall's lawyer to say 'no comment' but Will, the brave one out of both of us—because, in terms of what would have happened if they went through with the prosecution and it came to trial and we were convicted, Will would have faced the much harsher penalty and more likely a jail sentence—admitted to the police that we were in a sexual relationship. Will, extremely bravely, said, 'Well look, we've gone this far, we've achieved so much, it seems ridiculous to back down at this stage and deny it, and if we're going to change the law then this is going to be part of it.' So all credit to Will at that stage; very brave.

Going to Strasbourg was always part of the plan. The initial idea came from Stonewall; they were the absolute originators of the move to bring a test case. So we were scooped up to represent the campaign and to be involved in it. But the prime motivation, the prime driver, was Stonewall from the beginning. Was I involved in making the submission to Strasbourg? Very little, actually. I mean, our job was to make the arguments in the press and the media. Behind the scenes, our lawyers were representing us to Strasbourg. But, absolutely, I did have an understanding of the complaint and the European Convention on Human Rights. I forget which particular Articles it was now, but we were very much aware of the reasons behind it, but also the legal rationale as well.

Conceptually, at the time, the European Court of Human Rights seemed to offer a future model of democracy and freedom where rights were recognized and equality was enshrined. For me, as a rather idealistic nineteen year old, it did seem to offer a very striking and shining example of where Britain should be in 1993. Unlike today, when it certainly gets a bad press, I still think the European Convention on Human Rights is a fantastic and very valuable part of our legal tenets and also of how society is structured as well. Back in the 1990s, Britain was very, very different to what it's like nowadays. The one thing that the Blair government did from 1997 onwards was to civilize the UK. The Blair government absolutely—through various changes to laws governing sexuality, but also in terms of how people in society really recognized and treated each other—changed the nature of society. Back in 1993 we were still riven by class factions, hatred of minorities, and violence towards immigrants—well, I guess that hasn't much changed—and it was absolutely a fractured society. It was very common to suffer homophobic abuse in the street; it was very common to experience racism amongst your friends. I think Europe offered a beacon of hope to what was still, at that point, a very backwards-looking society.

If there hadn't been the overriding—to be perfectly blunt—threat of legal stricture that the European Court could impose, then the British government would probably have just ignored the age of consent campaign. There was a growing mood for change but that change would not have been realized until Tony Blair came into power in 1997. I really want to stress—I know Blair gets a hugely bad press nowadays and has an appalling reputation after the Iraq war—that he wholly, one hundred percent, believed in equal rights. Not just in gay rights, but in equal rights. He was absolutely behind the age of consent campaign, absolutely behind the campaign for gay marriage, absolutely behind the campaign for gays in the military. He was a fundamental democrat who believed that everybody's born equal and should be treated equally. So a change in the age of consent would have happened eventually, but not under Thatcher or Major because the Conservatives didn't have the will to effect change. If it hadn't been for the European Court of Human Rights, yes, we would have achieved equality but it would have probably been a decade later.

We would have won the case in Strasbourg. The noises we were getting through our lawyer, about the feeling in Europe, were that it was a no-brainer. Absolutely, it would have been pushed through. Society was on the cusp of change, not just in the UK but across Europe as well. There was the rise of gay rights activism on a national and international level. The issue of gay rights, which of course had been going on for decades, became more an issue of human rights. It got on the agenda at the United Nations and across Europe as well. We witnessed the morphing of gay rights and human rights and I think, at that stage, although we were far, far ahead of public opinion, on a policy or parliamentarian level, we were almost there. So that's why we thought the European Court would almost certainly rule in our favour.

The British government had to act at some stage before Europe effectively told them to. The pressure that was applied through the European Court of Human Rights was effective and necessary. That leverage, that threat—a very loaded, *Daily Mail* word to use but, in this context, quite a useful one—of having the European Court of Human Rights ruling against the UK nudged it in the direction of change. Not as quickly as it should have done; certainly when the age of consent went down to eighteen, rather than sixteen, that was a huge disappointment and a huge failure, not just of the campaign but of our lobbying effort to convince people and parliamentarians on a policy level and on an emotional and personal level. But without the European Court of Human Rights in the background, the conversation wouldn't have started.

I want to stress that the European Court of Human Rights represented hope for us. It represented a future that we could push our country to achieving. We wanted to change society, to change people's opinions, and to achieve equality. The campaign contributed to the fairer society in which we live today, to a greater understanding of difference, and a greater compassion for people being different and yet equal at the same time. You can draw parallels with the shifting nature of public sentiment towards difference, towards minorities, and the rise of interest in the transsexual issue at the moment. It hasn't been with the level of vitriol that there was back in the 1980s or early 1990s towards homosexuality. The reaction has been more a curiosity, with interest, with a sense of fairness, and understanding and compassion. I think there has been a progression towards this and certainly the European Court of Human Rights—which seemed this amazing, wonderful, shiny, beacon of equality and modernity—really did help us achieve a fairer society in 2015.

In material terms, did the case affect me negatively in any way, has it held me back in my career, has it boosted my career, has it helped in terms of gaining a public profile at quite an early age? I'm not sure. I was quite loath to use the platform that I'd gained to get a job or to put myself out there. I wanted to become a journalist at that stage and it's a slight regret now that I didn't use it as much as I could have done back then; I think I was just too proud and also a bit too embarrassed. The one thing I will say is that, throughout the campaign, I found the level of attention and publicity extremely uncomfortable. You'd go into a local bar and people would recognize you and would come up and say, 'Well done, keep going.' That's great, but that level of recognition I really just loathed. It's bizarre because you look at the reality TV stars nowadays and that's probably what we were back in the day, in terms of always popping up on tele. But I absolutely found that level of attention really, really uncomfortable and I was loath to use the publicity factor to generate more. It's helped me in terms of my career as a journalist because people still remember me from the campaign even twenty years later. So it has opened doors in that sense, but I wouldn't say that I've ever used it as much as I could have or should have done. But my intention was never to get famous or get a job; it was simply to become an activist and continue to be an activist.

In terms of personal and emotional impact, I can't really say not at all, but it didn't strike me as doing anything strange or weird. It just struck me as being perfectly normal. This is what one does, one fights for equality; this is an extension of who I am in the normal course of things. So it didn't really feel that I was doing anything particularly special, or amazing, or brilliant, or terrifying, or exciting. It was just a case of getting on with it and treating it as a job. I was at university at the time and it had a massive effect on my university life. In my third year of a four-year course, I pretty much missed the year because I was bombing about the country. But the university were very good and they let me do my third year in my fourth year, so I did the two years in one go. It could have had a negative effect in terms of my university career, but it was never going to. It was always part of—going back to being a teenage activist—what I wanted to do.

It was a remarkable part of my life and certainly a part of my life I look back on with immense pride. Immense pride both in having done it, but also in having the privilege of working alongside people like Will and Ralph, and Euan Sutherland and Chris Morris as well—really brave characters. Ralph and I were both doing well—two middle class kids at good universities—and Will had graduated. But for Euan and Chris, who were sixteen and seventeen, it really could have ruined absolutely everything. If you're looking for bravery and the impact that this had on people's lives, then I think it is Euan and Chris that it would have impacted on far more than the rest of us. We were on our way, as it were, and this wasn't a distraction or a detour, but was part of what we were doing in our lives anyway. This was part of our attempt to live normal lives.

Will Parry

At the time Hugo and I met I'd graduated from Edinburgh University, worked abroad in Zimbabwe for a few months, returned to Edinburgh and, eventually, come back down to London to try and get things off the ground career wise. Hugo would come down from Edinburgh to London during the university holidays and spend lots of time with me. There was one holiday that Hugo was down when I saw an article in a now long-defunct gay newspaper called *Capital Gay*. It had a silhouette of a head and it said that Stonewall was looking for a young gay man to take the government to the European Court of Human Rights over the gay age of consent. Because I was over the age of consent I never, for one moment, thought that I would get involved in this as anything other than a volunteer, helping out the campaign by stuffing envelopes and things like that. As a couple, we'd been on several demonstrations and actions before. I vividly remember standing in front of the altar at Westminster Cathedral during Sunday Mass with Peter Tatchell and Outrage!, holding up banners reading 'Homophobia Kills'.

We went to the Stonewall office to chat—I went along with Hugo just to find out how I could volunteer—and we were interviewed together. I subsequently found out that they had been looking for a couple to take the case but they hadn't found one. I didn't know they were interviewing us with that in mind and, had I known, I would have been incredibly shy and nervous and would have stuttered and stammered all over the place. At that stage, I had no experience of public speaking and was very shy. Maybe a month or six weeks later, I got a call from Stonewall, saying that they wanted to take us as a couple. Hugo was up in Edinburgh but I called him and said that this was what they wanted. I was extremely shocked but it was something that I felt incredibly happy about.

I had grown up, as many if not most men and women of that era had, in default homophobia. Being gay was something you were not expected to be. I had been sent to boarding school—I was packed away at the age of eight until eighteen—and at no point during my education, either from my family or from schooling, or from popular culture, was there any kind of positive messages that said it was OK to be gay. It was the period of Clause 28, of HIV, so there was an awful lot of negative publicity and inference about being gay and almost nothing that was positive. I had just turned twenty-one when I first kissed anybody. It happened to be a boy and I defined myself as bisexual for a while, had a girlfriend for six months, and finally realized that I was gay. I felt that I was really only beginning to have, in my early twenties, those sexual experiences that I should have had in adolescence and I was quite bitter about that in many ways. And I was insecure and nervous as I explored that world and emotionally settled into my sexuality. My motivation for getting involved with the case was that I wanted young gay men to see an image of a happy gay couple; to see a different image that the majority of the media were putting forward at the time. At that period, even to see a gay couple in bed together, whether or not they were having sex or kissing, was almost beyond the pale and made the front page of the *Daily Mail* every time it happened. So that was a prime motivation, to try and ensure that young gay men and women didn't face the same level of prejudice and ignorance that I had.

When we spoke to Stonewall, prior to taking the case, we were assured that, because it was a test case, there wasn't a risk of prosecution. I remember that Stonewall said, 'Look, we can talk to your parents, your families, to reassure them of this.' We went ahead with it but then encountered Adrian Rogers—who was Director of The Conservative Family Institute, based in Hugo's home town of Exeter—who called for our arrest live on radio and then said, 'I'm going to write to the Director of Public Prosecutions', which he duly did. So we were then facing a real risk that we could be prosecuted. We voluntarily agreed to attend a meeting with the police, and prior to that we met with Angela Mason and Stonewall's solicitor in their office. We were interviewed by a couple of policeman at a now defunct police station in Victoria. The solicitor had told us not to admit that we were having a sexual relationship. He said something along the lines of, 'Say you have a loving and consensual, loving and caring relationship but just say "no comment" if you're asked is it sexual.' We went into the police station and I was asked to wait in one of those old Victorian cells while they interviewed Hugo—which was slightly sobering, although it wasn't locked—and then I went in with Angela Mason and the solicitor.

Perhaps it was the folly of idealistic youth, but I just thought this is absolutely pointless; the whole point of our court case is that we are in a relationship, we are having sex, our sex is criminalized, and we believe this is wrong. So I said to the policemen, 'Yes we have a loving and consensual relationship' but then, very deliberately, I added 'and it is sexual.' I'm sure Angela Mason and the solicitor were just inwardly groaning. There was a part of me, because I was making a video diary for Channel 4, that was thinking that any trial would be a great scene for the film! That was such a stupid and naïve thing to think. I had no idea really that, if we had gone to court, if we had been prosecuted, if we had been found guilty—which we almost certainly would have done because we'd admitted it—then we would be sex offenders, could have gone to prison and, because I would have been convicted for having sex with an underage partner, I would have been classed as a paedophile. Fortunately, the Crown Prosecution Service decided prosecuting us wasn't in the public interest. I don't want to be too harsh on Stonewall, because I think they considered it so unlikely it hadn't been a priority to think about, but perhaps a little more thought should have been given to it. I think perhaps Stonewall could have factored it into their consideration of the factors that could have arisen during the court case because, ultimately, had it gone wrong it would have seriously damaged the lives of Hugo and I. In many respects, we dodged a bullet. I think if I had been more aware of the risks that we did face I wouldn't have been flippantly naïve when being interviewed by the police. That said, I'm pleased that I did what I did.

My mum was pretty old school. She was forty-five when she had me and had lived through the war in Norway. She was a very kind person, she knew gay people in the 1950s, but her attitude to homosexuality was very much that you kept it to yourself. She didn't want one of her children to be gay; she was very worried about social opprobrium and social distaste. She was concerned that I would never find somebody, that it was a life of loneliness, all of those 1950s clichés. One thing that made her very unhappy was the fact that we were making a fuss about it, were going on TV, were standing up in front of everybody and saying this law is wrong and we want to change it. I remember one incident when I had gone back to hers for Sunday lunch and suddenly, out of the blue, she said, 'I don't know why you're doing this, it's so embarrassing for me, you're making such a fuss about this, and I just don't understand, why are you doing it?' I tried to draw the closest analogy that I could, based on her experience of growing up as a teenager in Norway during the Nazi occupation. Many members of her family had been in the resistance and, although she wasn't in the resistance herself, she did occasionally run messages between certain cells in the resistance and her brother was arrested and put in a forced labour camp. So she did things that were far, far more significant and braver than anything around the age of consent campaign. I said to her, 'Look, I'm not in any way trying to draw a comparison between the Nazi occupation of Norway and the anti-gay laws in Britain today.' I said, 'There is no moral comparison whatsoever so before I say what I'm going to say I'll just make that point. However, when you were young, you fought against something you thought was wrong and for something you believed in and, now I'm young, I'm doing a similar thing in very different circumstances.' She just shut the conversation down and said, 'There is no comparison whatsoever.' So we had this slightly awkward thirty-second silence and then she started talking about the weather. She never really wanted to know about the case; even years later, she never wanted to know the details of it.

In terms of preparing the submission to Strasbourg we were interviewed in the Stonewall offices with the lawyers present and were asked about the discrimination that we faced, our motivations for taking the case, and how our relationship was affected, and this was translated into the complaint. Obviously there are very strict rules—applying to Strasbourg is a process—and the lawyers know how to do it. We weren't going to sit there writing it ourselves. It was done on our behalf, basically. We definitely had a sense of the European Convention on Human Rights and a sense that the reason we were taking the case to Europe was because, at that stage, the Convention hadn't been incorporated into British law. There had been a number of attempts to address the age of consent through the British legislative process but they'd all failed. So Strasbourg was the final port of call. We certainly had an understanding of the contents of the Convention as a result of talking to Stonewall. I think I'd be lying if I said we had a sense of it when we first turned up at the Stonewall office. However, we spoke, we talked a lot, about the right to privacy, and the right to equality. I think what is important to remember is that, whilst we were the figureheads of the case, the case had been planned by Stonewall. They advertised for people that they thought would be most suitable to get their case across and win both legally and in the court of public opinion.

The court case was part of a wider campaign by Stonewall to bring the issue into public discussion and to highlight the inequity of the issue. It seems nonsensical now and so outdated but so many of the arguments against change revolved around younger boys: boys matured later than girls; younger boys couldn't make up their mind; they needed to be protected. When you listen to the debate in Parliament, which resulted in the age of consent being reduced to the compromised measure of eighteen, you still hear all of those arguments being trotted out. There was a real sense, at that stage, of Europe being a force for good. In the dying days of the Conservative government, there were so many ways in which the government seemed out of touch and the only way that you could actually achieve some sort of recourse was to go to Europe. You went there when all the options had been exhausted here and certainly all options had been exhausted. I think we would have won if the case had gone to the European Court of Human Rights because Britain was in the minority in terms of not having an equal age of consent. Austria and Ireland didn't have one but Ireland actually changed during our case. Even Russia had repealed Article 121 of its criminal code so, purely in terms of what was on the statute books, Britain was a more homophobic state than Russia. The ultimate goal was to try and address the issue through the legislative system because, if for no other reason, complaints to Strasbourg take so long. The Strasbourg case was used as a tool to pressure the government and say, 'Look, you are going to lose in Strasbourg, far better to address this through the domestic legislative process and avoid embarrassment.'

It's something that I'm very proud to have done. I'm very proud that Hugo and I went along that day to Stonewall. Had we not done so, I don't know exactly where my life would be today. It certainly made me, in the broadest sense, very aware of the power of standing up for what you believe in, not being shy about articulating what you believe in, not underestimating what an individual can achieve, and how a well targeted campaign can raise awareness of issues and get things changed. I now work as a TV producer and the first job that I ever did came about because I wrote to Channel 4 and said, 'How about a video diary following this campaign?' Had it not been for that, I doubt that I would be working in TV. It gave me a lot of self-confidence that I didn't have before. It has also given me a real understanding of the importance of incorporating the European Convention on Human Rights into British law. I read, with absolute horror, that the current Conservative government wishes to undo that. I think it is a completely retrograde step. It was one of the best things the Blair administration did and I wouldn't want Britain to undo that and take a step backwards. I think everybody has to be vigilant about human rights because it's very, very easy, as we've seen, tragically in far too many places around the world, for human rights to be ignored. Having human rights codified in something like the European Convention on Human Rights is incredibly important and we dismiss and ridicule—as seems to be fashionable at the moment—institutions like the European Court of Human Rights at our peril.

We are in an incredibly fortunate position now in Britain. The legal and social context around gay rights has changed beyond all measure and we've pretty much got all we want. Of course, there are still issues around bullying and things aren't perfect, but if you had told me in 1993 that there would be gay marriage in Britain, and that you would see tabloid news stories that talked about gay couples in the same way as straight couples, I wouldn't have believed it. Things can change very quickly. That is one lesson to take away from the case. I think it's a positive lesson, I think it's a lesson that hopefully can give some encouragement to people in Uganda or Russia or wherever they are. I wouldn't say that people in Uganda are in the same situation that we were; Britain in 1993 was immeasurably better than what people in Uganda are facing. I would be immensely in awe of anyone in Uganda who challenged the law and say they were astonishingly brave; far, far braver than Hugo, Ralph or I, because we did not face the same level of legal sanction and opprobrium. One thing we always talked about—as gay rights activists had for many years—is the importance of coming out. Once you have a family member or friend who is out, suddenly it becomes much harder to demonize homosexuals because they're a real person. Obviously, the entrenched cultural homophobia that exists in somewhere like Uganda today is far more intense than existed in Britain in 1993, but I think the principle still holds true. I do think it is always worth standing up for what you believe and there are people in Uganda and Russia and in many places around the world who are doing that. They are putting their lives on the line, literally their lives on the line. They are astonishingly brave people who deserve all the support that we can give.

*

Sutherland v the United Kingdom (1994–2001)

In 1994, seventeen-year-old Euan Sutherland complained to the European Commission of Human Rights about the existence of law that maintained the 'age of consent' for male homosexual acts at eighteen years, which was higher than the minimum age set for most opposite-sex and female same-sex sexual acts. In 1997, the Commission expressed the opinion that Mr Sutherland's application disclosed discriminatory treatment in the exercise of his right to respect for his private life. As a consequence, in 2000 the UK Parliament—by way of a contentious legislative process that required the use of the Parliament Acts—'equalized' the minimum age for same-sex and opposite-sex sexual acts. In light of this, in 2001 the European Court of Human Rights decided to strike Mr Sutherland's application out of its list of cases.

Euan Sutherland

I was born and brought up in southeast London in a very nice, stable, supportive family. In many ways, it was a very conventional background: my mother's a nurse; my dad was working in state-education. Me and my brother went to private schools, just because of what the schools in our local area were like. As a schoolboy, I don't think I was going to be very happy anywhere. I didn't feel that I was fitting in. It was the very usual gay adolescence: I felt no one understands me, I'm special, I don't know what's going on, or I do know what's going on and I don't really want to face up to that. Then I kind of erupted from the closet quite spectacularly, with a lot of support from family. So I had a very good, solid family foundation, as well as all of the usual imbalance of teenage, emerging sexuality: not fear and loathing of one's self, but a lack of confidence and fumbling around towards whatever I wanted. I wasn't quite sure what it was that I was wanting at the time.

I found myself with the opportunity to be involved with the Stonewall age of consent campaign quite accidently by reading a copy of *Gay Times* magazine, which was talking about the chance that Edwina Currie would get a backbench amendment. It asked people to go to see their MPs and talk to them in their surgeries about what they would do if a vote came up. So I did. My MP was Tessa Jowell and she said that, in principle, if a free vote happened, she would vote in favour of an equal age of consent. A week or two later, I phoned Stonewall and the person who answered took the details of which MP I was phoning about. They offered for me to go on to the mailing list, but I didn't fit into their age brackets. It was their press officer who had picked up the phone—it wasn't a big operation at the time—and he took the opportunity to ask me lots of questions, but I wasn't quite sure why. They were looking for someone who would be able to rebut many of the worries, or many of the images, or clichés, that the press had at the time. They couldn't find any relatively normal sixteen or seventeen year olds who would be happy to have some sort of media involvement. They wanted someone that was going to be PR friendly. They kind of roped me in. Not roped me in; I was interested in meeting up with them. And I was always asked, 'Do you want to participate, are you happy to continue and go further with this?', so I never felt railroaded or pressured.

That was the autumn of 1993. I had left secondary school after my first term of A-levels. I was working part-time, faffing around, with a plan to go to college the following year. The press officer invited me up to Stonewall's office at Greycoat Place—it was grotty—and I got introduced to Angela Mason, who was Chief Executive—a very intelligent, sensible woman—and then I got introduced to Ian McKellen. I think the first thing we did was to go off and meet Neil Kinnock in Westminster. It was very interesting, there were some exciting opportunities, and it was kind of slightly bizarre. The campaign was very much about adding weight, adding momentum, to the case that we were hoping that Edwina Currie would make in Parliament. It was about building a public relations campaign to allay fears. I remember some of the backbench MPs: the right wing, crusty majors; the ladies with awful hair and Victorian attitudes towards sex and sexuality. There was very much a need to counter each and every one of their arguments and to create an environment in which Edwina Currie's amendment would be able to breathe, be debated fairly and given a fair chance.

At the time of the vote, I was up in the gallery, in the House of Commons, and I was quite upset. Someone from Stonewall put his arm around me, and one of the ushers came over and said, 'You can't touch each other, that would offend the MPs.' Absolutely awful! A couple of days after the vote, there was an opportunity to sit down and discuss tactical planning with Stonewall about what to do next. Obviously, I'd met Hugo Greenhalgh, Will Parry, and Ralph Wilde, and, with the change in British law that would be coming through with an age of consent of eighteen, it was thought that the cases that they had already lodged in Strasbourg could do with some reinforcement, because they had lodged their case whilst they were over the age of eighteen. It was thought that it would add real weight to the body of work going forwards with the European Court to have another case with somebody who was under the age of eighteen at the time.

With family support, the case was very much an obvious thing to say yes to. I was still living under my parents' roof and they had been kind and supportive enough to partake in television, radio and newspaper interviews in the build up to the Parliamentary vote. So there was a family stake in it; it wasn't just my decision to make, because it would involve more scrutiny for longer. I think my parents were aware that all the attention had not been balanced, fair and reasonable. There had been some letters to the home, not all the press was supportive, and not all commentators in debates and media had been supportive. So, they wanted it to be a well thought through decision. But it really was left up to me to make the final decision, and it was something I was very happy to continue with.

My overriding motivation was simple fairness. For no logical reason, that I could identify, there was a discrepancy with the law. There was obvious discrimination with the way in which the law was treating people solely on their sexual orientation. It was just totally unfair. My parents were very principled, relatively left of centre, *Guardian* reading professionals. Fairness, dignity and respect were values that me and my brother were brought up with as children. So this seemed a very good thing to be doing for society. Also, from a personal situation, as a sixteen year old, I was jailbait. If a neighbour of mine took offence with me coming home with another sixteen or seventeen-year-old guy, they could call the police and my parents and I would all be in trouble. So there was the threat of the police—real or not—and the question of whether they were really going to go after middle-class teenage kids that wanted to get off with each other. There was also a safety thing; there was the gay serial killer, Colin Ireland. The attitudes at the time made it very difficult to be out and proud and I didn't really see many people like me in the media. So there was this whole societal thing, as well as just the principle that doing something would be quite good.

I went to college in the Autumn of 1994 and started my A-levels and there were peaks and troughs with the case. As different parts of paperwork went through there'd be another flurry or an article would be published in the paper. I just remember it being a long journey, but with each of the bits being quite important and necessary links in the chain. In 1996, when the case got to one of the Commission stages, I was sitting my A-levels and my parents had gone away on holiday to Scotland. At my home address—and also at the solicitor, Stonewall, and my college addresses—I received a series of really nasty, very descriptive, very believable death threats, which completely gave me a wobbly. It was scary. My godmother took me down to our local police station in East Dulwich to log it. There was very little that they could do—I don't think they were ever able to trace anything or anyone—so it all fell by the wayside. The college were nice and supportive, but I had a complete wobble during my English exam. It was upsetting and worrying and distressing. It did throw me and worry me hugely, but it didn't put me off doing the case.

In terms of the Strasbourg application process, I did feel involved. I remember sitting in chambers with Peter Duffy, Angela Mason, and with other people. I don't know if I was able to alter, adjust or change the arguments, but I was able to offer personal stories that would help make points in law. Stories are very interesting. Peter Duffy brought those things very much alive. He had a great skill in narrating and articulating things; he could make things incredibly interesting and captivating. It was utterly fascinating to hear about how case law's interpreted and how we could argue our case by citing it. I met Richard Desmond at some event and we talked about how things had been interpreted differently twenty years before hand, what case law had happened since, where we had moved on to, and how the same word had been interpreted differently in the twenty years between the two cases. Fascinating! Certain bits of it felt quite surreal, sitting in jeans and a T-shirt in someone's posh, law-book encrusted office. But it was interesting catching a bus up there and having a gossip and then going back to do an afternoon of A-levels in politics and media.

In summer 1996, me and my dad went to Strasbourg with Angela Mason, Peter Duffy, Clare Montgomery and another barrister, followed by a camera crew from MTV. It was all quite bizarre but it also felt a very normal thing to be doing. The Commission was in an impressive building. I wouldn't exactly say it was like a National Trust historic house, because it was a very modern building. I wasn't in court as in, 'You've been arrested'; it was us sitting on our table, and Her Majesty's government on their table. David Pannick was quite pleasant and, although they wanted to win, I never got a sense that Her Majesty's government would be actively hostile to me or my family. The press might be, the nutters and the religious fanatics might be, but I never got the impression that Her Majesty's government would be malicious. I do remember speculating that I would probably have my phone tapped—jokingly—and that there would be some subversives file being generated. But I never felt that they were out to get me. I was a figurehead and, actually, they would want to get at the points that were underneath rather than at me at the top, so I never got a feeling of hostility from the case.

The Commission was not particularly friendly. I thought they were efficiently bureaucratic. They weren't personal. It was business. I knew this was not so much about me, but that I was being used to illustrate a point, and they needed to get to the argument underneath. So I didn't feel that the Commission were particularly interested in me, to be honest. To get the case in there you need someone to figurehead it. I had been used to replace or back-fill Ralph, Hugo and Will. Stonewall were then bringing in someone else; the new and improved, younger version of me was being lined up. It was business, for the greater good. I was an illustration being used to paint a picture.

Some of details of the case were very personal, but it seems less so in black and white, dressed up in legal language. It was relatively sanitized and it could have been equally applicable to most of my gay teenage friends who would have had a very similar background. It's generically personal. It doesn't mention the names of partners, locations—well it talks about the family home and the worries about parents and what the implications are for them—but it didn't seem that special a story. It was quite a generic and deliberately vanilla, middle-class story, because that's what was going to generate the most warm reception. It was a safe story, a safe case study to pick, and other bits of the story were whittled off. You could find thousands of teenagers around the country who would relate to the bare bones of the story.

The Commission's opinion was two months after New Labour came in. I remember being euphoric about the change in government, not just for the case, but because I couldn't remember anything pre-Thatcher. It was very exciting. I can't remember how far up the Labour agenda it was, but the age of consent was not going to be one of their top priorities. Messages were very clearly being put through to us that 'we will get there' but a decision was made that we weren't going to stop and withdraw the case. We were going to go on, and it would keep a little bit of pressure on in the background. I don't really remember receiving the Commission's opinion and I'm not sure why that does not stick out in my memory. Perhaps it is because it is all wrapped up with the election and the result. If the Conservatives had won they would have obstructed, delayed and procrastinated. I sincerely felt that with this combination of the Commission's opinion plus Labour, it was a matter of 'when' not 'if'. But there was still the question of how we would get this through, because it was still the 1990s, it wasn't universally popular in the House of Commons, and the House of Lords was still hereditary. So we needed to keep Labour on board; we needed to work with them.

I remember the argument at the time—I really did believe it and I still do—that it's more palatable if the change comes from Parliament than from being imposed. Coming through the British Parliament, even though they had to use the Parliament Act to get it through in the end, was better than having it come through Europe. We wouldn't have got it through Parliament without the European Court, but I'm pleased we didn't have Strasbourg impose this. Because that's how it would have been painted. It was already being painted that way by the *Daily Mail* and *Daily Express* but it would have been worse had it come from a final judgment at the European Court of Human Rights. We needed these cases to force Parliament to do their bit. I think, ultimately, the case would have won—I just might have been collecting my pension before it happened—and we needed that pressure. We needed the European Court to do that and thank god it's there. It's being attacked by so many different people, but it plays an important part in making us a better society. Whilst it's slow, what it does do is to allow the opportunity for nation states to engage in a debate within its legislature and also within its society. It's triggered those debates and, by using its framework, it's allowed us to sort our own house out, to get our house in order. I think it was in everyone's interest, and natural justice, that the change in legislation was by Parliament rather than judges in Strasbourg.

When the law changed, I felt utter relief. I don't think I'd appreciated when I signed on—teenagers and sense of timing is not very good—how long this would actually be a feature. And I think that, in a way, it did detract from an ability to have a smoother adolescence into young adulthood. Not that I regret doing it, but I don't think I appreciated the impact on education and relationships. Yes, some of it was detrimental; with hindsight I can say that. I do think I benefitted hugely from listening to arguments, participating in hugely important events of cultural history, but, actually, at the time, I really could have done without the opportunity to be door-stepped by the *Daily Mail* on my way to college, getting nasty, shitty letters from right-wing, Christian born-agains, or meeting columnists from newspapers at TV shows who were absolutely hideous. And, because of some of the events I was attending and people I was meeting, I had access to a very exciting social life but was very bad at boundaries, limits and self-control. It did distract me from my academic studies and wasn't really conducive to high grades. There were quite a few things which added distraction and imbalance and, I suppose, teenage life into young adulthood is bumpy enough without adding in all of these other, greatly exciting, things. Some stability would have been a useful thing. However, looking at the whole sum of it, I would still do it again. I view it all as a very important, very positive thing to have done. But I now know that, actually, there were some drawbacks.

I think about the case from time to time. It is now a bit more in the background. It was a very interesting adventure and it's one I look back on quite fondly and relatively objectively, not just through rose-tinted glasses. It was something I am very proud of participating in. I had the opportunity to experience things I never would have dreamed possible. To think that I have got paperwork that says Euan Sutherland versus United Kingdom government: wow, we got things changed! If we proposed to introduce an unequal age of consent now, it would not be tolerated; we've won that argument. There are enough freedoms for religion and personal expression in the world, but the principle of equality before the law, I think, we've won. Not every area of society will agree, but the law should not police morals, it should protect its citizens from persecution, crime and harm. We've got away from Victorian and 1950s law. I certainly learned a lot and met some incredible people and had some wonderful times but, actually, it was an interesting little bubble with peaks and troughs of activity. The case was part of the fabric and the patchwork that built up to here. So god knows where I would have been without it, but I'm quite happy with where I am now.

3

The Armed Forces

Lustig-Prean and Beckett v the United Kingdom (1996–2000)

In 1994, Duncan Lustig-Prean, a Lieutenant Commander in the Royal Navy, was investigated and subsequently discharged in pursuance of the then policy of the Ministry of Defence that homosexuality was incompatible with service in the armed forces. After becoming involved with Rank Outsiders and Stonewall, Mr Lustig-Prean sought to challenge the legality of his discharge and the policy on which it was based. Having been unsuccessful in the English courts, he complained to the European Commission of Human Rights that the investigation into his sexual orientation and discharge from the Royal Navy amounted to a violation of his right to respect for his private life. In 1999, the European Court of Human Rights upheld Mr Lustig-Prean's complaint and, as a consequence, in 2000 the UK government announced that homosexuality would no longer be a bar to service in the armed forces.

Duncan Lustig-Prean

I had a fabulous career. I was very lucky. I joined the Royal Navy—first via the Royal Naval Reservists in Birmingham as an ordinary sailor—because I missed the sea, having been brought up in the Isle of Wight. During my initial career in the Navy, I would have been defined as a training risk. I was slightly older than the average intake for officer and I had a very firm mind of my own. I suppose some would say I was eccentric in many ways and, thus, not ideal for the manipulation of mind that is Dartmouth. So I did struggle at first and it was only when I got to my first ship that I suddenly started to flourish, with a commanding officer who really understood me and, as I subsequently discovered, knew that I was gay. I had a love affair with the Navy and was close to the people I worked with, of all ranks. The only person who I ever spoke to about my sexuality when I was in the services was a Naval chaplain. He and I more or less discovered that we were both gay. He was a married man himself. We talked; we were honest. Most chaplains, frankly, were very, very hostile and were not people who maintained pastoral confidence very often, which is quite a shocking thing to say.

What led to my arrival at the door of the Special Investigation Branch was this: I had been to my appointer in London to discuss my next job and I came back to the ship absolutely on a high because I'd been offered three jobs, which was

Going to Strasbourg: An Oral History of Sexual Orientation Discrimination and the European Convention on Human Rights. First Edition. Paul Johnson. © Paul Johnson 2016. Published 2016 by Oxford University Press.

very unusual. We had a celebratory drink and there was a knock on the door: 'Your mother's rung, could you give her a call please.' So I rang home, with a sense of foreboding, and Mum said somebody had been ringing, quite frequently, to talk to me. So I rang this chap and he said he wanted to meet me in London to discuss an investigation. I played the blustering game and said, 'Well what the hell is all this about, I'm not travelling up to London to meet strange people.' 'You better meet me, it's about an investigation.' So I drove up to London on a Thursday night, met him under the clock in Waterloo station and, in the best John Le Carré style, we walked along the embankment and he told me that he had discovered that I was gay and, if I made it worth his while, he would keep quiet about it. I told him to get fucked—that's the first time I've said that out loud—and I told him it wasn't going to work that way because, before he got anywhere near the military police, I would be there. There was one thing that I was determined about and that was, if and when it happened to me, I was going to go with dignity and I was not going to betray the very principles that I fought all my life to sustain and uphold.

I drove back to the ship. It was a very sleepless night and, the next day, we went on weekend. Over that weekend I contacted my close friends, my partner at the time, and I also got in touch with the organization Rank Outsiders for some immediate advice. On the Monday I spoke to my captain, told him what I had to do, and he tried to stop me. He said, 'You don't need to do this.' I said, 'Actually, you don't have the full facts'—I didn't want to involve him in the full facts—and I then rang up the head of the Special Investigation Branch in Portsmouth, who had actually worked for me in my previous job. I arrived at his office, there were tea and biscuits on the table, and I said, 'I've got a problem.' 'OK, how can I help, what's the problem?' 'Someone's trying to blackmail me.' 'OK, give me the guy's details, we'll put a stop to this, why is he trying to blackmail you?' 'Because I'm gay.' It was like a knife had slashed across the room. He leant back and said, 'Are you telling me you're homosexual?' 'Yes, I am.' 'Well in that case, you're not obliged to say anything, but anything you do say …' The coffee cups were swept away, the interview stopped, and I was taken into the formal interview room where we started the taped interview. The moment I said blackmail and homosexuality, he named the blackmailer. He was well known to them, he outed several people, and the military, of course, used him. They inevitably wanted to do a search of my cabin; this was standard routine. I said, 'Well, what are you expecting to find?' 'We're looking for evidence that you're gay.' I said, 'Well I've provided that and if you think you're going to find pictures of my partner, letters from my partner, they've gone.' In fact, when I drove to London to meet my blackmailer, I had buried them just outside London in the woods to be collected later. That was the sort of paranoia that we all lived under in those days.

I certainly didn't leave the ship in mind to become a test case. I was acutely embarrassed, I was very private and I didn't feel comfortable talking about my own sexuality. When I left, there were two reasons that I felt it important to distance myself. One was pure embarrassment, and indoctrinated embarrassment. You have to understand that, in the services, as a gay man you are indoctrinated that you are wrong, you are dirty. The whole system makes you dirty and feel guilty. So you tend to withdraw and take yourself away from your former comrades. Secondly, I was aware that people who were close to me were likely to be in danger themselves. You have to remember that the atmosphere was very hostile to gays. I had no idea, until I had the courage to get back in touch with sailors in the last few months, what their feelings were towards me at the time. That has been one of the most surprising and tear-jerking things for me since I left.

It wasn't my inclination to scream and shout about it. I would have gone quietly. But I became involved with Rank Outsiders, where I had a use—because I was a very senior officer in comparison with everybody else in the organization, I had worked in personnel and in HQ, I had dealt with military police, I knew the service law—and, before I was even discharged, I was advising them. Very quickly I became co-opted Special Advisor, then Campaigns Director, and then Vice-Chairman. I was given the difficult cases to look after and, to give you some idea of the numbers, I had seventy or eighty people on my books, going through investigation or discharge, at any one time. People were being hurt and these were not people who had committed a crime or who had behaved inappropriately. They were invariably, if one looked at them, people who were outperforming the average in the services. My own belief is that they, like me, covered their tracks by being married to the job and performed better. So we were getting rid of some really, really good people and we were doing it in an extremely cruel way. The final straw for me happened in October or November 1994, when I was asked to go down to the Tamar Bridge because of a sailor who was there at two o'clock in morning, in the rain, surrounded by police, wanting to jump. That's when I decided, you have to stand up and say 'no' publically and it was the final persuader for me to take on the case. I felt, having shied away and being embarrassed about who I was, if I was worth the bloody commanders' rank, then I had to stand up for people like that. You cannot have people being hurt so severely that they are going to kill themselves at the age of nineteen just because they're gay. That was the final kick in the arse I needed.

Through Rank Outsiders we met Stonewall. Robert Ely, who was the founder of Rank Outsiders, and who had been a warrant officer in the Household Division Bands, had been the first to flag the issue and approach Stonewall. My first appearance at one of these meetings was hysterical because I turned up dressed in a suit—typical Naval officer—and I walked in on a group of people in jeans and dressed in typical activist style. When they were talking I, with my plummy tones, would come up with Article X, Y, Z or Queen's regulations, and there was a sense of, 'Oh my god, there's a man from the Ministry of Defence and he is spying on us.' The politics of the late 1980s and early 1990s in the gay community were extremely left wing and at the very first Pride that Rank Outsiders went on—and, indeed, my very first Pride—there were people who were spitting on us. So it wasn't just about persuading the law to change; we actually had to get the message over to our side. We had to persuade Stonewall, under Angela Mason—herself coming from a left-wing, activist background—and their board, that this was a cause that was worthy of funding. We focused on saying that this was not just a very narrow issue in the armed forces, but one of protection in employment generally. Our actions preceded changes in the age of consent, which was still a nervous one for people, and I think what turned them on was that, actually, the issues were so black and white. We were a nice clean case.

I think Stonewall rapidly realized I was quite useful. We agreed that action was worth taking and to select test cases. The lawyers and Stonewall had about seventy or eighty cases of people who had submitted their papers. I wasn't involved in the selection, didn't expect to be, and nor did I expect to come out of the woodwork. We wanted to cover all the bases and all the services, so that we shut every single potential door in the face of the opposition and had no loopholes. Those selected also had to have an absolutely clean record because, if you're going to be a test case, you don't want any other issues to become involved. You need an absolutely black and white case, where there's no dirt that can be raked up. So, I understand why I came out of the woodwork. In some ways it was beneficial, in other ways very difficult, because I was also leading the campaign at Rank Outsiders. Thus, the spokesman was also the subject. It made life a lot more difficult because you feel quite naked and exposed when you are the subject.

I expected my mother to be understanding and sympathetic. I expected to have huge difficulties with my father who was an Austrian catholic, had been to a military school, and was very conservative in his background. When I told him, I prevaricated and beat around the bush. I said, 'I'm going to have to leave the Navy.' 'Well why?' 'It's an issue of security.' 'Well, I don't understand, what security?' 'Well, it's a suspicion of homosexuality.' 'Is it true?' 'Yes, it is.' Then Dad, in his Austrian accent, instantly said, 'Well then you must sue them, it's unfair dismissal.' We became so close, because suddenly he was my strongest supporter. They were both very important, as was my then partner, Martin. The *Daily Express* were doorstepping my parents and ringing them up saying things like, 'Is it true you haven't spoken to your son since he came out to you?' Dad rang me straight up and said, 'I've told them not only is it untrue but that I speak to him everyday and they can publish that if they want but, if they do, I'll sue the arse off them.' The media were interesting. I was followed by the *Daily Mail* for six months. The neighbours would say, 'They're going through the bins again.'

We didn't choose David Pannick to represent us; he chose us. David had represented the government on various occasions and he was a very good gamekeeper-turned-poacher. He was entirely sympathetic and it was quite clear he was onside from the start. I didn't believe in being a client who sat idly by and allowed the experts to deal with the case. It was something I wanted to be intensely involved in. David was receptive to this because this was *pro bono* so, if you have a client who is going to take some of the heat off, you're going to welcome it, especially if the client is able to advise on military regulations. It was also important for me to be involved because, although I wanted to achieve an improvement in the services—a civilization in this one aspect which I thought the services had got wrong—I didn't want to end up in a situation where civvies interfered with something they didn't necessarily understand.

I'm not claiming to be a lawyer, but I had studied enough law and I had immersed myself in the case. I felt that our strongest point was always going to be Article 8 and looking at the level of State discretion, which I felt was unreasonable. Thus,

I drafted the initial skeleton argument for David Pannick. Jeanette Smith argued an additional item. She argued torture, Article 3. I was not comfortable with that, hence we didn't argue it. I felt that it's not very pleasant being interviewed by the police, but torture is water-boarding, thumb-screws and electric shocks, not an unpleasant time at the hands of service police asking difficult questions and looking through your private diaries. That is not, to my mind, what the Convention is there for. In terms of Article 10, I didn't feel that it was anything more than a distraction from the principle, core argument. No one in the armed forces has absolute freedom of expression. It is, sadly, in the real world, one of the rights you have to give up. What we don't give up is the right to be protected from an admiral staring through the privacy of our bedroom window at night. I felt much more comfortable arguing that they were intruding into my Article 8 rights. I didn't feel comfortable in giving opportunities to the opposition, or judges, to go down rabbit holes on points that were not so clearly winnable.

There was huge hope in this country that the European Court was the answer to every gay problem. The reality was that we also had the fall of the Soviet Union. We had former Soviet bloc nations now joining the Convention and becoming members of the Court, still with very strong conservative social views on this issue. We were aware that there were sympathies at Registrar's level in the European Court. To my mind, depending on the constitution of the final Court, it was not a sure bet that we would win. And anyone who bets on the law is an unwise gambler in my view; it can go either way. So I was trying to limit expectations. My view was that, if we lost, there was the inexorable pressure of change and, at some stage, we were going to prevail—even if it was not us—in the European courts, given the way that European law lives, breathes and grows. But I was not entirely convinced.

When we got the judgment we were standing around in Milbank, in BBC Studios. Graeme Grady had gone over to the Court—he was our representative in the Court—and the rest of us were with Angela Mason at the BBC. Up came the decision and there was this intense disbelief. I skim read it and I could see, yes, we've won on Article 8 and, where I felt uncomfortable on other people's arguments, on Jeanette's argument on Articles 3 and 10, I agreed with the decision. It was overwhelming, absolutely overwhelming, because it was such an outright victory. Geoff Hoon was in the building and he'd already instantly announced suspension of all discharges pending review. I just said to him, 'Thank you very much for that, Sir.' I have to say that the Ministry of Defence played a very decent and honourable game. I did not. I was quite happily leaking papers that were being given to me to do as much damage as possible to the government's stance. If I had been working for the Ministry of Defence, I would have been doing what governments do, to brief against you, to say, 'There's no smoke without fire, these guys are not all that pure.' You only needed a little whispering campaign with the *Daily Mail*. They didn't do that. It was done entirely honourably and I admire them for that.

I certainly have no regrets whatsoever about doing the case. I regret mistakes I made along the way, I regret errors I made in my own personal management of me, as an applicant and as a campaigner, in failing to recognize the personal attrition. One of the mistakes that I made was to fail to see that I needed as much support, and that arm around my shoulder, as everyone else. To some extent, as the senior officer, I felt it was my duty to shield the other three, so I took the lead and they were more than happy not to be the upfront campaigners. There was too much of the stoic, stiff upper lip, without showing emotion. I think it was only afterwards, when I bowed out—and that was a deliberate policy, not to carry on in overt gay rights—that I realized there was a price to pay for it. I had to find my own feet again, find my own happiness again, having lost something which was more than a job, which was a way of life, and lost all my friends in one fell swoop. You don't really recover from that. I would say the recovery process has only started in the last six months. It's taken that long. It's taken fifteen years.

What gives me more pleasure than anything is that the judgment is so often used in other cases. To find that some poor, little, helpless person is able to find something—nothing to do with a gay issue—that has been said in our judgment that assists them, I find hugely pleasurable. I am very fearful of proposals to remove this country from the influence of the European Court. I'm not so worried about removal of the Human Rights Act because, frankly, with Europe in the background the Human Rights Act was merely something nice to bring in. But I would be really worried, and would fear our lack of respect for history, were we to leave the Convention. This wasn't some left-wing ideal, this was actually Churchill's idea and he's hardly the great socialist of modern history. I do like the idea that, unlike our precedent based, almost immovable, system in the UK, the joy of the European Court is that it will live, breathe and develop. It will move along with society and will change society. That, to me, is a system that is responsive and better than what we have here, when it comes to dealing with issues where conscience is involved.

*

Smith and Grady v the United Kingdom (1996–2000)

Graeme Grady, a Sergeant in the Royal Air Force, was investigated and discharged in 1994 in pursuance of the then policy of the Ministry of Defence that homosexuality was incompatible with service in the armed forces. Following unsuccessful attempts to challenge this in the English courts, Mr Grady complained to the European Commission of Human Rights that the investigation into his sexual orientation and subsequent discharge amounted to a violation of his right to respect for his private life and, in addition, that he had no effective remedy before a national authority. In 1999, the European Court of Human Rights upheld these complaints and, as a consequence, in 2000 the UK government announced that homosexuality would no longer be a bar to service in the armed forces. The Court rejected Mr Grady's complaint that the treatment to which he had been subjected was degrading and did not examine his complaint that the Ministry of Defence policy on homosexuality had interfered with his freedom of expression.

Graeme Grady

I'd always suppressed my sexuality. I've known that I was gay since I was about twelve or younger but, because I thought it was wrong, I just shut it away and tried not to think about it. It sounds silly, but I thought that if I joined the Royal Air Force that it might knock it out of me, it might take these feelings away, which is a really bizarre attitude to have when you are putting yourself in an institution full of men. But when I was in the RAF, I led a straight life and had fantasies more than anything. There had been one or two guys, but nothing major. There was a flutter at RAF Lyneham in the early 1980s, which totally took me by surprise. It was just a one night thing and then it was never discussed; we just carried on as normal. Certainly, when I got married, I wasn't somebody who was sneaking off to see men. I didn't do that. I just hid it and tried not to think about it.

I was in Washington, DC, at the British Defence Intelligence Liaison Service North America, where I was the chief clerk. I was married with two children; my son was four, my daughter was just a baby. Everything was going well and my wife decided that she wanted to come back to the UK for a holiday, to see her family, and so she took the children. It was 1993, the year of my thirtieth birthday, and I just knew that I was going to have a relationship with a man. So, when my wife went back to the UK, I did meet somebody. I just knew that once I'd gone down that road the marriage was going to be over. We were very amicable about the situation. I mean, she didn't go mad and try to attack me or anything like that. She was very calm and collected. At first, she suggested we had a life where we did what we wanted but stayed together for the children's sake. To me, that was always the wrong idea and I felt that children are more aware than you think they are at an early age. So we decided we'd divorce.

My wife then joined a group for the wives of gay married men—America being all about therapy and all the rest of it—and I thought what a load of bollocks. She said that I should go to a group called GAMMA, which was for gay married men, and I said no. Then I thought, perhaps it could be interesting. So I did go along and I was surprised that I was one of the youngest people there. There were all these gentlemen—some were grandfathers—and they'd had relationships with men all their married life. Sometimes their wives knew, sometimes they didn't. It just fascinated me. They introduced me to the gay scene in DC and my life sort of changed.

At the GAMMA group, I gave my name and said I worked in the Embassy—there was a non-disclosure agreement between members of GAMMA which meant that no one was supposed to discuss attendees outside the group. There was somebody who went to GAMMA who also went to another group, the Dulles Triangles, and mentioned me there to the nanny of my Officer Commanding, an Army colonel. The nanny then went and mentioned me to the colonel's wife. She had no idea you couldn't be gay in the forces, so it was in all innocence that she mentioned it. My colonel called me to a meeting at the Embassy and he said, 'There's a problem with your security clearance', and 'You're going to have to go back and answer some questions.' This was at one o'clock in the afternoon and at seven o'clock that night

I was put on a flight from Washington back to the UK. I was met at Brize Norton and told, 'You aren't under arrest; you are coming back voluntarily.'

I was taken to RAF Uxbridge and the RAF police security services came to interview me. It wasn't very nice because they treated you like a criminal. You were interviewed under PACE and they asked really derogatory questions like, 'How do you get on with your son?' That was really hurtful and bizarre, you know, that mentality: they assumed that if you're gay you must be a kiddy fiddler. I denied everything at that stage and I was saying, 'No comment', on the advice of my solicitor. There was one RAF officer there who was my boss at the time. I trusted him and I asked him whether, if I admitted this, would I lose my pension. He said he didn't think so. I just thought, I can't be bothered to fight this anymore, so I said, 'Yeah, I'm gay.' But it didn't stop there and that's when they asked, 'Who did you go with, who did you see in the US, how old were they, did you know any people in the RAF or US servicemen?' I just said, 'No, no, it was civilians I was seeing, that's all you need to know.' It wasn't very nice.

I got on to Stonewall because I went to see them about an immigration case—somebody in the States wanted to come across to the UK—and I mentioned that I was in the RAF and that sort of clicked with them. They said they'd got this case going forward about trying to change the law about gays in the military. I went along to this meeting and there were some barristers there. I was just chatting away and then, low and behold, they said, 'Well, we'd like to take you as one of the cases', and I said, 'Okay.' All my life, I've always thought that if I'm going to fight for something it's got to be something I believe in. They explained I might get some funding but that I might be looking at paying the expenses myself. I was the only one out of the four people in our cases that was employed and wasn't getting legal aid. So I did know there was a chance that if we did lose, I could be looking at humongous fees. I just thought to myself, I'm going to do this, because we're going to win. I didn't understand half of what was going to go on, or how long it would take, but in the back of my mind I just thought, no, I'm not going to let them get away with this, because why should I have been thrown out of the RAF after a successful career. My service was exemplary through the whole fourteen years I was in there. That was one of the reasons why Stonewall thought mine was a good case to go forward.

Going to court was all a bit bizarre in a way. I'd never had anything to do with the law before or the courts. So it was all a whole new thing, sitting there with these judges with their robes on and all the jargon going on that meant absolutely nothing to me. People tried to explain it to me—I'm not the brightest spark, so I didn't understand all of it—but it felt like I was going to achieve something. On the very first day in court, one of the things the judge said to the Ministry of Defence was that he didn't want to hear anything derogatory about us because he'd seen our service careers and they were all exemplary. One of the first things that one of the Ministry of Defence guys said was, 'Mr Grady is a liar', and the judge said, 'You can stop right there, I'm not interested in that, because I've told you, I've seen their records.' They wanted to try and blacken everyone's names. They were thinking, we'll blacken their names, get the public on our side, and discredit them. They tapped our phones, which was pretty bad. They were obviously trying to find anything to try and discredit us.

It was very disappointing when we lost in the different levels of the UK courts. I remember the Master of the Rolls saying, 'I'm sorry Mr. Grady, I have to award costs against you, however I would not expect the Ministry of Defence to follow you up for it.' It was £75,000 and I had a little laugh when he said that, and I thought to myself, where would I get that money? Then I thought, I'll say that I'll pay them a pound a week! But, in the back of my mind, I still thought that we were going to win. We had to take it to Europe but I thought, well, the European Court of Human Rights has got to see it right, because there were other forces in Europe that allowed gays to serve, so how could the European Court of Human Rights say the UK could carry on with the ban?

I imagined the European Court of Human Rights as this huge, modern, stuffy institution, with European judges, or judiciary people, all over the place. I didn't realize that we'd actually physically go there. I thought we'd just sit in the background and the case would go there. But we did go there and that was just an amazing experience, to see this huge chamber and think, oh my god, this place exists and these people are going to decide something that is not just going to affect me. I was happy to go to Strasbourg. One of the QCs, Laura Cox, who was part of the initial meeting to decide which cases should go forward, had asked would I be willing to give up the Strasbourg case and go to an industrial tribunal, because she felt I could win there with no problem at all. I said to her, 'Well, what's the difference?' and she said, 'Well, at the tribunal you'll get compensation and that will be it.' I said, 'But will it change anything?' and she said, 'Well, not necessarily.' I said, 'Well, I'm really sorry then, in that case, I'd rather go to Strasbourg to have the change take effect.' It had dawned on me that, if we won, this was going to change the employment law for all lesbians, gays and transgender people. That's when I thought, Strasbourg's where I'm going to go, because I don't want it to be just about me, I want to try and change something for everybody else as well. That was my big thing; it wasn't just about me, it was something that could help other people as well.

The legal arguments were all done by the legal team and, I've got to be honest, I didn't have a great understanding of them. Don't get me wrong, I'm sure the lawyers told me what they were going to say but, not being a legal person, it would go in one ear and out of the other. I had a very, very basic understanding of the Convention. I do remember the argument about degrading treatment. I think that was about when we were interviewed under PACE and the standard of the questions about what I got up to sexually and how I got on with my son. That was a degrading question; it's disgusting to assume that because I'm gay that I'd want to sexually abuse my son. It's abhorrent. The Court said that didn't reach their minimum threshold to constitute degrading treatment? Well god knows what their threshold is. How could they not feel that that was derogatory and degrading?

I'd said to my mother, 'I'm going to take this to court', and she said, 'It's not going to be in the papers is it?' I said, 'Oh god, no, nothing like that.' I had no idea. And then there you are, that first day, on the tube, seeing your photo splashed on the *Evening Standard*, and the next day, on every newspaper. I had people who knew me in the forces writing to me from South Africa and globally, from all over the place, sending me clippings about the court case. I couldn't believe it; it was beyond my comprehension. I had a very good relationship with Stonewall and I found them very helpful. At that time, Angela Mason was the director of Stonewall and I got on very well with her and the whole team. In hindsight now, it would have been good if they'd given us some sort of idea about what you do in front of the media. I'd never been in front of the media before and on that very first day, when we got to the High Court, there were all these film crews, camera people, news people, getting you to say things. I ended up saying stupid things because I didn't know what to say; I didn't really understand it all myself. I do remember on the first day suggesting that we wear rainbow ribbons and, sure enough, lots of reporters asked what they symbolized. In hindsight, Stonewall could have said what was going to happen and, perhaps, told us what we needed to learn to say.

Because I had started my life in London, and was just mixing with the gay community and didn't have many straight friends, nobody shunned me. I never had any aggression in the street or anything like that. My mother struggled with it big time. She struggled with my sexual orientation to the point where she said to me one day, 'It hurt me worse than if you had cancer.' I found that a really hurtful thing to say, but she tried to explain she didn't mean she wanted me to have cancer but that the shock was so much for her. In terms of the case, she told me a few years later that she had some friends who called her up and said, 'I've seen this in a newspaper and I can't believe Graeme has done this to you.' My mother knows I've got quite a strong personality and I said, 'Look, if you want me to stop visiting or to stay away', but she never wanted that. She was worried for me more than anything. Don't get me wrong she has said to me, 'I'm very proud of you Graeme.' So the publicity didn't worry me, but it did worry other people.

If it wasn't for the European Court of Human Rights we would never have won and we would still be in the dark ages here. Let's face it, when Labour got into government they could have lifted the ban if they wanted to. I mean, we knew with the Conservatives there was no chance that Nicholas Soames was going to lift the ban. With Tony Blair, we thought perhaps he's going to lift it, but he just let it run and carry on into the European Court of Human Rights and let them make the decision. He was too scared to make a decision about it and that really pissed me off, to tell you the truth. If it hadn't been for the European Court of Human Rights we wouldn't have won and nothing would have changed. And I would be looking at a huge fortune to pay! I'd be paying it until this day, a pound a week.

I think there is a good argument to keep the European Court of Human Rights there, so we have got somebody else that can say, 'No, you're actually doing this wrong.' I'd be totally against the UK pulling out because it would be like going back to the dark ages. Especially if you get some total right wing in, who then repeals a lot of laws on homosexuality. No, that's the last thing we want to happen. There are some cases in Strasbourg where you think, that is ridiculous. Prisoner voting, I'm totally against that. I think if you're in prison, you're there to be punished, so why should you have the right to vote? I know some people say it's all about rehabilitation, but I think you lose your right to vote as soon as you're locked up. But, to me, it defeats the object if you sign up to the Convention and you don't enforce it because you don't like the Court's decision. It's that catch twenty-two thing where, although I disagree with it, I think if we've signed up to it we have to do it.

I do still think about the case. I actually still miss the RAF, even though it was twenty years ago, because I really enjoyed myself in there. It was a great career, great camaraderie, and I loved the work life and the social life. At the time of the case, I was adamant that if they had offered me to go back in I would say no, because of how I was treated. But as time wears off, I think it would have been nice to go back and finish my career. Yeah, it is in the back of my mind a lot, it's never going to go. And, because we won, they're good memories. This is going to sound bizarre, but for years I wondered, 'Why am I here, what am I here to achieve, what am I on this earth for, what do I do?' and then one day, I thought, oh my god, perhaps that's what I was here for, perhaps that's me done my bit, I can go, I can pass away, I've done my bit.

We changed things and it meant that people now can't be discriminated against in the workplace. People who were dishonourably discharged from the forces for being homosexual managed to get their pensions back. And we changed other things, too; it wasn't just the legal side. It opened things up socially and it seemed to open up the media. It made people more aware, and it brought in more gay characters on TV and in films. Even the Archers have got gay characters! The one thing I do regret is that I never had the courage to come out many, many years earlier. It's only a slight regret. Health wise, I used to suffer from tremendous migraines and once I came out, touch wood, I've not had a migraine to this day. It was obviously the stress of holding it all in. Would I change anything? I don't know. Even though I regret it, I wouldn't go back and change it. What I would say is, if you believe in it, fight for it.

*

Perkins and R. v the United Kingdom (1998–2002)

Terence Perkins, a Leading Medical Assistant in the Royal Navy, was investigated and discharged in 1995 in pursuance of the then policy of the Ministry of Defence that homosexuality was incompatible with service in the armed forces. Emma Riley, a Radio Operator First Class in the Royal Navy, was similarly investigated and discharged in 1993. Following unsuccessful attempts in the English courts to challenge their treatment by the Royal Navy, Mr Perkins and Ms Riley complained to the European Commission of Human Rights that the investigations into a most intimate part of their private lives—which, in Ms Riley's case, included the search and confiscation of her personal belongings—and their subsequent discharges constituted a violation of their right to respect for their private lives. In 2002, the European Court of Human Rights upheld their complaints.

Terence Perkins

I joined the Royal Naval Reserves in 1989 as a Probationary Medical Support Assistant. It was a new branch they had started. I worked with computers before that, in a very small company, and the boss had a father who was an ex-captain in the Reserves and he thought it would be a wonderful idea if I joined to become a communicator, to improve my communication skills with customers. I wasn't very keen on the idea to be quite honest, but thought I'd go along just to keep them happy. I had my colour perception tested that day—there just happened to be a nursing officer walking past—and they said, 'Oh, it's bad isn't it', and I said, 'I don't know, I was just told I was colour blind when I was a kid at school.' They said, 'Well, you can't be a communicator but we've just started a new branch.' I said, 'I don't know anything about medicine', and they said, 'We'll train you.' So I thought, okay, there's something new and you get paid for it as well. So I joined the Reserves and I was in for three and a half years. The last thing I did with the Reserves was on exercise with the Royal Marines in Norway. I was having a great time and I thought, this is great, I'll do it full time, so I joined up.

When you join the Navy—it's different from the Army and Air Force—you sign up for twenty-two years, so that's what I did. At that point in time, I hadn't really thought about my sexuality. I'd had no sexual experiences at all, so it wasn't an issue. Looking back, I was very confused I suppose, but left it at that. I think I always had an inkling, but never acted on it. They ask you when you join, 'Are you gay?' I thought, I'm not anything, so I joined up for twenty-two years. They put me in as a Probationary Medical Assistant but, because of my time served in the Reserves, I insisted that I become straight away an Acting Medical Assistant. When you first join the Navy you do seven weeks basic training—general Naval knowledge—and there were four classes of twenty-five people. My class was Nelson 07 and it was a really good class. We won the guard, so on our passing out parade we marched at the front in full rig and gatters. Somebody from our class won the shooting cup. I won the Owen Cup, which was for the highest marks of the entry.

From the basic training I went to the Royal Naval Medical Staff School, which was at the Royal Naval Hospital Haslar. They made me the class leader straight away. That training, intense training, was for thirteen months and I'd have to march my class around the hospital to wherever we were going. From the medical training, I got the highest marks again in the class. At the end of the first three stages of the training we were asked where we wanted to go for our Part 4 training, which was training in a proper sick bay, working with trained staff out in the field, so I volunteered for 45 Commando in Scotland. At the time, my grandma was very ill—she died of cancer—and I went off on compassionate leave. When I got back, I was called in to the Divisional Officer's office and he said, 'Perkins, get a request form and put in for grat issue of tropical rig, you're not going to 45 Commando, you're going on HMS Cornwall.' I thought, oh my god, I'm going on a ship. I went to the Caribbean for five months and when I got back I worked in sick bays, went back to the hospital to do more work, and then I went to Commando Logistics Regiment Royal Marines. I wanted to go on the Commando course at CTCRM Lympstone, which I did at a later date.

While I was on the Commando course, I met somebody, and that's when I realized for sure that I was gay. We were both serving and we both knew that we couldn't do that. So we would just meet at weekends, away from the base, and just be together. Then we'd just go back and live the Navy life. I was leading two lives and it just carried on. My family didn't know; they just knew about my Navy life. I split up with the guy because I met somebody, a civilian, when I was back home in Nottingham. If I went away for the weekend it would be back up to Nottingham, but I wouldn't even go and see my family, I went to stay with this guy. It was awful, not seeing your family because they didn't know.

One day, when I was working in the hospital, I got a call from the Regulating Petty Officer, and he said, 'LMA Perkins, can you please come to my office?' I immediately knew what it was about. A couple of days before, I was crying on the shoulder of another medic. She'd been in the Navy longer than me and she'd just split up with her boyfriend. I'd split up with my partner and I told her. She went and told her boss. So the next thing I got was this phone call and I went to his office and, when I got there, there were two guys in civilian clothes from the Special Investigations Branch. They said, 'We have reason to believe you are homosexual.' I just thought, yes, yes I am. I thought, why should I deny, why should I have to deny, who I am. Then I burst into tears. They said that I'd have to have a recorded interview. At the end of the interview they said, off tape, 'We don't like doing this.' But they had to, that was their job at the time.

There was a Red Cross civilian person acting as a counselor and, after the interview, I was sort of handed over to her. She was a brilliant woman. She gave me the details of a solicitor, Stephen Grosz, who I contacted. He was already dealing with two other people, Duncan Lustig-Prean and someone else, who went on to win their cases. He said, 'Right, well there's nothing I can do to stop you being kicked out, all you can do is to, within twenty-four hours, tell them that you think that the decision is unfair, unjust and unlawful.' So I put it all in writing and gave it to the Medical Officer in Charge of the hospital. He knew me and his words to me were, 'Terry, don't waste your money on solicitors fighting such a huge organization.' He was concerned for me; he was a lovely guy. From there, I had another forty-eight hours to put forward something else, knowing that I was going to be discharged.

They got rid of me very quickly—there's none of the eighteen months notice or any of that—and I think I was there for maybe another month at most, probably not even that. I went back home, back to Nottingham. I was brought up by my grandparents—although, as I said, my grandma had died—and when I was back in Nottingham something came on the TV that really upset me. I said to my grandfather—he's passed away now as well—'Look, I told you that I was leaving the Navy and they let me go early, that's not true. I was kicked out of the Navy because I'm gay.' I thought there was going to be explosions because of the generation gap, but there wasn't. He turned around and said, 'That's their loss.' He was great. I thought, I've got to tell the rest of my family and my assumptions of how they would react were completely wrong, all of them. They were all brilliant. Yes, there was so much support from my family; they were great. Even from my parents, who I wasn't brought up by, but I still get on with. In terms of my friends, one guy

I had lived with had quite often joked about me being gay and said things like, 'Oi, Perkins stop mincing; Oi, Perkins are you gay?' He'd kind of guessed but didn't know for sure, so I did tell him, and he was upset with me for not telling him earlier. I still get on with him now, twenty years later; he's a great, brilliant guy.

I had to tell my family, before it snowballed. I didn't realize it was going to snowball as much. I had no idea it was going to get so much publicity. I had so much support from everybody. Even *The Sun* and the *Daily Mail* were just reporting it; as you read it, you can see it's quite clear they're not particular happy about it, but they didn't bother me. Everything was quite positive. I think everybody realized that something had to be done and it was wrong, even if they didn't particularly agree with it. I kept all the press clips, just for history I suppose. They've just been stuffed under the bed in a suitcase. I had to deal with the case separately from going to work, because I had to carry on my life. I kind of had to deal with leading two lives again, I suppose, because I had to focus on what I was doing otherwise I wouldn't have been kept on in any job, it would have interfered with it, so I had to try and push it to one side and let my solicitor deal with it, which he was doing a brilliant job with.

The question my solicitor asked me was, 'What do you want to get out of this case? Do you want compensation? Do you want your job back?' I said, 'I don't want anyone to have to go through this.' I didn't care about the money. After I left the Navy I went back to computing and I was being paid a lot more than I would ever have been paid in the Navy, even if I had been an officer. I wasn't interested in the money, that wasn't my issue at all. And I didn't want my job back on principle, after what they'd done to me. According to the people at the top, there weren't any homosexuals in the armed forces. Obviously there were, I was one of them. But as soon as they found out, there was one less.

I remember one day I sat down with my solicitor, Angela Mason from Stonewall—she was great—and my barrister representing me, Peter Duffy QC, who was really pro what we were after. I wasn't talking much. They knew what they were talking about so did all the talking between themselves really. Because I didn't really understand what they were talking about, I thought I'll leave it to them, they know what they're doing. I was trying to focus on getting my life back on track, I was young, and just not really interested in any of the politics really. I think my solicitor saw it as a slightly different argument to the two that he was already dealing with and he saw my case as an opportunity. I think that's why it went to the High Court and they said we think you've got a very good case and we'll give you leave to go to the European Court of Justice, based on *Lisa Grant v South West Trains*. Unfortunately, they lost that case so I couldn't then go to the European Court of Justice, so I had to go back to the High Court and then to the European Court of Human Rights. But because the other four—Smith and Grady, and Lustig-Prean and Beckett—were waiting to go to the European Court of Human Rights they, based on my case, leap-frogged and went ahead of me. They won in December 1999 and the law was changed in January 2000. My case was still ongoing and it got joined up with 'R.' and that took another two years.

I never went to any of the courts. I never went to the High Court, I couldn't go to the European Court of Justice, and I never went to the European Court of

Human Rights when it got there. I went back into computing and I was working. But on the day that the four others were in the European Court of Human Rights, I actually took the day off work and was sitting in the Stonewall office answering phone calls from reporters. I was trying to help Stonewall. I thought their aims were exactly what I wanted to achieve, just to get everything changed. Another thing I did was to put something on the Internet—the Internet was still in its early stages then—which was a questionnaire. I was getting replies from all over the world, Australia and America, and it was incredible just hearing about people in the armed forces. I knew the European Court of Human Rights was huge and that was as far as it could go. I knew it was a big deal and it was going to be amazing if we won. I suppose I was ever hopeful. The other four won first, but all the way through those cases my name is mentioned, it's quite funny. Even my High Court judgment is mentioned. It would have been interesting if my case had gone forward first. Maybe it would have been a different result, I don't know.

In terms of the impact on my life, I can be open now. I can be who I want to be. So I don't have that hurt anymore. I don't have to live a double life. I don't think about the case at all now. If I'm out on an evening, and I'm in a pub, and somebody asks me what I've done, it might come up, and I'll show them that if you do a Google search for my name and Royal Navy you'll see it. So I can't help but be public, if you like, because it's there as general knowledge. But I don't have a problem with that because it's part of who I am now. I've still got my friends who I was in the Navy with, but we talk about now not about back then.

I didn't think talking about it would bother me like this, the way it has. Just looking back on it, brings it back. I knew I'd kept all those pieces of paper, I just didn't realize that talking about it would upset me. I don't know why it does. Maybe I tried to brush it aside, but those feelings are still in there. I said I had some counselling with the Red Cross, but that's as far as it went. I've never had any other counselling or anything. I suppose that's maybe the way I deal with my emotions, I'm quite soft and I do cry at a lot of things.

A few years ago the armed forces put together a group for LGBT meetings. I saw it—I just came across it on the Internet—and I contacted them. I explained who I was, what I'd gone through, and I said it would be interesting if they could let me know the outcome of the meeting. They invited me along and they also had the police force and the fire service there as well, which was quite interesting. I thought the meeting just showed how much it had progressed since I got kicked out and it was just great. People can serve being who they want to be. There are transsexuals in the armed forces; that would never have been thought of when I was serving. It's great and why not? It shows that the case had an impact and it has changed things for the better. I think if I hadn't gone to the solicitor in the first place, I don't know who else would have done. I mean, yes, there were the four going to the European Court of Human Rights, but I don't know where their case had got before my case had been heard. Maybe if I hadn't gone, maybe their case wouldn't have had the same impact. I don't know, I'll never know. But the way it happened, I'm so pleased, so pleased. Keeping those press cuttings, I can look back and think, yeah, I did that, that was me, and it has made a change. I'm proud of that.

Emma Riley

I joined the Royal Navy in 1990. Up until that point, I'd been doing A-levels and failing miserably at them. They weren't really important to me; I'd got five GCSEs at B and C levels, so I had enough to get into the Navy. I'd had a very clear view of what I wanted to do since about the age of twelve, when an armed forces careers fair came to my school. That's when I remember saying to myself, this is the career that I want and this is what I believe I will be good at. I thought I would enjoy the camaraderie, the work, the fact that you can travel, and it was to do with the sea. I'd always sailed with my family, so I had a lot of sea background.

I joined the Navy at the time when they were making the change to allow women to serve at sea. So I was in the last class of women to have their basic training separate to the men, on HMS Sirius, and when I did my specialization training, as a radio operator on HMS Mercury, I was in the first mixed sex classes. In fact, I became the class leader of that class. Being in the Navy felt very natural. I was good at everything they were throwing at me during basic training, from stripping and putting together an SA80 gun and doing all that practical stuff, to examinations about ranks and all the stuff you have to learn. I passed out with high grades, as far as I remember. In secondary training, again, I also did very well. They were talking about me going on to be officer material, just months after I'd joined, so it felt right.

One of the first things you do, when you get there, is go for a big meeting with your class and they give you this booklet of stuff that you have to read and a contract to sign. I remember reading those clauses, which say something along the lines that homosexuality is strictly forbidden in the Royal Navy and is a ground for discharge. At that time, I had already been questioning my sexuality. I was fairly sure that I was attracted to women, but stronger in me was the want and need to serve my country and to be part of the Navy. At that point in my life, I was completely prepared to give up any kind of relationship—something I'd not had before anyway—to serve that purpose. I clearly remember pausing before I signed and thinking to myself, I know there is something potentially in me that is conflicting with this, but I'm prepared to put that to one side to serve my country and do the job I want to do. So I made my decision; I said to myself, put those feelings in a box and forget about them. Effectively, I became a priest in the Navy, in a weird kind of way; I suppressed all of my natural feelings in order to follow my calling.

Once I'd finished my secondary training I got the opportunity to volunteer for sea, which I did. So I went straight back to HMS Raleigh to do the basic sea training. I was lucky enough to get drafted to a frigate, HMS Cornwall, and we went out to do West Indies Guardship, which meant I got to see a lot of really amazing places. So I did get to travel and I was good at what I was doing. That's not to say it was a smooth ride. When I joined the Navy, I thought I would be part of the group, rather than be outside of the group, but unfortunately it didn't work out that way. There was bullying, there was name calling, and all of the usual kind of crap you get when people are in confined spaces and they clique and go into little groups. So not everything was as good as I hoped.

I started thinking about the issue of my sexuality again when I was on board the ship. I had feelings for other people on the ship, which was difficult to deal with. Then, when we were in America, there was an incident where we got royally drunk, and, at one point in the loos, one of the ratings was, for a prank, trying to get underneath the door of a stall that some other girl was in. I was horrified because I can't stand that kind of thing and was trying to stop her getting in there. When we got back to the ship it all got changed around and I was said to have been deliberately trying to get into the stall with this woman. I got taken across the coals for it. I was interviewed and got 'the talk' from the Chief Officer who said, 'Some people are like this, and you may find later on that you meet somebody and you will become a lesbian.' I said, no, that's nothing to do with me. So that kind of thing would go on. But, at the same time, I continued to pass my examinations. I knew I was totally fit for the job, that I was absolutely the right person to do that work, but that aspect of my personality was not allowed. And, as much as you would think that you can put something in a box and not think about it, it doesn't work like that.

After the ship, I got drafted to a communications centre in Scotland for six months and then to Faslane. During that time, I went to London with a couple of women who I'd served on the ship with. At that point I thought, I really need to test myself and find out if all of these feelings, all of these thoughts, is really who I am. So I took myself out, without my friends, and did what many people probably do: I went to a bar and got myself picked up by a woman and went home with her. I found out that, yes, that's who I am and confirmed what sex I wanted to be with. That didn't change the fact that I was still prepared not to have a relationship, because I still didn't want to leave the Navy. But it at least put to bed that question, in my head, about whether I was a lesbian or not. It was a clear moment.

In the midst of all this my father, who was sixty-seven, went through a quadruple bypass. I was sent home on compassionate leave so I could support my mum, take him to hospital, and be there when he was having his chest cracked open. It was extremely distressing and I came back from that experience pretty traumatized. These days I probably would have gone for counselling but, as far as the Navy were concerned, you just came back and kept going with your work. I'd got friendly with the person I was sharing a room with in the block. I thought that she was my friend, so I confessed to her that I'd had this one night when I'd gone out and confirmed to myself that I was gay. At the time, the reaction she gave was very supportive; she said she was fine about it, and that she wouldn't tell anyone. Then she reported me to the Special Investigation Branch.

They knocked on the door and woke me up at some ridiculous time in the morning. I was asleep and they woke me up saying, 'Get dressed, come downstairs, you're being arrested.' They asked me a whole slew of questions and it was immensely distressing; I was crying a lot of the time. At one point they stopped the interview, the interviewers went out, and I was left in the room with the Chief Wren who was supposed to be supporting me. She started asking me, 'Are you sure there's nothing else that you need to say?' I was so distressed I started to tell her stuff and mentioned the fact that I'd been with a woman in London. As soon as the interviewers came back into the room and the recorder was switched back on the Chief Wren reported what I had said. It was classic manipulation. There was no compassion or thought for the kind of distress I was going through. They treated me like a criminal. As far as they were concerned I had broken their laws, so I was a criminal. They took me up to my room and said they were going to search all my belongings. Before they went in to do the search they asked, in a rather lurid tone, 'So, do you have any electrical items?' I said something along the lines of, 'Well, if you mean dildos and vibrators, no.' But, frankly, if they'd searched any locker in that block I'm sure they would have come up with loads of that kind of stuff; they're not exclusive to lesbians! Nothing was sacred; they went through everything.

They moved me out of the room with the person who had dobbed me in, but they didn't actually move me very far, so I saw her every day. I wasn't discharged for three months, so I was stuck on a base with everybody knowing what was happening. I had people who were very supportive; there was a Naval photographer who was very good to me. They sent me home to tell my parents, which was a very difficult conversation. They were completely supportive; they always have been and they always will be. I am extremely lucky to have such wonderful parents. I was massively distressed; I was feeling such a disappointment to them. Sorry, I wasn't expecting to find talking about this so upsetting, but it takes me right back to being in the room with my parents and apologizing for being such a disappointment. That was horrendous. God, if they hadn't been supportive I don't know what I would have done, I really don't. That's not a place I would wish to visit again; nor would I wish it on anyone to have to do that.

I came back to base to wait and eventually they said that I was discharged shore, had to leave the base in forty-eight hours, and give all my stuff back. When you leave, there's lots of things you have to sign: you have to sign all the statements that people have made against you, you have to read the transcript of everything you've said in the interview and sign that, and they also make you sign something that says you will not take them to court later. I remember that I specifically wrote, 'The only reason that I am not going to take this further at this point in time is because my father is so ill, but I reserve the right to be able to do so later.' I am absolutely sure that they burned that. They also mysteriously mislaid or destroyed the transcript of the interview and also the master data tape. I was immensely traumatized. My dream to support and serve my country was gone. I was completely lost.

It was five years later, in 1998, when I first spoke to Stephen Grosz, who became my solicitor. I'd phoned up Stonewall and they gave me his number and set me on the path to exactly where I needed to be. By that time, I'd got enough confidence in my own self and felt secure enough in my own person to face looking at this question of whether people who are homosexual should be allowed to serve in the armed services or not. My motivation for contacting a solicitor was that I wanted to change the law. I wanted, also, a validation that I should have been able to stay in the Navy and build my career and be Chief Petty Officer or an officer, or whatever

I would have been at the end. So I wanted to, at least, register my protest about gay people not being allowed to serve in the armed forces. To get to the point where the law actually changed was the golden goal. It wasn't about money; it never was, it never will be.

In March 1998, I went to an Industrial Tribunal hearing, which was a very strange experience. As well as my barrister and I, there were three QCs lined up on the other side for the Ministry of Defence. It was an open public hearing, there were journalists in there, and when I came out there was a camera in my face. It was the weirdest sensation ever and I didn't enjoy it, to say the least. We didn't succeed in the Industrial Tribunal and, because there were some other cases that were likely to scupper us, we decided not to continue in the UK court system and instead go to the European Court of Human Rights. So there was more gathering of data and meetings to develop exactly what was going to happen. I didn't have an understanding of the Convention and I trusted the solicitor to put the complaint in under the right Articles. I didn't read the Convention, which is pretty poor of me really! My view of the European Court of Human Rights was that it existed to defend basic human rights, whether that's the right for gay men and women to be allowed to serve in the armed services, or any other small or large human right. I saw the European Court of Human Rights as the defender of my soul; or at least that is what I was hoping it was going to be.

I was asked at this point whether I wanted to be anonymous or not. I felt that, whilst I'd had no choice about anonymity in the UK courts, I did have a choice in the European Court of Human Rights. It was such a large and potentially high profile case and I'd already had this Lady Diana experience of having a camera stuck in my face. I had my parents and my brother to consider, and I had also started a relationship with a woman that was only four or five months old. I wanted to protect my family and my new girlfriend from any kind of repercussion or scrutiny. I also didn't want anything to affect the new career that I was building. So, for those reasons, I decided that I would prefer to be anonymous in the European Court. What's interesting is that I now look back and regret that my name isn't on it.

I had no involvement with Stonewall other than that sole phone call and I didn't have any contact with any other organization, like Rank Outsiders. You would have thought that I would have done but, no, I was totally on my own. I didn't do the case as part of an organization. I didn't even think to align myself with something like that. It was about me; it was my way of making a protest and, hopefully, trying to change the law for others. It never occurred to me to be part of a group or to look for support in other areas.

I'm not sure I knew what to expect from Strasbourg. At the beginning, I didn't think I'd win. As time went on, once Duncan Lustig-Prean and the others' complaints were deemed admissible and they won, I had more confidence that my case would follow that precedent. But until that happened, it was up in the air. Also, I thought I might win my case but that they might just compensate the people who had been thrown out but not change the law. So it was only really in January 2000, when the law was changed to allow homosexuals to serve in the armed forces, that I thought I must be able to win my case.

At the time of the case, it was empowering to feel that I had taken that stand; that I had followed up effectively on what I had written on my exit papers. It felt like a very personal victory when the law was changed. Although my case wasn't the one that turned the law over, it added weight and I felt I was part of a movement, a small cog, which was helping further the rights of gay men and women in the UK. I didn't really think about the case once it was won and closed. It's only really been in the last few years that, when I meet people and explain something about my life, I talk about it. More recently, I've realized the importance of what I did. One thing that really brought it home to me was at this year's Gay Pride in Brighton, which I went to for the first time in seventeen years—the first time since around the time I started the case. I couldn't believe that the Army had a stand at Gay Pride and, not only that, but it was a recruitment stand. To go from being woken up, investigated, interrogated, having all your stuff gone through, and being thrown out, to finding the Army recruiting gay men and women was completely mind boggling. It really brought it home to me that if I hadn't done what I did, seventeen years later gay men and women would not be being recruited into the armed services, but would still be persecuted and thrown out. The fact that I had an integral part to play in that journey is a source of immense pride to me.

Some people are quite shocked and amazed that I would go to the lengths of taking something to the European Court of Human Rights. It's no small task; it took four years in total. At the time, as I said, being anonymous made me feel more comfortable about doing it. Now, I'm very grateful that I can put my name to something that's my little stamp on history. I would rather have my name there, as a human face to the case, than just an initial, if that helps somebody who is looking at it from the other side of the fence, where that's not possible for them.

*

Beck, Copp and Bazeley v the United Kingdom (1999–2002)

Kevin Bazeley, a Flight Lieutenant in the Royal Air Force, was investigated and discharged in 1995 in pursuance of the then policy of the Ministry of Defence that homosexuality was incompatible with service in the armed forces. Following an unsuccessful attempt to challenge the decision of the Air Force authorities, in 1999, Mr Bazeley complained to the European Court of Human Rights about the intrusive investigation into a most intimate part of his private life and his discharge from the armed forces. He also complained that he had no effective remedy before a national authority. In 2002, the Court upheld these complaints.

Kevin Bazeley

I'd always wanted to be in the Royal Air Force and to fly. I joined the Air Cadets as soon as I could at thirteen and went straight into the RAF from school. I went to RAF Cranwell in November 1985, graduated from there in March 1986, and started initial pilot training at RAF Linton-on-Ouse. I was redirected to navigator training and, when I passed out, I went to RAF Leuchars to be a navigator on Phantom aircraft. It was there that I met my wife. Up until that point I had thought that I was possibly gay. I had been conflicted throughout much of my youth and my early sexual history was non-existent. I bought some magazines as I was growing up as a teenager, both heterosexual and homosexual magazines, so I knew I had some thought about being gay. But there was the conflict of knowing that, although I wanted to fly in the RAF more than anything else, homosexuality was still criminalized at the time that I joined. So I pushed it out of my mind and tried to carry on with the professional side of things. I couldn't let that side of me become public and I would do everything I could to forget about it. I'd try to be asexual or, if there were parties in the Officers' Mess, I'd flirt with the nurses that got invited, just to do the thing that everyone expects of you. When I met my wife and it developed into a physical relationship I thought the feeling that I might be gay was just a phase I was going through. Initially, it was a huge relief and I thought, I am just like everyone else, I am just a slow starter.

We got married and I moved to RAF Brize Norton. My wife came with me and by then we'd just had our first daughter. I started to realize that things weren't right and that I wasn't getting from the relationship what I needed. At the end of my time at Brize Norton I was ready to sit my wife down and say things weren't working and needed to end. There was no easy way out of the situation without someone getting hurt. I could have done what other people did, I could have gone cottaging or whatever behind her back, but, for my own integrity, I wasn't prepared to do that to her. She didn't deserve it and both of us deserved to be happy. So there was one of those discussions where I said, 'I've got something to say', and she said, 'I've got something to say', and I said, 'You first', and she said, 'I'm expecting again.' So I thought, okay, let's make this work. But it got progressively worse and I felt completely and utterly trapped. I didn't want to hurt her but at the same time I was desperately unhappy. It got to the point where, when my wife would touch me, I would be physically recoiling from her, which must have been horrific for her.

I couldn't come clean with my wife because, since the armed forces weren't accepting of homosexuality, my biggest fear was that I would tell her and, quite understandably, in a fit of rage she would lash out and tell the Air Force. Not only would the relationship end but my career would be over as well. So eventually I just said things weren't working and that we had to separate. It was a horrific decision and I spent a lot of time and angst coming to it. My wife was, understandably, very upset and angry. After a few years, I did eventually tell her the reason and it didn't necessarily smooth things over but perhaps she had a better understanding. I lost contact with my two daughters for about the first fifteen years of their lives. I had very little contact with them, other than Christmas and birthdays cards. They're obviously mature adults now and they have progressed to the point where they want to make contact with me. I wouldn't say it's the closest of relationships, but we are slowly getting there.

I really don't recall any significant incidents of overtly homophobic behaviour in the RAF. The only thing I recall is that every now and again someone like myself would be discovered—outed or whatever—and obviously the news would ripple very quickly through the ranks. For a period afterwards there would be jokes about that squadron and people would say things like, 'They're all a bunch of bandits over there.' Nothing really sticks out in my mind as being overtly aggressive but there's no such thing as harmless banter; it can always impact on someone. And obviously it impacted on me because the banter I did hear, as low level as it was, was still sufficient to reinforce the message that there was no way on earth that I could be open, even with people I thought I knew exceptionally well. In the RAF, in the officer corps—this sounds a bit snobbish—the people tend to have a higher level of education and that higher level of education, which generally and historically has been more accepting of homosexuality, has conditioned them in social acceptance. So I'd think, well, perhaps I could be quietly open with someone. But then some throwaway comment would be made and I just thought, no, I can't do it. And, obviously, there were no outwardly gay role models that you could point to.

I think the constant battle to hide part of yourself and not take your whole self to work was the reason that I didn't do as well as I believe I should have been able to do in the Air Force. My performance suffered and I wasn't the officer that I believed I could have been, because twenty-five or thirty percent of my capacity was being diverted to maintain my cover. Obviously, whilst I was married, I had cover, and it was all perfectly okay. After we separated, I hoped that I could make it to the point where the armed forces would come to their own senses about homosexuality. In my head, I thought it couldn't be long before they had to come in line with the rest of society. I thought I had a few years to just hang on in there, focusing on my career, becoming the best navigator I could be, and if a relationship happened I would make sure that it was maintained away from the eyes of my colleagues until such time as legislation was changed.

I thought things would change because I'd seen the way that the military had handled bringing women into more frontline roles within the armed forces. There had been exactly the same types of arguments against that—it will be damaging to morale and to discipline; there will be fraternization and relationships—and all of these arguments were thrown out and eventually people realized they were nonsense. So, in the back of my head, knowing that the rest of society—although there was a long way to go—was becoming more accepting of homosexuality, I couldn't see that the armed forces could last much longer as this bastion of anti-gay regulation. It just wasn't consistent with being part of the European Union, the European Court of Human Rights, and so many things that were coming out in the press at the time. I knew it was only a matter of time and I was just trying to hold on long enough.

I had started talking with a guy before I actually separated from my wife. I'd met him on one of those chat lines that used to exist. When I separated from my wife I met him and a relationship developed—we are still together now and we've been happily married for six years. We joined the Gay Bikers Motorcycle Club together and we went out clubbing and things like that. Unfortunately, in 1994, I lost my wallet somewhere and the membership card for the Gay Bikers Motorcycle Club and a nightclub in Wolverhampton were in it. From the moment I realized I'd lost it I panicked and, about a week later, after we'd been on a training sortie and landed from a ten hour flight, the wing commander met the aircraft, came up the steps and, whilst I was filling in the post-flight paperwork, said, 'You don't need to fill that in, just come with me.' He drove me to the RAF police station and I was taken away to an interview room and went through the process of being interviewed by the RAF police. They presented me with my wallet, said it had been handed in, showed me the two membership cards and said, 'Are these yours?' I think my response was something along the lines of, 'The signature on the back would seem to indicate it wouldn't it.' They spent a short while trying to confirm details, asked me did I know anyone else who was gay, did I understand that it was against the regulations, and then I was immediately suspended at that point.

In a lot of ways, it was a huge relief. I was no longer hiding things and I was able to be honest with my colleagues, who I did respect. They had no issues at all. They were young people of my age, they knew what society was like, and it was all quite amiable. The only negative feedback I received whilst I was still on the station was that someone threw my coffee mug away. So, on the face of it, if my peers and colleagues could be understanding, I felt that if I could hang on in there and argue my case well enough that perhaps I could overturn the decision and get to stay. It was in August 1994 that I was met off the plane, and I was finally discharged in September 1995. After the first four or five weeks of that period they sent me away from the station and I sought every avenue I could to fight the situation. I went through various stages of discussions and interviews with senior ranking guys in London but eventually it got to the point where no one in the Air Force was going to do anything. A good part of me knew it was probably a hiding to nothing so I started day college, doing accountancy studies, knowing that I needed to secure some sort of professional future, because I had very few relevant qualifications or directly transferable skills.

I had started going to the support group Rank Outsiders and had met a few of the other people from the time, Duncan Lustig-Prean and so on. We had obviously discussed the issues and what could be done to change legislation. I eventually went to solicitors in Birmingham on the recommendation of some of the other people from Rank Outsiders. By then I was under no illusion that I was going to get the decision turned round and get readmitted. It was very much a case of me saying you shouldn't have done this to me and it was wrong to have thrown me out of a job for something that was not job related. In terms of my motivation, I would love to say it was totally altruistic, that I wanted to change the world and force a legislative change to create a better environment for anyone following in the armed forces. But, at the time, there was an awful lot of financial pressure on me—I'd gone from a fairly good salary to being a temp working in a finance office—and I had childcare to pay. I was in a very difficult place financially. So I will be totally honest and say, of course, there was a financial aspect to the case I was bringing. I could see that I had lost the potential for considerable future earnings and pension. But I did want things to change, because I did not believe that it was right for anybody to be discriminated against. I knew that I was perfectly good at my job and as good as the next person, whether they be gay, straight, lesbian, transsexual, transgender or whatever label anyone wanted to apply.

It was my solicitor's idea to go to the European Court of Human Rights. We had initially gone through the UK courts and that decision was mine—I had gone to them to pursue the case, they hadn't sought me out. I had heard of the European Court of Human Rights, yes, although I couldn't tell you specifically what cases I had heard of. I saw Europe as a huge bureaucracy that had grand visions of trying to regulate across a raft of very different nations and populations. There were the usual horror stories at the time, of the European Union trying to force this and that on us, trying to straighten our bananas. Did I read the European Convention on Human Rights? I'll be honest, no! I understood the basic concept of what they were trying to achieve, in that everyone was equal, no one should be discriminated against on grounds of race, sexuality, colour, creed, or whatever. In that respect, I understood the goals that the Convention was indented for and fully agreed with what they were trying to achieve.

The solicitors tended to deal with the majority of it. I met with them on a number of occasions and I listened to them and their recommendations. At the end of the day, my understanding of employment law was slight and they were the experts. At the start, I would say I was probably fifty-fifty on whether we would win in Europe. Personally, I couldn't see an argument to maintain the ban and everything I had read about human rights suggested that the European Court of Human Rights would come down in favour of me but, as with any legal case, surprises can happen. I was certainly very hopeful but I really had no definite sense that we were going to win. When the first rulings came through from the Court in 1999, I then knew that we were going to win. There was nothing different in any of the cases that followed and I couldn't see anything that would change the mind of the Court; they had effectively made the ruling for all future cases.

I would say that my solicitors were a little optimistic on the amount of recompense that would be forthcoming. I mean, certainly the claim that we put in was considerably higher than the monies paid out. When the solicitors first started talking about the sum of money with regard to the pension that I was owed I wasn't under any illusion that I was going to get anything like that. The final recompense was a small percentage of the initial claim so, in that respect, I think my solicitors had overestimated the will of the European Court of Human Rights to make recompense for any wrongdoing. The real goal for the Court is getting the laws changed, getting the society changed, to get rid of those issues. Yes, they recognize that certain individuals who have claimed are owed something for what they've been through, but I guess what they think is that if they pay out millions to everybody then the floodgates would be open, and who would pay that money?

When I got the judgment, I felt hugely vindicated. It came a few years too late perhaps, but better late than never! Initially, when the ruling came out, there was a two-page spread in the *Mail on Sunday*, with names mentioned, and I remember going to work on the Monday morning, sitting in my car shaking, wondering if I should go into the office, because I wasn't out with the people I worked with. But it was a complete non-event and, since then, my civil partnership has happened and, as with any other marriage of anyone in the office, everybody chipped in and they bought presents and gave wishes in cards, and the atmosphere is great. My understanding of the armed forces is that they have got to the point where being gay is a non-issue. It is amazing what change can happen within such a short space of time. The armed forces would probably argue that the change was effectively forced on them, but they have embraced it fully and lost none of their capability as a result. I would like to think that, in some way, the cases that myself and the rest brought did something to kick start that change and make life better for hundreds or thousands of soldiers, sailors and airmen who have gone through in the last twenty years and who have been able to express themselves as openly as they wanted to.

I don't think about the case very often anymore; my life has moved on. I'm pleased I took the case because if I hadn't pursued it as far as I could then I would have been forever thinking, what if? It was a shame that it had to get as far as the European Court of Human Rights—I would have liked to have thought that the UK, the House of Lords and so on, could have found in my favour without taking things to Europe—but I'm very pleased we took it that far and won. I would have been really pleased to take it that far even if we had lost, because I would know that I had tried as much as I could.

In terms of the future of the European Court of Human Rights, I think it would be a huge shame if people in the UK were to have the ability removed from them to go to an independent body, plead their case, and for any ruling to be rolled back into our UK legislation. Yes, I know there have been so many horror stories that the European Court of Human Rights has made us have five hundred thousand refugees living in the town next door and we have no choice but to accept it—all of those kinds of stories are constantly being made in the press. But I genuinely believe that the Court is there to ensure the human rights of everyone within Europe and the good that they have done is tangible. People can't always see the benefits but to not have that facility to go to, to ask for an independent decision on the facts presented, would be a very sad day. I think it's very easy if you're just going through the courts of your own country for the institutional beliefs of that country to be reflected by the courts and for that to override the right thing. Sometimes you need that third party to say, 'Well, no, hang on, that's not right, this is the right thing.' And sometimes that makes it easier for the national country to then turn around and say, 'Yes, you're right, we'll accept it, because you've made us.' The country can then back down and save face at the same time. So it's politics at the end of the day—and politics can be a treacherous place—but, in my view, leaving the European Court of Human Rights would be a retrograde step for the UK.

4

Family Life

Simpson v the United Kingdom (1985–1986)

In 1984, Mary Simpson's female partner, Nicky, died. Prior to that, the couple had lived together for several years in a council house of which Nicky was the secure tenant. Following Nicky's death, Harrogate Borough Council sought to possess the house and evict Ms Simpson from it. The English courts would not accept Ms Simpson's claim that, because she had lived with her partner in a manner akin to the state of living as husband and wife, she should be able to succeed to her late partner's tenancy in the same way that the survivor of an unmarried opposite-sex cohabiting couple was able to. Ms Simpson complained to the European Commission of Human Rights that evicting her from the house violated her right to respect for her private and family life, her right to respect for her home, and was discriminatory. In 1986, the Commission declared Ms Simpson's application inadmissible.

Mary Simpson

I met Nicky through a friend of mine in Southampton and she said, 'Why don't you come up and live with me?' so I said yes. I arrived in Harrogate, everything was all right, but I knew she wasn't well. She had an alcoholic problem. It was a snowy day and she just literally went on the floor, she fell out of the bed. I got her back into bed and I phoned the ambulance and the ambulance men said, 'No, there's not going to be much hope.' They took her to the hospital, which was just across the road, and she was only in there maybe a day and she passed over. The morning she passed over, they told me to go home and get some rest. My friend said, 'No, come and have a drink at the pub.' We got to the pub and the hospital phoned the pub and said, 'Come back immediately', so we went back and she had gone.

Within maybe less than an hour a housing official turned up and said, 'Your name's not on the housing book, the rent book, we're going to evict you.' I said, 'She just died.' He said, 'It doesn't matter, your name isn't on the rent book, we're going to evict you.' That happened within a couple of hours, less than that, of her dying. I don't know how they knew. It might have been the hospital phoning them up, I don't know. Somebody tipped them off, because they were there saying, 'You're being evicted.' They didn't say anything about my relationship with Nicky, they just said, 'You're not allowed to live here.' So I looked at my two dogs, I looked at my

Going to Strasbourg: An Oral History of Sexual Orientation Discrimination and the European Convention on Human Rights. First Edition. Paul Johnson. © Paul Johnson 2016. Published 2016 by Oxford University Press.

cats, and I said, 'Right, we've got to fight it.' I phoned *Gay News* and told them and they said, 'Right, we'll see what we can do.' I contacted them straight away, because I was fuming. Because it's like being dictated to: 'You can't do this, we'll tell you what to do, if you won't toe the line, we'll do this or do that.' But it's not toeing the line; you just want your life.

In the meantime, the kids in the street found out I was gay and they broke every window in that house. They thought that was fun. Even the police couldn't stop it. Because being gay wasn't 'normal', was it? But I still stayed put. I had no electric; they cut the electric off. There was broken windows, toilet just worked, just a little drop of running water, it was a right mess. I still stuck it out. My motivation was: why should I be dictated to because I didn't have my name on a bit of paper? So I thought, if I make a stand something might get done. And I made a stand. I was holed up there until we went to court and it was horrendous. But I thought, I'm not going to let them downtrodden you, you've got a right, you're still a human being, it doesn't matter what your sexual orientation is, you've still got a right to live, it doesn't matter what they try to do to you. They tried to knock me down but, although I'll get really down, I'll come back fighting. I've got an inner fight in me.

Gay News got hold of a solicitor for me. The County Court wasn't too bad. You just say 'yes, no' to the judge in the right places and you're all right. They said, 'Oh no, we can't do this', and 'You'll have to go to the appeal court.' The appeal court was horrendous. They couldn't do anything. There were only two judges sitting that day, I'll always remember, because if there was a third judge it might have been different. It is a great big building, with all these people in these robes and their wigs. It's a scary place, especially if you don't want to go there. I felt daunted with all these wigs and wotsits but I thought underneath it they're still human, hopefully. I thought, I've got to do this, it's not right, we should have rights, we've got to have rights. If we don't stick our necks above the parapet we don't get anywhere. It was hard, really hard. A friend of mine in Harrogate bleached my hair blonde—it was horrible—they were trying to make me look different, make me look sort of 'please help me', more respectable. Yes, it was frightening, but I kept thinking I've got to do it because if I don't do it nobody else is going to do it. Nobody else is going to say, 'Right, we've got to have some rights.' They'd just give up. I never give up.

I wasn't talking to my family by then. My brother went home with the newspapers, which said, 'Lesbian in High Court.' He said, 'Look, it's Mary.' I didn't know that I was in the Yorkshire paper, that I was in *The Times* next door to Princess Diana. It was absolutely everywhere. The next thing I knew there was a letter from Dad saying, 'What's all this about, what's going on, do you need some money?' So I had to go to the callbox and phone them up and say, 'It's all right, it's all been sorted.' Seeing as my father threw me out and said he didn't want anything more to do with me, they started being very supportive. Did I want any money? That's all they ever thought about, was money. No, I get by. He threw me out because I was lesbian. Mum wouldn't stand up to him. No, what he said went. I spoke to Mum on the phone after I'd been to court and she said, 'You're sticking your neck out a bit aren't you.' I don't care; I always put my neck on the block. That's me.

We went to the court of human rights and they couldn't do anything. It was the lawyer's idea. He didn't charge much for his fees. The chap from *Gay News* said, 'He hasn't charged us anything, or he's only added a small charge.' The lawyer said, 'Right, we're going to try the court of human rights.' He said, 'You don't have to go to Strasbourg, we just send the papers over.' I said, 'Go for it.' 'Sign this bit of paper, sign this bit of paper', that's all he kept saying. Did I have an idea about the kinds of arguments that they were making in the application? Not really. I know it was because same-sex persons couldn't take on the house without their name being on the rent book. But I thought, go for it. If we can do something, go for it. I thought, if we can just do something to make people understand: you cannot be cruel to other human beings, that's what it is. Doesn't matter if they want to be with a same-sex person, that's their business, it's nobody else's. We just have to open up their minds and tell them: look, you can't knock us about, we're real!

When the lawyer made the application to Strasbourg and sent the papers off, there was a long wait. Did I feel I was going to win? No, I just shut it out. It was going ahead, going ahead, that's all I kept thinking. It was hard; you don't realize how hard it is. But I thought, something has got to come out of it. I was hoping the law would change. So that if people lived as a couple and one decides to pee-off they still keep the house or, if the other one kicks the bucket, they can still keep the house. I did it for the freedom of being gay. Because there are a lot of people that are gay that won't admit it. In those days a lot of them never came out. They shut the door and kept the closet locked. But if you can just express yourself and say, right, I've done it for freedom… Freedom's a great thing. It's hard getting it, but it's a real good thing when you've got it.

They had a fund at *Gay News*, the Mary Simpson Appeal, just to get some money in to help us go through all the procedures. I thought it was really good of them. Because in those days you couldn't even say the word lesbian, or gay, without people turning their backs on you and walking off. You had to be really, really careful. They knew what they were doing. Without them I wouldn't have had the fight, because I wouldn't know how to have gone to solicitors and go on like that. You've got to go to solicitors and they have to look for a barrister, and then you've got to go to the High Court, and the appeal court, and the court of human rights. It's a lot of rigmarole. I wouldn't have had the know-how. It's having the know-how and the wherefore about how to start it going. Because you've got to get the ball going before it starts rolling haven't you, and you've got to know what to do.

In terms of the Convention, I know we've got human rights but I don't know what it's all about. All I know is that we've got to have rights and its got to be on equal par. It doesn't matter if you are gay, straight or peculiar, you've still got to be on equal par. The Articles in the Convention… No, no, it's too complicated. But as long as I could put my case saying, 'Look, something's got to be done.' I thought there were some judges there and they'll read the paperwork and they'll think, 'Ah, right, yes, I think they should change the law and let same-sex people keep their homes.' That's what I was hoping they'd do. I know they've got a load of jargon in between, but I thought they'd go, 'Oh yes, I can see the problem, yes, yes, I think same-sex people should keep the house even if one goes off, one dies; one should keep the house, the person who's living there.' That's what I thought it would be.

When I got the decision I felt gutted, really gutted. I felt deflated because I fought all that way. You know, you put all your heart and soul into it and they turn around and say they can't do anything. I was absolutely gobsmacked because it would have helped a lot of people. I was just trying to make the law different. But at least I did try. I tried to put my case, which was that everybody's got a right to live how they want to live, and not be dictated to. I thought the court of human rights would be a big building, with some dithery old blokes sitting in there, with their wigs on and their gowns, passing judgment on people they've never met, or never likely ever to meet, and thinking, 'Oh right, yeah, that should be alright, we'll let that one go… Oh, but just a minute, there's two women living together, one dies, ah, don't like the look of that, two women together, no they really need a man, dismiss it.' I reckon that's what they said. Or, 'Two blokes, two chaps living together, no, dismiss it, they need a woman.' Sorry, but that's what I think. They've got narrow views. They haven't lived. They haven't lived like I have anyway. They're so narrow-minded; they haven't seen the world.

The decision says, 'The applicant dressed as a woman and Mrs R. dressed as a man.' Well she's supposed to be the butch, you see. No, she didn't dress as a man. But they have this idea in their heads. You know, two woman can't be two women, they've got to be… That's bonkers. She always used to wear jeans and a T-shirt, she never did have a shirt, it was always a T-shirt and a pair of jeans. Their idea is stereotyped, isn't it. If they can't fit you in a box, that they think is the right box, they are completely foxed. Yeah, they've got to fit everybody into little boxes.

Afterwards, I kept my head down. Not many people know what happened thirty years ago. I just kept my head down; I kept trying to be normal. Because being gay in the 1980s was hard. I was at the Car Boot the other week and a nice young gay person come up—gaydar still works!—and I said to her that I was going to have an interview about what it was like thirty years ago and how you couldn't be openly gay. And she went, 'You couldn't?' and I said, 'No.' I said, 'You had to keep everything kind of normal.' I didn't tell her that the gay boys used to take you out to make sure they were normal; so it was two girls, two boys, and we were couples, so it was all normal. She was literally shocked. She said, 'It's not that bad!' And I thought, no, but it can be, and it still is in some parts. In those days you weren't supposed to be gay, you were supposed to be normal. Now, what is normal? Oh, it was terrible. You couldn't admit you were gay because if you went out and they knew you were gay they would beat you up. You had to keep so quiet all the time. So that's what I've done, I've been quiet. I've drawn myself in.

A lot of people around here I think know what I am. I don't care, I'm me. There are no two people like me. *I* am *me*. I will fight for my rights and I will keep on fighting until everybody gets their share of their rights, because it's not fair. Overseas, some places overseas, they're literally penalized for their sexual orientation all the time. And it's heart breaking to see what they go through. I've been through it and I know what it's like. You see, kids today think it's great walking about being openly gay, but there is still a lot of suppression. There are a lot of gay people that haven't come out. They've got married, but they've got married to sort of be normal. But they won't admit what they are. They sort of keep sweeping it under the carpet.

Over the years I've thought about the case now and again. I think about how hard it was. Sometimes you think 'if only'. And you think, no, forget it, that was years ago, shut the door, forget about it, move on. Him upstairs keeps us going. I'm a great believer that he'll always sort us out. I've got some type of inner strength, because I've been through so much in those thirty years. I've still got a fire in my belly. I would do it again. Now the law's changed a lot, but I would still do it. Because it's still not right how gay people are treated. There's still a lot of it going on in England, there is a lot of homophobia. Even in the whole world, there is lots of homophobia. So you've just got to keep toeing the line, but sometimes that line can break, and that's when it gets bad, so you just keep going. You've got to just keep on trying. You've got to make the government realize that they can't just ride roughshod over everyone. You've got to put your fight up and just concentrate on what you want to do. If you're being persecuted, don't let them get the better of you. Just keep on fighting. If they've downtrodden you, just keep going. You can't let people put you down. Sometimes it's really hard, but we've got to keep going, we've got to show them who's right. If you put your neck on the block you get somewhere. You've got to keep chipping away at the paintwork, bit by bit, until you break through.

I'm proud I did it. They walk about with gay pride, but I've got pride inside. I'm proud that I stuck my neck on the block and tried to get something done. It makes people realize that we can't be trodden on. Because a lot of people think gays are the riff-raff of society, they're the queer lot of society—it used to be queers, not gay—and I thought, no, I'm not having it, I've got to do something to make people realize we're still human beings. No matter which side of the fence we sit, we're still human beings. I just can't understand why people have to be so horrible to people, that's what gets me. Because if you don't do what they want, or toe the line, what do you do? You become a rebel. But I wasn't a rebel without a cause, I had a cause. I always make sure I've got a cause before I'm a rebel, because that way you're trying to help other people. That's what I've always been trying to do, is help other people. If I've helped somebody on the way, you know, I'm glad. It's better to do a good turn than a bad turn. It was hard going, but I think I have done something.

*

Parry v the United Kingdom (2005–2006)

In 2005, Wena Parry applied for a gender recognition certificate in order to gain legal recognition of her transition from male to female gender. In order to be issued with a full certificate, Ms Parry was required to annul her existing opposite-sex marriage because English law did not, at that time, recognize same-sex marriage. Ms Parry and her wife, Anita, did not wish to annul their marriage, not least because of their religious beliefs. Ms Parry and her wife complained to the European Court of Human Rights that requiring them to annul their marriage in order that Ms Parry could be legally recognized as a woman violated a number of their human rights including the right to marry which, they argued, must include the right to ongoing recognition of their marriage. In 2006, the Court declared the application inadmissible.

Wena Parry

Life had been a struggle for me. I felt my femininity and my masculinity. On the one hand, I was attempting to be masculine and behave masculine. I was an ardent do-it-yourself man, even banging a wall down in the house. But then, privately, with my wife, Anita, or earlier on when I was at home with my mam and dad, I would cross-dress and, immediately afterwards, feel very guilty. I was in a tug-of-war, you know. Anita was a lovely person. When I first told her about my cross-dressing she said, 'I thought you were too nice to be a man.'

When I went through the process of the transsexual change, the surgery, something happened. While Anita and I were very happy—we were often referred to as lovebirds—I realized that I wasn't fully a man as far as our marriage was concerned. Although, normally, it doesn't happen that your sexual attraction changes, it did for me, which made life terrible. I thought, when I was married, that I was one hundred percent heterosexual, but I wasn't. I remember seeing this hulk, where I was working in a commercial dairy, and I thought, wow. With my change of gender, I realized that I was attracted to men—but not gay, not gay, because now I am a woman. For some years it exploded my mind, but I've calmed down now.

In the late 1990s, I was given the cold shoulder as a minister because of my gender change. They couldn't understand it. There was also a chapel which, despite me having had the gender surgery, insisted that I use the men's toilet rather than the ladies' toilet. The chapel had a car park at the back of the building and, instead of going to the toilet, I'd go out through the back door into the car park and, when I wanted to empty my bladder, I used a bottle in my car. They also refused to let me go to the ladies' prayer meeting. They really put the thumb-screws on me. I had to take the chapel to court because I had to make it public that chapels and churches, like this particular one, were not sympathetic and couldn't understand it. I also had a case against the college that I went to when I was in transition. I went there, immediately after I started my transition, to learn a trade that I could use as a woman. I went to learn skin care and beauty and, part way through, they started saying, 'Well we can't do this with you, and we can't do that with you, and you've got to get your own client to do the beauty treatment on.' They lost the case; they capitulated.

I made a submission to the House of Commons at the time that the Gender Recognition Bill was going into Parliament about why I was for it. Then later on, of course, we found out that the Gender Recognition Act told us that we had to have an annulment of our marriage. That was a knock-back because, since Anita and I weren't prepared to have an annulment, we, or I, could not have a full gender recognition certificate; I had a temporary one. That's when Anita and I started fighting the Strasbourg case. When we were talking to the barrister who was doing the work, we told him that Anita and I had got married in church and that we made a declaration before God and the congregation that we would stay together until death do us part. That was basically our grounds for the complaint. I was prepared to go on without a gender recognition certificate, a change of birth certificate, or anything. I wouldn't annul the marriage, certainly not. It wouldn't be fair for Anita, for a start.

I was in a group, mainly on the Internet, called Press for Change. We all needed to play our part. Any newspaper that came along, I would speak to them. As part of the group, I knew that many, many people were frightened of the press. I am used to speaking in public and it was on my shoulders to do so. The barrister that dealt with the Strasbourg case found out about me refusing to take the annulment—I think he had a student, or worked with someone, who was a transsexual and possibly was in touch with Press for Change. I had posted it on the forum of the Press for Change website and he might have seen it there. The barrister offered to do the case *pro bono*. Another member of Press for Change was also going down that road but he was actually doing all the documentation himself, which is not a wise thing.

I met up with the barrister on, I think, two occasions. I took Anita with me as well because one of the documents concerned Anita agreeing to fight the case. He asked me about my feelings, emotions and so on. At that time, there was the so-called gay marriage, civil partnership, but we both felt that it would betray our marriage to simply have an annulment and then go and have a civil partnership. The barrister was very helpful. He was supportive, in as much as he could understand it for some reason.

I read the Convention and I considered that it should be one hundred percent for me because it was about human rights and my human rights were being trodden on with hobnail boots. The law relating to transsexuals had been to the European Court of Human Rights before, and two or three people had had their problems solved. The barrister asked me about the Articles in the Convention and he was very thorough, I think. He even put in the submission that I was a minister, when I got ordained, what denomination I'm with, and how my ministry had involved working behind the Iron Curtain. I was very involved in making the application.

In terms of my motivation, I was prepared to take the case because there were other people, other transsexuals, who had the same problem as me. I literally had to fight for them. I know how frightened you can get, when everybody turns against you. As a minister, I've always been in difficult situations. So I was doing it for other people, and for myself and my wife. If you're in a corner and there's a lion wanting to bite your head off, what do you do? Kick him? That's how it was with us. I was not prepared to break up my marriage. It would have made my children bastards, and I'm not going to have that. If we could have stayed together and had everything working all right, then that would have been smashing.

There was a personal cost. It made the persecution a lot worse. One particular fellow came across from his house and smashed the car up and started on the windows of the house. Anita got up and we went to face him. He had a hood on his face. Anita said to him, 'You want to fight women do you? You want to fight old age pensioners do you?' She was strong. He came up to me afterwards and said, 'I'm better now, I'm not the same man.' He didn't actually say, 'I'm sorry.' Our ordinary people, on council estates, didn't know the difference between a paedophile and a transsexual. The *News of the World* didn't help either. The biggest problem, even now, is still our chapels.

My family wasn't supportive and they're still not. When I first started my transition, I went to one of my three daughters' houses and told her, 'Look, let me tell you something, it's something really shocking and will frighten you probably.' I haven't seen my seven grandchildren ever since. I cry about it sometimes. But that same daughter has now started calling me Dad again. She says, 'Look, do you mind me calling you Dad, because you are my dad after all.' I do believe that I will see all three of them and my grandchildren before I go in that box in the ground. I don't blame them, let me say that I don't blame my children. It took me fifty years or so to come to terms with my feelings and emotions. I can't expect them to do much better than that. It's more explosive to them than it was for me.

When the case went to Strasbourg, I expected to win. I felt that this was the top, this was the Goliath, of human rights law. I felt that because of my right to privacy, and my home, and my rights in every other way—my family, and religious freedom—that we would win. But they failed me. When I got the decision I felt, well, that's a battle lost. I mean, all my life I've had battles; they're there to fight. Not with guns and bombs; I'm a Christian solider, I was brought up in the Salvation Army. While I wouldn't go and fight in the army—I was a conscientious objector and wouldn't do national service—I will fight for people's rights, even if I have to fight it for myself, because I am part of the human family. I would still do so. If Jesus was here now, he would do exactly the same. Anita was disappointed with the decision. But, you know, when you campaign, everything is part of the same fight and we were in the fight before the Gender Recognition Act and the Strasbourg case. Anita said, 'What are we going to do?' I said, 'Well, I'm not going to annul our marriage.'

The Court said the complaint was manifestly ill-founded. I don't think it was. There are the family rights between my wife and I and my children, plus the religious side. It might be thought to be ill-founded by chapels and churches, possibly. The weakness of the decision was that they sent it back to Britain, to the very same people that had made the law, the Gender Recognition Act. So, it was—I can't explain it—it was a cop-out. The decision of the European Court of Human Rights was a cop-out. The problem that the Gender Recognition Act created for Anita and I, and other people like us, is not a problem anymore because transsexuals can remain married. That's an admission that they did wrong with us. It's an open admission.

I'm beginning to see why the government wants to come out of the human rights thing. I'm not surprised. I think, even though I was disappointed with the European Court of Human Rights, they could make a better job if each of the countries were prepared to give up control of their own human rights to Strasbourg. But it would be a bit hit and miss because they wouldn't know us Welsh people. They wouldn't know how religious we are. They wouldn't understand the sociology of our people. They have that difficulty. However, one of the problems that arose for me, that meant I had to go to Strasbourg rather than to British law, was that I had a barrister that was prepared to do *pro bono* work for me and take it direct to the European Court of Human Rights. Where would I get the funds to take that same matter through British courts? It would have cost me a fortune, that I don't have. The British human rights system is failing people by not having a court of human rights. I think we should have a UK human rights court that would consider a case until, at the end, it said, 'Well, we can't take this any further, so you can now go to Strasbourg.' That would be by far the best thing. I mean the politicians are talking about this at the moment. As it is now, and as it has been, well, it's a waste of time. It's a waste of money. Another great weakness in Britain is that, in human rights matters, the courts should not be pressing for costs whether or not a case has failed.

It wasn't long after the Strasbourg decision that Anita died. Now, for me as a Christian, and for my wife as a Christian, death means being in heaven with our saviour. So, there is no fear of death at all, except pain of course. I was very reliant on Anita for all sorts of things. When you start transitioning as a transsexual, you get quite frightened because people have got daggers after you—not literally, of course—and Anita was my support. If I found somebody else now, it would have to be a real radical Christian. I couldn't imagine that, because even evangelicals in my own denomination can't accept my transsexuality very well. So I've come to the conclusion that, at seventy-six, I don't want to get married. Some great prince would have to come along and sweep me off my feet, but I can't think that is going to happen. Also, if that was to happen and I was marrying a man somewhere, it would cause another problem for the religious people that are around me. They would think, 'You are still a man, so you're gay then', which is not so, because the Gender Recognition Act declared that I am a woman 'for all purposes'.

People confuse homosexuality with transsexuality, or at least they did. I think the Gender Recognition Act has overcome that greatly. It's ten years since the Act and it has done a lot of good. I don't understand gays, I don't indeed. I used to preach against gays at one time. I can't understand them, neither do they understand my transsexuality. I met them in different places, like on Welsh television which did a programme on gays, lesbians and transsexuals. Let's be fair, the gays and lesbians were much more friendly to us than the ordinary people. They were in the same sort of battle, but not the same one. People think that the transsexual is gay and I'm trying to get away from that. These days, I prefer to keep quiet, because I don't understand. I have realized that sexuality is something far deeper than just human relationships between one person and another. I can't say I approve, but I can understand from my own feelings, from my own emotions, that some things are very unexplainable. In a chapel I am associated with, we had a vote on whether we should allow gays to be members of the chapel. There are some bible verses to stop me voting for it. The minister was all for it and we crossed swords. On the one hand there is the scripture and, on the other hand, I can't understand the mentality of men with men.

*

Courten v the United Kingdom (2006–2008)

In 2005, Andrew Courten's partner of twenty-seven years, Punch, died suddenly. Mr Courten was not married to his partner—because English law did not then recognize the marriage of same-sex couples—and he was unable to benefit from the exemption from inheritance tax available to a surviving spouse. Mr Courten's partner died prior to the commencement of the Civil Partnership Act 2004 that provided same-sex couples with a formal mechanism for recognising and giving legal effect to their relationships, including exemption from inheritance tax. Mr Courten complained to the European Court of Human Rights that denying him the exemption from inheritance tax that was available to married couples, when he and his partner had been unable to enter into a legally-binding arrangement akin to marriage, was discriminatory. In 2008, the Court declared the application inadmissible.

Andrew Courten

Punch and I were together for twenty-seven years. Before that, he had been married, in South Africa, and, like myself, had never thought of himself as gay. In those days, any portrayal of gay was this horrible, over the top, caricature. He knew that that was nothing to do with him and, therefore, thought he couldn't be gay. Like an awful lot of gay boys it was very easy for him to go out with really beautiful women and he married the biggest catch in Cape Town, the daughter of the Norwegian Ambassador. After six months they knew the marriage wasn't working and, then, very sadly his wife was killed in a car accident. For Punch, it was a big shock and he wasn't sure what to do. He ended up leaving the country to make a new start in England. About eight years after his wife had died, he went on a business trip to Chicago and, as he often liked doing, he went out in the evening and was walking along Lake Superior, where the moon was out. He noticed there was a whole set of men around the shores—very handsome, butch men—and they weren't looking at the moon! He worked out what was going on and thought well, if gay men are actually like that, maybe I might be gay. When he came back to London he phoned up the Gay Switchboard and asked about the main clubs in London and found out, in a very precise and rational way, all the information he could. The main club in London at the time was called Bangs, so he decided to go there and see what was going on.

I had also led a very sheltered life. I didn't even know what gay was. There were some people that were portrayed on television that were über theatrical, but I had no concept of what gay meant. When I went to university, I saw this thing called Gay Society and I said to my friend, 'Look, they have a society for people that just want to be happy' and, seriously, that's what I thought it was. I had no idea at all and I just assumed I'd get married and settle down like 'normal' people. But then, when I was at university, I began to realize that there was this other world around. My first job was in London, but for two nights a week I also started working at Bangs—it was a good way to try and understand and meet people, and was a bit of fun. One night at eight-thirty, when Bangs opened, Punch came in and, because it was quiet, I was reading. He spotted what I was reading—the *Critique of Pure Reason* by Emmanuel Kant!—and we had a long conversation. It was very nice and the next week he came back and we agreed to meet. We went out to a little place called Annabel's on the Fulham Road for our first meal and it just went from there. He had a place that he was renting in Clapham so, after a few months, I moved in with him and it blossomed.

Over a few years, outside our professional careers, we bought, upgraded and sold several properties. When we bought the house, which I still live in, it was in a very poor state and we had to do an awful lot of things to it. Every day, as soon as we finished our day jobs, we were straight into our work clothes and we worked non-stop, every evening and every weekend, on the house. We were up until two o'clock in the morning sometimes. Because we had stretched ourselves to buy the place, we couldn't really afford to get workmen in, so we learned carpentry and plumbing skills ourselves. We absolutely slogged to build the house and the garden. The house became part of us, really. We were very much in love. People say couples have their ups and downs but I can honestly say that there wasn't a single day in the twenty-seven years I was with Punch that I wanted to be with anyone else. We never argued. We had disagreements, but never once did we raise our voices in anger to one another.

It was New Year's Day 2005 and we had lots of plans about what we were going to do during the holidays. We'd been in the garden and I'd made a lovely pie for the evening with Happy New Year on it. We ate and then Punch went upstairs and was lying in the bedroom watching the TV. I was working in the library and I heard his voice from the other room saying, 'Andrew, can you come in here please?' So I went through and he said, 'I don't feel very well.' It didn't feel right and I phoned a friend who was a GP and described what was going on and he said to tell Punch to relax and take an aspirin and to see how he was in ten minutes. But within five minutes the pain was intensifying and within just fifteen minutes he was dead in my arms. From absolutely normal life, in fifteen minutes, he was dead. There was no indication at all; it was unbelievable. The ambulance took him to the hospital and in the mortuary I lay on top of his dead body and wept uncontrollably for over an hour. It was just too much to bear; I was traumatized.

Soon after Punch died, I got a letter from the government saying that I had to pay £800,000 inheritance tax. Any married couple, in the same situation, wouldn't have had to pay a penny. Basically, what they were saying was: because the person that you have loved and lived with for twenty-seven years has died, we think that this is a good reason to tax you to such an extent that you've got to sell the house that the two of you have spent twenty years building up together. My reaction was complete, and almost naïve, incredulity. I have a natural sense of fairness and thought that this was so blatantly and obviously wrong. We'd spent fifteen years campaigning for civil partnership rights and, just after the Civil Partnership Act was passed in Parliament, old homophobic laws were cruelly punishing us.

The reason that we were denied the rights and privileges available to married couples wasn't fundamentally because of sexuality; it was because one of us wasn't a woman. It was pure sex discrimination and it was sexuality as well; it was both. I had spent fifteen years campaigning for civil partnerships. When civil partnerships got the Queen's assent, we had a party at our house with Ann Keen MP and various members of the House of Commons and the House of Lords. Ann said that she would make room in the House of Commons so that we could actually get married there on the first day that civil partnership became legal. As she left, the last thing that Punch said to her, with his usual lively humour, was, 'Well, we'll have to make sure that Andrew and I stay alive until next Autumn.' A week later he was dead.

We'd kept our own independent bank accounts, because Punch didn't want his company to know he was in a relationship—a typical gay scenario of those years—so all the funds went into an account with his name on it. I gave all of my spare money to him and he invested it. He was an accountant and knew better than me; and we were one unit, one person. I also travelled a lot overseas with work and Punch often needed to do speedy investments which, in those pre-Internet years, would be lost if he had to wait for my return to sign papers.

I knew his account would be closed when he died but they also closed my account as well because, although it was in my name, he was named on it as a signatory. So at that point in time, when everything was going wrong, and I had all the funeral costs, I literally had access to no money at all. I had to live on nothing and it was six months before I could actually get them to open my account. I was so fortunate that, as an accountant, he had hand written on so many documents and I was able to show that money in his account had come from mine. So, although originally I was asked for £800,000, the government accepted that, because we'd been living together as a couple, I'd been taxed on my own funds and, two years later, just before Christmas, I got a cheque returning my money.

That I didn't qualify for the exemption from inheritance tax available to married couples seemed an obvious unfairness. Everybody was saying, 'That's outrageous, how can they possible do that.' I tend to be a bit pig headed and, rather than disappear into a corner, I thought I want to actually do something. My only previous involvement with the law was getting our mortgage signed and when we did our wills. Because I'd never been involved and knew so little, I'd assumed the legal system was about right and wrong. So, at the start, I just thought I'm not going to sit on my arse and do nothing but, rather, see what can be done to help all people suffering in my situation. So it started off with me doing it all myself and then I realized that it was getting big. I was on the TV, the radio, and in the national press. I was trying to find people in the same situation as me but one of the problems was that a lot of people in the same situation were much older than me and had more hang-ups. A lot of them absolutely shunned the idea of being involved in anything where their names might be published, because they had deep shame issues about being gay. They had resigned themselves to the fact that when their partner died they'd have to pay tax and would do so quietly.

I knew about the European Court of Human Rights and when I realized that there wouldn't be success within the UK courts, it just seemed a logical avenue to explore. I spoke to lots of people and they confirmed that that would be a possible route. But first I had to go through all the UK courts; a very long and costly process.

Lord Lester, pre-eminent in the field of human rights for three decades, wrote a beautifully crafted letter that laid out the reasons why it was not possible for me to succeed in the hierarchy of UK courts and, *ipso facto*, why I could go straight to Strasbourg.

I saw fifteen solicitors and every single one of them asked me, 'How big is the estate?' It was either the very first thing they said or they asked it within two minutes of meeting. It was like asking a builder to quote for an extension and the first thing they say is, 'How much is your income?' Would you trust them? It was just outrageous; there was no sensitivity. They also didn't show much enthusiasm and one of the reasons for that was, if you're a lawyer, you want to pursue your career and the way you do that is to say, look at me, I have changed the law, I was the person that took something unfair and made it fair. But, in my case, the law had already been changed, civil partnerships had got the Queen's assent, and what I had suffered was in the period between the Queen's assent and the law coming into force. So a lot of the lawyers didn't have an incentive and thought, why bother with that one, I'm not going to get the kudos. I mean, they didn't blatantly say that but you can read between the lines.

There had been an article in the Guardian about me and a friend of mine who saw it emailed a lawyer he knew and said, 'Look, I know you've got a lot of gay clients, maybe you should go and speak to Andrew.' Initially, Richard, the lawyer, thought that it seemed a bit weird, me trying to go to the European Court of Human Rights on my own, and that I must be a bit of an oddball. But he did contact me, we arranged a meeting and, when he opened the door, both of us thought that we'd met before. We had our business meeting and, when we met a few days later, we worked out that six years previously, in a hotel in Provincetown in America, him and his partner, and me and my partner, had shared adjacent rooms, had cocktails in the evening at a group event, and had had breakfast together the next morning. Richard is now my husband. Because we realized quite early on that there was something between us, he said it wasn't right for him to act for me—he's a very honourable man—so we found somebody else: first, Mr Margave-Jones and then, when he decided that he no longer wanted to continue with the case because it was getting bigger than he'd expected and he was approaching retirement, Mr Hamlin from Withers, a firm that Richard had done a lot of work for.

I'd read the Convention and my understanding of it was helped a lot by the fact that the guy I was now going out with was a lawyer who knew a lot about that field. Richard could explain it to me on a casual basis, so I learned a lot in a non-formal way. I trusted Mr Hamlin as well so, if there were certain aspects that I didn't understand myself, I could see his competence and was quite happy to go with that. I didn't help prepare the submission, because Mr Hamlin did all that, but we had lots of meetings. I just read the submission and listened to what he said, and what Richard said, and understood that way. I was hoping I would win but, by the time I'd got to that stage, one of the lessons I'd learned is that the law is not about what's right and wrong, it's about precedent. But I still hoped, at least in the European Court of Human Rights, that right and wrong would be important.

So I was hoping I'd win, and I didn't think I wouldn't, but there were too many unknowns in the situation.

When I got the decision, I felt angry about it because it was so obviously wrong. I mean, why have we got this thing called the European Court of Human Rights in Strasbourg if they're not interested in human rights? Human rights isn't really about what's written on a piece of paper; it's about being humanistic and treating people as equal human beings. I'm very happy to accept someone else's opinion if they have a logical argument, even if it's not where I come from, and am happy to agree to disagree. What really annoys me is when someone makes a decision and they can't justify it; when they just say no. The reason the Court gave was that we were in an informal relationship. In fact, that was true, but the whole point of going to Strasbourg was to say that it was wrong for our relationship to be treated as informal and that we had desperately wanted it not to be treated as informal. So don't tell me it's informal—I already knew that—because I wouldn't have had to go to Strasbourg if we had been allowed to make our relationship formal in the way that we had wanted. It was such a damn stupid thing to say.

My understanding, from an insider who spoke with the decision making judges, was that the problem was basically that, were the Court to find in my favour, there would then be big pressure in all of the countries in the Council of Europe to implement civil partnership laws. But the Council of Europe contained many homophobic countries. With countries like Poland, can you see them putting in civil partnership? Someone said to me, 'Forget whether your case is right or wrong, there is no way that you can possibly win in Strasbourg because there are so many homophobic countries in Europe and, because of that, the Court will not be allowed to say yes to you, irrespective of whether your case is right or wrong, because the consequences will be so displeasing to governments.' It's realpolitik, isn't it, and that's when you realize the European Court of Human Rights isn't really about human rights.

Although Punch and I had tended not to be involved in groups like Stonewall—just, because of our personalities, we were more independent and used to do lots of things around the edges, like sending letters off ourselves—I was quite disappointed with Stonewall. At Punch's funeral, I told people not to bring flowers but that we would give money to Stonewall and I collected £8000 for them. Later on, when I was trying to find people in the same situation as me, I asked if I could use their records to find people and they refused. They were happy to take my money but not to help me. The law on civil partnerships had been passed and they weren't really interested. I was very disappointed that they had no interest in me at all, after the work I'd done for fifteen years to try and help the same cause. I was left on my own.

The Strasbourg case was incredibly stressful. I recognized, through direct experience, just how unfair the world is. Anyone that looks at the case can see that the way I was treated was so obviously wrong. The Court says it's about human rights but it's not humanistic at all; it's not interested in the human condition, it's got its own agenda. It's quite sad to realize that that is the case. While the case was going on I couldn't move on properly with my life because I didn't know what on earth was happening. It was a time of incredible confusion. The one good thing that came out of it was meeting my husband, Richard.

I'm pleased I took the case because I know that if I hadn't done it I would have been permanently saying I wonder what would have happened if I had. I just find it very sad that it was stopped for the reason it was stopped, which wasn't a logical reason at all. The home that Punch and I had struggled to build up, literally with blood and sweat, which had risen in value over the years, could have been taken away. And why? Because one of us had died. What's 'human rights' about punishing someone because the person they love has died? How is that right? There's nothing I can do about it now and I only tend to worry about things I can do something about. It's very sad, it was wrong, but worrying won't help me or anyone else. I can tell other people, but nothing can be done. It's just terribly sad that is how it is.

*

J.M. v the United Kingdom (2006–2010)

In 1998, J.M. began living with her female partner. She shared the care of her two children with the children's father, with whom they mainly lived. In 2001, Ms M. had her child maintenance obligation assessed. The assessment was made according to regulations that would have taken into account any new opposite-sex relationship that Ms M. had formed but took no account of her same-sex relationship. Ms M. successfully appealed against the maintenance assessment in the Appeals Tribunal but the Secretary of State repeatedly appealed until the decision was overturned by the House of Lords. In 2006, Ms M. complained to the European Court of Human Rights that the manner in which her financial liability had been determined was discriminatory and, in 2010, the Court upheld her complaint.

J.M.

In 1998, I started a degree. I'd been married up until that time, for sixteen years. I had two small children, two sons. Within that period of doing the degree I met a group of girls—all of the cohort were female—and I met a particular person called Sarah. It was something that came totally out of the blue and my life just changed. I fell totally head-over-heels in love with this person. I wouldn't have known why or how. I'd never thought of myself as anything other than heterosexual. But I wasn't and, obviously, I can love whomever I fall in love with. It just blew my world apart, basically.

I completed the degree—it was a very stressful time doing the degree anyway, particularly with two young children—and the pair of us thought we would live our existing lives and have this relationship. Actually, our lives were mirror images; we both had a husband, a detached house, two cars, two children, and professional lives. But I'm not a duplicitous person—I'm not a liar, I can't deceive, I'm an open book—and one thing led to another and we decided that we would be together. Our respective partners, our husbands, were just absolutely blown apart, and I suppose our children were as well. It was quite an emotional journey; we went from one extreme to the other.

I wish I'd had a husband that didn't want to be with his kids but I'd picked a good 'un, if you know what I mean, and he wanted to be in his children's lives. Sarah and I decided that the best thing was, because our husbands were participating partners, to leave the children in their family homes. Looking back, that was a big, big mistake—but life is a big mistake sometimes. Things then went into an Indiana Jones situation; like the big ball running after you. We ended up where the children lived with the men primarily. We went to court and we ended up with shared care, to a degree. My husband got the majority of the time with our sons.

Then it became all about finances really. The thing about the Child Support Agency at the time was that the less time you had with your children, the more you paid. I provided for my children while they were with my husband and also while they were with me. So I was paying him a large lump of money, and still providing everything for my children whilst they were with me. But if I had more time with them, the payment would have reduced. That was the thing about the Child Support Agency at that time: even though you were providing for your child it didn't promote children having both their parents in their lives, because it was all money focused. My younger son was saying, 'I want the week to be eight days, four and four', but it was never going to be like that. Why would my husband give me more time with the boys if I was going to give him less money? I was experiencing financial hardship. Because of what the Child Support Agency expected to come out of the pot, even though me and Sarah had good salaries, we didn't have a lot of money for us as a family—for all four children and both of us together.

But don't get me wrong, it wasn't about money, it was just about it being fair. Sarah was also dealing with the Child Support Agency—she was paying for her children, and I was paying for mine—but we weren't seen as being together. That was the whole issue. We weren't living in separate houses, but we were being treated separately. If I'd gone and lived with a man, they would have taken that into consideration. I would have been happy for them to take what they wanted from me, if they'd recognized that we were together. But they wouldn't recognize us as being a family. I could have been paying more, if they recognized us as a family. That didn't matter; it was about it being fair. You don't know what it's like until it happens to you. We were trying to maintain our income—not a high lifestyle—by getting by through hard work. And the issue was about us not being treated fairly; about the bureaucracy of not recognizing people as being together.

Before the first tribunal against the Child Support Agency, I contacted Liberty and approached James Welch and asked if he would be interested in attending and representing me. He did and we won. The lady who sat on the first tribunal was like a head mistress; you would be frightened of her. But the way she conducted herself—her arguments were so pro-family life—I was in awe of her. She wasn't concerned about the finances at all, she was just so positive about family. But the government wouldn't let it go. The support of James was important in me deciding to go to Strasbourg. He felt, as I felt, that it was just wrong that people should not be recognized. I felt that the way that we had put the case forward—and the barrister felt this too—was that it was viable. The problem was with our bureaucracy—who had their heads up their arses—whereas we perceived Strasbourg as being able to step away from that, being able to look in an objective way at the actual issue.

I suppose, truthfully, I was angry at the Child Support Agency. People have no idea how the Child Support Agency was; they were deviants themselves. It was torture; it was absolutely torturous. I suppose that was what pushed me on. I was angry; I wanted them to recognize that same-sex partners could have a fruitful relationship, a healthy relationship, a family relationship. I wanted to make that point. I had heard about the European Court of Human Rights from the Liberty website. I'd done a bit of reading around it and the Convention. I know in my heart it was the Child Support Agency that drove me because they were determined they were not in the wrong. And I also wanted to take the House of Lords to task. You look at the judges who were sitting in that House of Lords, probably 243 years of age, and that's two of them! They were never going to find in my favour.

So, truthfully, it wasn't about the money, it really, really wasn't. It was about fairness. People have these images in their mind about what you're actually doing. It all comes down to sexual acts; it's not about the person. There are more deviant heterosexuals, but people don't see that. You get treated differently and that's what it was about. I went and sat in the court and the guy said, 'But you realize you could pay more money?', and I said, 'Yes.' It was about the principle that we were treated differently. I was saying, 'What about our household?' I was totally in love with this person, wanted to have a family life with her, and wanted to provide for both our children. Not at the expense of our husbands, but they had partners. So it was just about everybody being able to have a life and being recognized as being together; like same-sex partners now, who have the same rights as everyone else.

It was such a traumatic time in our lives. It was a special time, but quite a traumatic time. Life, identity; it was all life changing stuff. My family disowned me originally, after leaving my husband, whereas Sarah's family totally accepted me. I remember her mam, who is now ninety years old, and was seventy-five then, told Sarah to bring me around to hers. That woman saved me, because it was such a big life change. I went from being 'normal' to being, well, you know. I'd never come across that. I'd never, as a heterosexual, been treated in any way different before. I'd worked in a women dominated profession and I'd never, ever had to cope with that. I'd always been seen, and perceived, as strong. I can't cope with unfairness. You explain to me why I am being treated differently and I'll try to understand it. But I couldn't understand it. I'd never come across being discriminated against, and I couldn't understand it. Because, to me, being in that relationship was normal; why wouldn't it be normal? You love someone; you want to be with them. It's not about what you do in the bed; it's about what you do as a family. Our children were healthy, they were well educated, and they weren't struggling. There was nothing wrong with our family unit. And they, the Child Support Agency and the government, were sort of disgracing that, by saying, 'How could you be a family? How could you, how dare you?'

Although I wasn't aligned socially with anyone particularly—I wasn't going to gay bars or anything—I just thought this is so unfair and, at the end of the day, this was a sort of vehicle that could make a change for people. That's what it was about.

But really the vehicle was too slow because, by the time the judgment came, time had moved on and society had moved on. This country knew that once they said 'yes' to me it would set a precedent, but as time went on the door was creaking open anyway. We were on the cusp of things. Because the case dragged on, the world changed dramatically during that period of time.

I was absolutely over the moon when I got the judgment. I was no longer with my partner, because time had moved on, so it was a bit of an anti-climax because it came after the horse had bolted, kind of thing. I was pleased a lot for Liberty, to actually have a judgment that was in place so that people could refer back to it and use it as a reference. It put in stone that this is how people should be treated; they can be recognized as a family, they are entitled to that. So I was over the moon. James was delighted, and I was delighted for them, because they had worked so hard on my behalf. So at least it wasn't futile. Not being with my partner, I couldn't go out and celebrate; that was the bit that was missing, you know, the glass of champagne. But it was good for people who could have their rights recognized. And I must admit, there was a little bit of me thinking, 'Yeah, we did it.' We combatted that discrimination really, for other people. People are entitled not to be discriminated against in law. People will always be discriminated against for lots of different reasons, but in law it was written in stone. So I was like, 'Yeah, we did it.' It was a nice feeling.

Although my partner knew about the case, because of how long ago it started, she wasn't aware of it at the end. I only told a couple of people, like my best friends, but wider than that, I didn't tell anyone. Truthfully, I've never discussed it with my children, because it was a painful time. The anonymity really was because, at that time, it was a stressful time for my children. I didn't need for someone to pick it up; people can be cruel. At that time, because I was with a woman it was like, 'She's different.' I'm not; I'm just the same person. But at that time you got treated differently. There's still that prejudice there, but not like it was then.

For all I was with Sarah, I would never have seen myself as gay, because I didn't think I was. I don't identify as gay. I think my first choice would be men now—maybe that's an easy way out! But it would probably be easier being gay, because if I go out with men now—again, I'm an open book—I'm not going to not say I've had a relationship with a woman. But when I do, it's like, 'Do you really know who you are, do you really know what you want?' People like you to be in a box. Being in a box makes people feel so much more comfortable, rather than being fluid, in between or whatever. I can remember all of my colleagues were supportive when I got together with Sarah but they all had this idea that I was gay. I used to say, 'I'm not, it's just a Sarah thing.' I wasn't looking at other women, it wasn't like that; it was definitely a thing about chemistry with someone. I've been in a couple of relationships with guys since then, but nothing long-term, and I'm not actively seeking anyone now. So I don't know what the hell I am really! But I'm comfortable with who I am.

The case going forward would never have happened without Liberty, because I didn't have the know-how, the knowledge or understanding. I owe everything to them. But they wanted me as a vehicle as well, and I wanted to be that. They represented me for free and got the barrister to take the case to the House of Lords and to Strasbourg. And I did get some money from the Court. Liberty got the whole costs awarded, and I also made a contribution.

I think that the way that things have changed, equality is now on the table. But there are new things that are happening. There's lot of children who are being born now who feel that they are not in the right body. I mean there are three year olds now—a little boy dressing as a girl, or a little girl dressing as a boy—and there's still people in this world who do not get it, do not want to get it, do not want to understand it, and will not protect their rights. Strasbourg is objective. I don't see it as being in a country. I see it as a body that happens to live in Strasbourg. I don't see it as country-related. It's not bothered by the financial implications of what it is deliberating on. It's just about people's rights; it just wants fairness. And our human rights could change beyond our understanding in the future. What if the UK decided that we could only have one child, like China did? Who knows how our human rights are going to change?

5

Legal Professionals and Campaigners

William Nash on *X. v the United Kingdom* (1975–1979) and Going to Strasbourg in the 1970s

In 1975, a man in his late twenties submitted an application to the European Commission of Human Rights from prison. He complained about his conviction for buggery, in respect of acts committed with two eighteen-year-old men, for which he had been sentenced to two-and-a-half years' imprisonment. William Nash became the applicant's legal representative after the Commission declared the application admissible—the first application relating to sexual orientation discrimination to pass this stage of review. The focus of the application was the minimum age for male homosexual acts, which, at twenty-one years, was five years higher than the 'age of consent' for most opposite-sex and female same-sex sexual acts. The Commission rejected the applicant's claim that his conviction and the law under which it was secured amounted to a violation of his right to respect for his private life, a violation of his right to freedom of expression, and was discriminatory. As a consequence of the Commission's opinion, the application never reached the European Court of Human Rights. 'X.' died in 1979.

This case was slightly odd in the sense that he actually submitted it. I only picked it up after it had started going through its paces at the Commission. I think it had been declared admissible without any legal advice from anyone. He had petitioned the Commission, as people sometimes did. In those days, it was quite common for the Commission to deal with admissibility on paper and then invite submissions on the merits and hold an oral hearing. At the time, it was not uncommon for people to know that you could write to Strasbourg. When I was legal officer of the National Council for Civil Liberties we used to get, as a matter of routine, a postbag from various prisoners who would complain about the correctness of their conviction or whatever. I think a few of them got to know about the European Commission and started writing to it, treating it as some form of ombudsman or court of appeal beyond the UK.

I don't quite remember how savvy he was about the Convention, but he obviously knew something about it because he'd put it forward. I presume it was after he was released from prison, but he might even have petitioned from in prison. I certainly didn't meet him until he'd been released. There had been some toing and froing between him and the Commission and they declared it admissible. At that point, he contacted the National Council for Civil Liberties and they asked me if I would take it on. The case was referred to me because there was a worker at

Going to Strasbourg: An Oral History of Sexual Orientation Discrimination and the European Convention on Human Rights. First Edition. Paul Johnson. © Paul Johnson 2016. Published 2016 by Oxford University Press.

the National Council for Civil Liberties who processed, what might be described as, the gay rights work, and who cottoned on to the letter and suggested my name. So I drafted the full submissions on the merits and then went to Strasbourg and presented the case.

As I remember, he was an accountant by training. I didn't get to know him terribly well. I can remember he took me out for a meal on New Year's Day and I met his partner/victim on that occasion. I didn't get to know much about him personally but, to me, he was intelligent. I particularly recall that. I think I was quite impressed with the fact that he had got as far as he had and hadn't done too bad a job on the paperwork at that point. His motivation is fairly obvious. I think he felt deeply aggrieved that he should be imprisoned for what he regarded as, or certainly presented to me as, a basic relationship that I could have had with a girl and nobody would have objected to. One has to accept that if you said now, to one man over twenty-one and one man between eighteen and twenty-one, 'you can't have a relationship, physically', you might expect something to be thrown in your face. I think he genuinely felt deeply aggrieved and I have a lot of sympathy with that, obviously. This was not a case that was heavily backed or inspired by one of the gay organizations; it was very much his own effort. I don't think he had any particular links with any gay organizations.

What I don't remember about this particular case is how sophisticated the initial argument was. Because the client himself was quite bright, it probably wouldn't have been past him to put together—and, indeed, I suspect he did put together—something which looked halfway reasonable on the various issues. Certainly, he raised the right to freedom of expression. I don't remember thinking of that one on my own. It sort of smacks to me of something he thought up. It's not the one that would hit you immediately. It's not impossible that I'm more inventive than I give myself credit for, but my guess is that he'd put it in the mix somewhere at an early stage. And when they declared it admissible, they probably added it in as one of the grounds on which they'd declared it admissible. Any argument that found favour at the point of admissibility is one that he'd thought up, rather than one I had, and anything that was declared admissible I would have gone along with and done my best to argue on the merits later.

I had been very surprised that this particular case had managed to get through admissibility, because there was an ambiguity on the facts about the degree of possible sado-masochism and/or coercive behaviour. One of the counts on which he had been convicted was, in fact, with the guy I met when I had dinner with him. He had maintained his complaint during the criminal proceedings in the UK. So it wasn't quite as simple a set of facts as: here are two men, one of who happens to be under the age of twenty-one, engaging in pure consensual sex. It was a little more murky than that and I can remember being quite surprised that they'd got it through. I mean, there were cases around at that stage when one might have had a cleaner, more 'acceptable' set of facts.

I didn't come to any personal decisions. I had my instructions and my instructions were that it was a consensual relationship. And, indeed, I submitted a statement from the other chap saying that. It's not the advocate's role to judge whether the instructions he's been given are true. And the forum I was in was not one of those places where you go and call witnesses and invite the court to think of them as truthful witnesses, or cross examine them and invite the court to say that they're lying, as one might in a standard criminal court. It was entirely done on paper—I mean in terms of the facts of the case—and I seem to recall that we had a full transcript of the relevant portions of the domestic court hearing. So the judge's sentencing remarks would all have been there, in front of the Commission.

I made the point in the Commission that they shouldn't regard it as a murky set of facts because he was convicted on the basis of consensual acts. That was, so to speak, my get out of jail card on the fact that the facts were not particularly nice in my favour. There could not have been an indictment against a heterosexual couple of those ages—transposing the facts into the heterosexual context—based entirely on consent, that's true. But there was always the problem that there was a bit of an issue about whether that was really the case, and that's what the Commission referred to. I'd always been a bit worried that the facts were going to come home and bite me, and I think in fact they did a little bit in the end. It was always a bit hopeful because, simply on the mechanics, the Commission was not a place that was there to find facts contrary to those found in the domestic hearing. Its role was much more to take the domestic hearing's result and test it against the provisions and the jurisprudence of the European human rights environment.

The merits were essentially drafted by me, with help from various places. The paperwork for the merits went into some detail. Not only things like our own Wolfenden Report, but also the Dutch Speijer Report, and also some other similar academic stuff that we drew upon. I didn't find all of the stuff that I put in the merits argument on my own. There was one particular academic who contributed quite a lot to the argument. He was incredibly helpful. He helped me develop the arguments on the merits and pointed me in the right direction of the sort of materials that I was quoting. For instance, I don't think I would have known of the Speijer Report. I mean, I'm a lawyer, I'm not a single-issue campaigner. But people who were more like single-issue campaigners, who were around, knew about these things. I had left the National Council for Civil Liberties but I was fairly well in touch with most of the campaigning groups in the civil liberties field. I certainly had links with the gay rights organizations that were around at the time, and it wouldn't have been difficult for me to contact one of them and say: what do you think of this?

The case was a matter of considerable interest. There's been a lot of stuff recently about the Paedophile Information Exchange and all the rest of it, but one has to remember that at that time it was only ten years since the first tentative steps towards liberalizing the law on adult homosexuality had taken place. An awful lot of people were questioning the age of consent issues that surrounded male homosexual behaviour, because it was an area where there was an obvious disparity between that and the heterosexual equivalent or even the lesbian equivalent. There was quite a bit of debate about how far the law should go and whether—actually it sounds quite frightening now—homosexuality could be inculcated into you, into the young. There was a sort of obvious, basic presumption that that would be a bad thing.

Indeed I recall, when I was preparing the case, discussing the issue with a consultant psychiatrist I knew, who was an expert in psychosexual disorders. I had been helped by him in an earlier European case on a different topic. I went to him and he was very reluctant to assist me because he took the view that young men were not particularly fixed in their sexual preferences and it would be unfortunate if the age of consent was young enough to divert them into homosexuality. I can remember being very surprised he took that view, because it was already beginning to sound a very conservative view; but it was around. The whole climate was quite different.

It's difficult to say what the government's position was. I think the British government tended to look at cases like this and say: this is a piece of litigation, it's against us, and we have to try and win it. I don't think they were very pleased. The level I was engaged with—which is not the top political level—was the sort of civil service, treasury solicitor level. I don't think they thought it was a very good idea that some whippersnapper could come along and force them to change the law. The thing I will say—whether this is fair or not—is that for the one I did on the Irish case, McVeigh and Others, Vincent Evans was the person who presented the case, with Nic Bratza as his junior. Nic Bratza, at the time, was an up and coming junior barrister and it was long before he himself got appointed judicially to Europe. His predecessor, as the British judge, was Vincent Evans. Now, whether you read anything in to the fact that they sent Nic on his own for this case, and when it got to the prevention of terrorism stuff in the Irish case they brought in the big guns, I don't know. I don't know whether that's the way they thought. I mean, whenever you go over there the British government always sends a delegation of about fifty people—that's an exaggeration—and if you look at the opening remarks it says, 'On behalf of the government we welcome' and then there is a whole list of people, and then, 'On behalf of the applicant we welcome Mr Nash and we welcome the applicant.' You feel outnumbered. I think if we had won they would have had fairly good grace. But that's not to say that they didn't fight to win, I think they definitely wanted to win it. I can remember being really annoyed that the government came up with the argument that because anal intercourse was still unlawful between heterosexuals that this couldn't be considered to be discrimination if it was unlawful between consenting males. I can remember jokingly saying: I'm going to try and find one of those to take to Strasbourg.

We had a good hearing out of it, and there were some good people on the Commission in those days. Though I say it myself, it was presented with some care and I rehearsed the arguments with a number of people. I'm not gay myself and I went to a number of gay friends and asked them to consider the written application on the merits and check that they thought it a correct approach, one that they would approve of. I was quite concerned to do that because it is always possible to tread on toes and make arguments that people don't really like. I wanted to make sure that it sounded right on all sides, so to speak. I can remember being quite pleased with the written argument on the merits. It wasn't just simply a rant about the law. It was quite a difficult and closely reasoned argument as I recall it. My first involvement with the Commission had been with the Isle of Man birching issue and I might have gone back to how that was presented as a template for how to do it this time round, or it may have been my idea generally. But I plead guilty for producing the format and presentation of the merits.

I often wondered whether I was really right. What I do remember worrying about in my own head was whether to pick the age of eighteen as the basis of my argument, or whether I should be going the whole hog and saying sixteen and equating male homosexual acts with heterosexual acts in the way that they would now be regarded. I can remember worrying about that and thinking maybe I was going to be too radical for them if I did that. That's why I picked eighteen. I did sometimes wonder whether there wasn't a little bit of inconsistency in the argument. Because essentially what I was saying was these guys are being discriminated against, they're not being allowed to express themselves sexually in the way the rest of us are and, if I as a heterosexual male can have affairs with girls of sixteen, why can't my homosexual friends do the same with boys or young men of sixteen. I do remember worrying and thinking, no, it would actually be going too far in the present climate. And that was very definitely a political—with a medium sized 'p'—decision, to base the argument around the age of eighteen.

It was convenient that the age of majority had been reduced to eighteen. You see, in 1967 the age of majority was twenty-one. I know to my own cost, because my parents died when I was eighteen and, being under the age of majority, it had all sorts of strange consequences. So I would have been quite conscious of that, on a personal level, and I was acutely aware of the differences between twenty-one and eighteen that had changed during the course of my, at that stage, not particularly long life. It was very convenient that there was a peg to hang it on. But I do remember thinking that it's not necessarily a wholly consistent argument if you don't go down to sixteen. And there were, I suspect, people who were trying to persuade me to argue it on the basis of sixteen. There were people who knew I was involved in the case and would have put in their two penny worth as to how I should argue it. I can remember taking it round and just arguing it with friends and acquaintances, just trying arguments. I mean it was a very interesting case to do. I probably got paid about tuppence-happeny an hour but I wouldn't have given it up for the world.

As far as I'm aware, this was the first attempt to make a serious stab at lowering the age of consent. I had forgotten that it was a split decision. But that's typical isn't it, you get a split decision and then, like the American Supreme Court, it wavers and then it goes, in one direction or another. Sometimes that's to do with changes in persona, but on other occasions it's simply getting a further refinement of the argument. Obviously in anti-discrimination terms, I deeply regret I didn't win it. I took on the case because it was an obvious issue where I felt that we were lagging in this country and I felt might be something that the Europeans would grab. I do remember being quite disappointed about the fact that we did lose, although I think we did soften up the territory a bit, so to speak, for subsequent cases. I certainly remember feeling that, having had the opportunity to do a bit of ground breaking, it was rather sad that the ground wasn't broken. I would like to have been able to put as part of my epitaph that I had succeeded in that case, certainly.

*

Nigel Warner on Going to Strasbourg in the 1980s

Nigel Warner, currently ILGA-Europe's Council of Europe adviser, previously worked as a volunteer at the Campaign for Homosexual Equality and, in 1977, helped set up its Law Reform Committee. As a member of that Committee, he collaborated closely with the human rights lawyer Peter Ashman during the 1980s in respect of a number of applications to the European Commission of Human Rights about sexual orientation discrimination. These applications were the first of their kind and, although they were unsuccessful, they laid the foundation for future similar applications. Mr Warner describes how, in frustration at the Commission's consistent rejection of applications concerning sexual orientation discrimination, efforts were made to advance gay and lesbian human rights via the Parliamentary Assembly of the Council of Europe. Peter Ashman died in 2014.

In the mid-1970s the Campaign for Homosexual Equality launched a major law reform campaign, the idea being to try to eliminate the many areas of legal discrimination not corrected by the 1967 Sexual Offences Act. They drafted a monumental Bill and lobbied MPs. But supportive MPs came back with the advice that the time was not right and that CHE needed to do a much bigger, longer term, grassroots campaign to change people's minds. So a pressure group was set up within CHE called Gay Lobby. The idea was that this group would coordinate the 70 or so member organizations around the UK in lobbying MPs at the constituency level. I was an accountant, working in the oil industry, and was already involved with CHE. I joined Gay Lobby and eventually became its coordinator.

We could also see the need for a committee involving the gay groups within the political parties to push forward with political work at Westminster. So, in 1977, several of us organized a meeting at the CHE London office, which was in Soho in a dark basement in Great Windmill Street, just by the Raymond Revuebar. CHE operated a helpline from that office. One of the volunteers on the switchboard overheard our conversation and came over and joined us. He was Peter Ashman. And at that meeting we set up the CHE Law Reform Committee which continued until 1989. Over that period the Committee had many different members but Peter and I were there throughout. The Conservative Group for Homosexual Equality was represented much of the time, first by Christian Elliott, and then by Peter Campbell, but the representatives of the other political party gay groups soon dropped out. Trevor Pearcy and Nick Billingham were two other people who contributed a lot over time. The main purpose of the Committee was to promote pro-lesbian and gay legislation by responding to Parliamentary Committees, putting forward amendments, and preparing speeches and reports. It also became the focus for international work. The Committee met more or less monthly.

In early 1978, COC—the Dutch Association for Integration of Homosexuality—wrote to CHE suggesting that we host a joint meeting and try to set up an international organization. So, in 1978, in the margins of CHE's Annual Conference in Coventry, we organized that meeting out of which the International Gay Association was set up. I think it was at that meeting that Peter first got to know Jeff

Dudgeon, who was one of the co-founders of the IGA. The idea of taking further complaints to Strasbourg emerged from the Dudgeon case. Peter was by then the legal officer of Justice. He was a very expert human rights lawyer who knew all the possibilities of human rights law. Jeff already had his lawyers in Northern Ireland who had represented him at the Commission stage, but he wanted someone who was going to take a stronger stand when it came to the Court. He'd got to know and like Peter and he wanted an out gay lawyer to take his case—someone with whom he could communicate about the principles of gay rights and someone who would present the case from a gay rights perspective. That involved going beyond what Jeff's lawyers had done at the Commission stage; they had focused on the issue of private life, under Article 8 of the Convention, and Jeff wanted to put more emphasis on discrimination, under Article 14. There was also the idea of trying to bring in the issue of discrimination in the age of consent. I think that was Peter's idea. We had quite a discussion about it and, although I was in no position to advise—being completely inexpert—I liked the idea that they should be extending the case in these ways.

Peter wasn't Jeff's lawyer in the Court hearing, but he drafted the submissions. He showed them to me and I have a vivid memory of the drafts with Peter's handwriting all over them. About a month before Peter died, in 2014, we were talking about this and he told me that Jeff was terribly keen that Peter should represent him before the Court. Peter had said no and it took him and Paul Crane, Jeff's solicitor, many hours to persuade Jeff that he needed a top QC. That's how Lord Gifford came into the case, and he was supported by Terry Munyard, who at the time was a member of our Law Reform Committee. So Peter didn't represent Jeff in the Court and his name is nowhere in the case documentation but, actually, he contributed a lot to it.

So, we knew of Jeff's case and we also knew that David Norris—who was also involved in the early days of IGA—was preparing his case in Ireland. Those cases were therefore very much in the air at that time. So that's where the idea of taking a series of cases to Strasbourg came from. It grew out of Peter's involvement with the Dudgeon case.

Jeff's case led to the decriminalisation of sex between men in Northern Ireland, but with the same limitations as for England and Wales under the 1967 Act. Discrimination remained in areas like the age of consent, the armed forces, and in the definition of 'in private'. It had by now become completely clear that the Thatcher government was not open to further changes and, from our work in Gay Lobby, we knew that even the most supportive Conservatives were no longer willing to actively support us. So the European Court of Human Rights seemed to be the only way of achieving further progress.

But it wasn't going to be easy. The complaints raised in Jeff's case about discrimination under Article 14 of the Convention—including on the age of consent—had been rejected by the Commission and the Court. However, other developments at the Council of Europe offered a glimmer of hope. In parallel with the last stages of Jeff's case, the Parliamentary Assembly of the Council of Europe had been considering a report on the rights of homosexuals—the 1981 Voogd Report. Through the

IGA we were involved in lobbying delegates to the Assembly. Crucially, the draft Recommendation in the Voogd Report proposed that Article 14 of the Convention be amended to include a reference to 'sexual preference'. But when it came to the debate, the Legal Affairs Committee of the Assembly were against that on the basis that amending the Convention was a long and difficult process. They recommended that it was better to see how the case law of the Commission and the Court evolved, and try to amend Article 14 only if it was unfavourable. Peter said, 'Okay, if they won't do it, we'll have to take the cases to force the issue.'

Peter was an exceptional lawyer but he was also very practical. He had a very good understanding of how organizations worked and how you could make them work. He followed everything and seemed to know everything. My role was to try and jolly him along, because he was very busy and had so many other cases. I didn't know anything about this stuff but after the Dudgeon judgment I was very excited and was always saying to Peter, 'Come on, we must go for the next round.' His response was, 'Okay, if you can find the victims, I'll take the cases.' That was the start point for the Desmond, Bruce, Johnson and Simpson cases that Peter handled in the 1980s. I was the auditor of the London Gay Teenage Group and found Richard Desmond through that connection. But, actually, Peter found the others—John Bruce, Martin Johnson and Mary Simpson—from reports in *Capital Gay*, or from contacts within CHE. The Martin Johnson case, for instance, resulted from a member of our Law Reform Committee, Laurence Brown, contacting Martin, who was a friend of his, and asking him if he wanted to do a case.

At the beginning, when we started the Strasbourg cases, we really didn't know whether we would win. Peter was an extraordinary optimist, but he was also someone who just went forward. You know, even ten years into Thatcherism, when so many people had lost heart, he would methodically, year after year, step by step, carry on the work. For example, in terms of the Strasbourg complaints about discrimination in the criminal law—particularly differences in the age of consent—the Commission had previously relied on old German research from the 1950s that emphasized that homosexuality was a threat to young people. For several years Peter followed closely the work of a Council of Europe expert committee on decriminalisation, maintaining contact with its chairman, and other members. This bore fruit in 1982, when a rapporteur for the Council of Europe Criminological Research Conference concluded that there was no clear reason to have different ages of consent for homosexual and heterosexual sex. Peter was a great believer that if the Council of Europe, through its own expert committee, had come out against the need for a higher age of consent in the criminal law, and had refuted the old German research that the Commission had previously relied on, that it would be possible to change the view of the Commission.

The Criminological Research Conference happened while the Commission was considering the Desmond submission. So, given what the experts were saying, he was optimistic. Also, when we looked at the situation in Europe in the early 1980s, there were plenty of countries that didn't have discriminatory age of consent laws and some countries that had recently repealed them. But, as the decision in the Desmond case showed, the Commission ignored the new evidence. On the issue of the age of consent, which also came up in the Bruce case because there was a twenty year old involved, the Commission refused to change its view.

By 1987, the Commission had rejected out of hand all four of Peter's cases—Desmond, Bruce, Simpson, and Johnson—and two or three others besides. They weren't even willing *to consider* whether there was a violation of the Convention. Gay rights were not human rights! And they were not going to change their mind. We were very angry. So Peter followed up with the idea of putting forward a Protocol to the Convention that would explicitly ban sexual orientation discrimination. There seemed to be no other way forward. He thought we should present this to the Assembly's Legal Affairs Committee and say, 'In 1981 you said case law would change and it hasn't. Now you, the Parliamentary Assembly, should start the process of creating a Protocol to change the Convention.'

Peter prepared a draft and we went through a couple of years of discussion within the International Lesbian and Gay Association before it was agreed. This ended in 1990 with a meeting of experts organized in Copenhagen by Steffen Jensen of the Danish ILGA member, LBL-F48. They then asked a Danish member of the Assembly, Bjorn Elmquist, to propose the Protocol in the Assembly. He did, but this was rejected in 1992 after the Legal Affairs Committee advised that it was 'unnecessary'. The fact that the Commission saw nothing wrong with the continuing discrimination against lesbians and gays does not seem to have counted for anything with the Committee. It was very disappointing.

Laurence Helfer, an academic lawyer, argued at the time against the Protocol on the grounds that it could increase animosity towards lesbians and gays by seeming to give us a privileged status. Well, you can argue that, but when all other avenues for progress are closed, what do you do? Although the Protocol would probably never have gone through, it would have been useful if it had been pushed a bit further, got on the agenda of the Committee of Ministers of the Council of Europe, and there had been some kind of reaction to it. It would have opened up the debate and put pressure on the Commission.

Seven years later, in 1999, when Protocol 12 of the Convention was being developed, ILGA-Europe campaigned on that and did finally get the Parliamentary Assembly to support sexual orientation being included explicitly. But this was not taken up by the member states. We later heard that Council of Europe staff were worried that we were campaigning about it and it was clear that they had decided to play safe, and not put sexual orientation in, even though by then the Court itself had said that Article 14 covered sexual orientation. Instead, the approach they took was to explain in the Protocol's explanatory memorandum that sexual orientation discrimination was now covered by the case law, and so there was no need to mention it. They worried that if we made too much noise about including sexual orientation in the Protocol's text itself, not only would it not be included but that some hostile states would also try to take out the explanation from the memorandum. If they were right then there never had been any prospect of getting sexual orientation into the Convention in the early 1990s.

Around the same time as the Copenhagen conference we had applied for the ILGA to be granted consultative status at the Council of Europe. I'd drafted the application with Peter's help, but it was rejected. So that was another indication that, quite simply, for the Council of Europe, gay rights were not human rights. There was no support for going beyond the very minimal rights established in the Dudgeon case.

In the cases Peter took to the Commission—the Desmond, Bruce, Johnson and Simpson cases—the applicants were all quite indignant about their situations but were not much involved in the complaint process. There wasn't a political campaign around the cases. Looking back, perhaps there should have been. But we were in a situation that is a bit like the situation in parts of Eastern Europe today. We were looking outside, to the Commission, to try and find a solution, because political action in the country was not working. We were in the world of the Thatcher government. Until we had a positive judgment from Strasbourg, no one would take serious notice. That isn't to say that we didn't keep trying. For example, on the age of consent, we made submissions to government review bodies and lobbied MPs. On the armed forces, we lobbied MPs, we had a press conference and we did research. But the situation was hopeless. Every five years, when the Armed Forces Act came up for review in Parliament we tried unsuccessfully to get an amendment into it to decriminalize homosexuality. When it came up in 1986, we produced a report—which documented a dozen cases of people who had been kicked out of the armed forces, the horrible experiences they'd had, and the suicides and other ghastly things that had happened—and we sent it to the Select Committee. The Conservative MP chairing the Committee said, 'We've got this report on homosexuality, any comments?', and then quickly moved on to the next agenda item, preventing any discussion. The horrible treatment of lesbian and gay service personnel didn't even get an airing.

The idea that we were going to get a real political debate in this country, without a victory in Strasbourg, just wasn't realistic. That wasn't true with the Dudgeon case where there had been a political debate, because total criminalization was so extreme and there was also the extraordinary situation in which we had discrimination based on territorial differences between England and Wales and the rest of the UK. But there was really no political support for going beyond what was achieved in the Dudgeon case. During the 1979 election, we had sent out questionnaires to MPs and got quite a few positive responses from some Conservative MPs. Then, after Thatcher was elected, within a very short period of time, they withdrew their support. You couldn't get them to do anything and the message came back that 'there is no mileage in this now'. So the 1980s was really a holding operation. We were trying to stop things like police entrapment and raids on Gay's the Word bookshop. We were in a defensive situation, rather than being able to change things for the better.

It's quite interesting to compare our efforts in the 1980s with the Stonewall campaigns that Angela Mason did so expertly in the 1990s. By then, things had changed so much. There had been the growth of the mass movement—that was visible with so many more people on Pride marches—and then, after Section 28, Michael Cashman and Ian McKellen came on board with Stonewall. In the 1980s, we had very limited resources, we were all volunteers who worked in full time jobs—CHE had one paid employee—and we only met once a month. We were doing the international work, law reform work, monitoring Parliament, and making submissions to government bodies. It was a slow, slow process and we were not equipped, as an organization, to undertake the scale of things that Stonewall did in the 1990s. We were kept going by our anger. And Strasbourg seemed to offer a sort of lifeline. But we helped lay the ground. Indeed, several of those involved in our activities joined in founding Stonewall, and for its first six months it operated from Peter's house.

*

Angela Mason on Going to Strasbourg in the 1990s

Angela Mason was Executive Director of Stonewall from 1992 until 2002. During that time she orchestrated significant law reform campaigns in the UK in respect of the higher 'age of consent' for male homosexual acts and the 'ban' on homosexuals serving in the armed forces. At the heart of these campaigns were a series of applications to the European Commission of Human Rights. Ms Mason describes the process of identifying and working with individuals to take complaints to the Commission and the role that these complaints played in encouraging law reform. She reflects on the contribution that going to Strasbourg has made to establishing sexual orientation equality in the UK.

When I became Director of Stonewall in 1992, we were fairly hopeful of a debate in the House of Commons on the age of consent. John Major did come up with that in 1994 but, although the vote was pretty close, it wasn't successful. Stonewall had run a very big campaign. I think that campaign really put the issue of the age of consent on the map and in the public arena. I remember Roy Hattersley said to me once, 'You say the age of consent is very important, but I've never received a single letter about it.' I said, 'You will Roy, you will.' So we did a massive letter writing campaign. Part of that was trying to let young men's voices speak in the public arena. It partially succeeded, in that the age of consent went down to eighteen, but we had campaigned on the basis of equality. So clearly, changing the age of consent was going to be difficult to get through Parliament. That was true of other issues too, like those relating to the armed forces.

The idea of litigating in Strasbourg came partly from the lawyer, Peter Duffy. Peter rang me up and said, 'You really ought to think about taking it to Europe.' I didn't know Peter at the time, but we got to know him and he was instrumental in helping us develop that strategy of litigation. I had the idea that we should advertise for applicants. It was quite novel but we had to find applicants. As it was before the web, we advertised in the gay press. The main criterion for selection was the person's ability to make the case for equality. That meant making the case in the media, which we knew was going to be very important. We wanted someone whose family wouldn't mind them coming forward and someone who could make the case coherently.

I think we were just looking for one applicant, originally. We wanted someone who people could identify with and think, 'That could be my son.' We got Ralph Wilde—that was nice, because *Wilde v UK* seemed like Oscar's revenge—and Hugo Greenhalgh and Will Parry. They helped the campaign a great deal; they gave a public face to the campaign for equality. Gay men, and young gay men, especially identified with the boys and saw them as the spearhead of the campaign. It made the campaign human.

The first Strasbourg complaint was primarily a means of getting more publicity as we were trying very hard to persuade Parliament to change the age of consent law. Also, I suppose, the complaint was a way of questioning the legitimacy of the English law. That was quite hard to do, at the time. It sounds very strange now, but there was a widespread acceptance that a higher age of consent for gay men was perfectly okay. The majority feeling was that we'd dealt with decriminalization and this issue of the age of consent was *de minimis*. We weren't relying on Strasbourg but then, of course, when we didn't succeed in Parliament in 1994, we lodged the second age of consent case, with Euan Sutherland. We didn't have to advertise for Euan, we'd already got to know him during the course of the campaign. And it was Euan's case that actually went forward.

I think Peter Duffy thought the age of consent complaints were strong cases. The success in Strasbourg was easier than we thought. The Sutherland case didn't go to the final stage because we agreed to stay it. Perhaps wrongly, but we did. I think Peter Ashman and Nigel Warner thought that we should have taken the Sutherland case the whole way, because that would have had implications for the rest of Europe. But our thinking was that we should work with the Labour government to ensure that the law was passed in Parliament. It was the Stonewall position that it was better to have legal change through Parliament, through democratic means, rather than through the courts, because it gave the change greater legitimacy. It also probably put us in better stead with the Government.

Working with the applicants was very exciting in lots of ways, because these were big cases, big trials. There were difficulties though, which I'm sure the applicants would talk about. We were interested in the cause and in building Stonewall through these cases. The applicants were, naturally, interested in their own circumstances. So there were some tensions. For instance, Will and Hugo once appeared on a radio show with a very homophobic Tory and they really wanted to say that they were committing gross indecency et cetera and be arrested. We thought that was a bad tactic. I thought it would cause difficulties with their families as well. In that instance, they followed our advice. But there was sometimes a tension between what we were trying to do and some of the applicants' personal wishes.

I think it was difficult for some of the applicants. Some of them, particularly in the armed forces cases, had been through a particularly bad and pretty traumatic time. I mean, they'd lost their careers and they'd been treated very badly—in a really shameful way—and they had to cope with all that. And then they were suddenly catapulted into the public eye. So I think it was a difficult process for them. To help them, we did quite a lot of media training. Some of them had economic problems and we tried to provide support where appropriate. Will Parry made a long television documentary so, in a sense, he did quite well out of it. And Ralph Wilde went into law himself. I don't think it was a damaging experience for anyone. I hope not.

When we started the Strasbourg litigation I had a bit of an understanding of Convention law—I was a solicitor before Stonewall, so I did obviously know something about it—and that knowledge deepened. Our guiding legal light was Peter Duffy, who was absolutely brilliant. It was such a tragedy that he died young. He was terribly hard working, sincere, and clever; a fantastic person. We owe him a great debt. I also worked with Stephen Grosz at Bindmans a great deal. Peter Ashman's role should also be applauded. He was always immensely helpful and persuaded people like me to pursue cases under the Convention; he and Nigel Warner were very enthusiastic about Europe.

When we went to the Commission I didn't get any sense that they were hostile towards us. I thought they were sympathetic—or neutral-sympathetic—and not at all hostile. I always felt they admired who we had representing us. Having Peter Duffy was helpful because he knew the Commission very, very well and was a respected figure there. Peter and Stephen Grosz had both studied with the Commission and were well known there. So I think that aided us; it smoothed our path. It was quite clear that we were not just campaigners, or cross victims, but that people of substance were saying that these were important issues that the Commission had to address. I always thought that was a key factor. And I remember the care with which Peter prepared for the cases. I think the Sutherland case was the first time I went over to Strasbourg and we stayed in a hotel, in a small room, all day while Peter prepared his speech. I had to entertain Euan and take him to dinner because he was getting a bit suffocated, bored and a bit overwhelmed by it all.

In terms of Stonewall's involvement with the armed forces cases, well, Stonewall had always done a bit of campaigning in respect of the armed forces. Parliament is required to periodically renew the right to have a standing army and we had previously been involved in that. Before I got to Stonewall in 1992, Stonewall had submitted evidence to the Select Committee examining the Armed Forces Bill 1991 and the Select Committee had gone on to recommend that homosexual activity should no longer be an offence under service law. So that had been a change in relation to the position of homosexuality in the armed forces that Stonewall had been involved in. Stonewall had also been quite involved in supporting Rank Outsiders.

I personally wasn't all that keen on doing the armed forces cases. I took the view, initially, that it was a minority issue. However, I met people who were involved in Rank Outsiders, like Robert Ely, and they had been treated so disgracefully—and with taxpayers' money—in ways that I thought was completely shocking. I changed my mind and was persuaded to have a go at it. Not everyone in Stonewall thought we should have done it. It wasn't always our most popular thing and there was some anti-military feeling. Usually, progressive causes are associated with the Left—Stonewall was slightly different because it was not against the Left but it was slightly disassociated with the Left—and those with a Left-progressive viewpoint weren't that sympathetic to what was happening in the military. But that changed when people saw and found out more about it—about people being hounded out of the armed forces, asked all these terrible questions, their diaries taken away, and their contacts followed up. It was a witch-hunt; there's no question about it. In the main, these were deserving young people, seeking to serve their country, being treated like this.

The contribution of Strasbourg to the development of gay and lesbian rights in the UK is that it eased the passage of law reform. It made things happen slightly more quickly—although it did seem to take an awfully long time at the time, because we had to wait so long for these cases to go through. We thought we might have won in the armed forces cases in the High Court. This was before the Human Rights Act and we had to argue on the grounds of unreasonableness. I know David Pannick, who acted for us, thought we had a chance. And our judge, Simon Brown, was very sympathetic. That was interesting because, when the trial started off, Brown was quite against us and then, when he looked at the affidavits and the evidence, he came out for us; he just changed. So it was quite clear Brown was sympathetic, as were the Court of Appeal, but they couldn't quite do it under the existing state of the law before the passing of the Human Rights Act and, therefore, we were required to go off to Strasbourg—where it was absolutely clear we were going to win.

It's interesting, in retrospect, to think about how Labour was elected with a very big majority in 1997, and was completely sympathetic to our aims, but was still nervous about whole-scale change. I think the armed forces change was always going to be more difficult for any government, but there was also a great nervousness about repealing Section 28—that didn't happen immediately—and the Parliament Act was required to equalize the age of consent. I think we shifted opinion to a great extent, but politicians were nervous.

Strasbourg was important for gay and lesbians rights because it gave us a legal arena in which to argue about the right of young gay men to have sex with each other. That was helpful because it was such an emotive issue. Winning the age of consent argument was what burst the dam. Public opinion was in advance of Parliament—so many people had come out and the gay scene was quite open in Britain—and it was because we had a long period of Conservative rule that change was held up. And so, when change did come, it appeared to come quite fast because society had changed and it was the establishment catching up on what had already happened. Which is not to say they didn't dig their heels in and fight quite hard—they were quite big fights. But, by the time we got to the A.D.T. case, the gross indecency case, it was very easy because the government caved in before it even got off the ground. I remember we all went out for dinner with the Home Office people, because everybody knew we'd win. Views had changed and it was clear that we were going to start winning these things.

It was, in fact, much easier to sell same-sex partnership rights in the UK. There was much more public sympathy for and identification with partnership rights. I was involved in the Mendoza case from 2002—by that time we had the Human Rights Act—which changed succession rights for same-sex partners. That was an applicant who I never met. His barrister had taken the case to the County Court and, at a Stonewall lecture, told me about it and we took it from there. The applicant didn't want any publicity at all, but it was quite an important case dealt with by our courts. The European Convention and the Human Rights Act, together with the changes in public opinion that came about from Stonewall's campaigns, made it far more possible to win changes through Parliament. However, without Strasbourg the doctrine of parliamentary sovereignty would have made it far more difficult to win lesbian and gay rights.

*

Robert Wintemute on Third Party Interventions in Strasbourg since 2000

Robert Wintemute, Professor of Human Rights Law at King's College London, pioneered the practice of making third party interventions in cases before the European Court of Human Rights about sexual orientation discrimination. He describes the historical development of these interventions and the significant role that they now play in litigation. Professor Wintemute reflects on the ways in which third party interventions are used by non-governmental organizations as a vehicle to further their aims of challenging and eliminating sexual orientation discrimination in Europe. He considers how this can complement—and perhaps conflict with—the aims of the individual applicants who make complaints to the Court about sexual orientation discrimination.

My involvement with litigation in the European Court of Human Rights came about over a fifteen-year process, which I'll try to summarise briefly. I worked in a New York law firm from 1982 to 1987 and, in 1984, I was given my first research assignment by Lambda Legal Defence—an NGO that worked on strategic litigation in US courts and was doing a fifty state survey of criminal laws affecting gay men and lesbians—which was on the criminal law in Tennessee. I was in the law firm library, pulling cases off the shelf, reading about cunnilingus in Tennessee and worrying about whether someone might come in and read it over my shoulder, thereby outing me. I thought about that feeling and I thought, this isn't right, why should I have to sneak around a library and do this surreptitiously? So, in 1985, I came out and I told my firm that I would like to do *pro bono* work for Lambda Legal Defence. That year, I worked on a case on lesbian and gays in the armed forces that involved assisting with the preparation of an *amicus curiae*, friend of the court, brief. In 1986, I wrote another one for a case of HIV-related employment discrimination. So these were my first experiences of, what we call in the European Court, a third party intervention.

My first experience of litigation in Europe, after I came to work as a lecturer at King's College London, was in 1996, in the case of *Lisa Grant v South West Trains* in the employment tribunal. I wrote a letter to Cherie Booth, who was the barrister, and asked her if she was planning to ask for a reference to the Court of Justice of the EU. To my surprise, I got a phone call and was invited to a meeting to discuss the case. My advice to her was that this was not a good case to go to the Court of Justice, because it dealt essentially with a question of family law and there was no precedent to build on. We made the best arguments we could, I attended the hearing and tried to advise the legal team, but the judgment came out in 1998 and we lost. Subsequently, in 1999, one barrister and one solicitor consulted me about the cases concerning gays and lesbians in the armed forces that were before the European Court of Human Rights and I commented on their arguments. When the judgment came out, with the violation found, it was a huge success.

One thing had struck me about the barrister's submission in the armed forces cases and it was that he used the word 'homosexual'. That jarred with me because I thought, if this case is about the entire lesbian, gay and bisexual community in Europe, why aren't you using the language they would use? I suppose it was the result of a heterosexual barrister using particular language and also having quite a narrow perspective on the case. An English barrister's goal is to win a specific case for their client, using whichever arguments will achieve that goal. They're not thinking about changing the law, necessarily, for all of the Member States of the Council of Europe. During a celebratory drink on the armed forces cases in a gay bar in Soho, I said to Nigel Warner that I thought it would be a good idea for ILGA-Europe to intervene in cases in the European Court that concerned sexual orientation discrimination in order to offer the Court a broader perspective.

In 1999 I met, through Nigel Warner, Philippe Fretté, whose complaint against France about sexual orientation discrimination in the process of applying for authorisation to adopt a child was pending before the European Court. Mr Fretté, who didn't like lawyers, was representing himself. In 2000, I made a third party intervention on behalf of ILGA-Europe in support of his case. In 2001, when the Court asked him to find a lawyer for the hearing, we agreed that I was familiar with all the issues in the case. So I argued his case and I thought the hearing went well. When the judgment came out, I was in my office at King's. I got an email from the Court and opening it, to find out the verdict, was a bit like opening your exam results. I opened the email and read that the Court finds, by four votes to three, that there has not been discrimination. I was disappointed for about thirty to sixty seconds and then I focused on the three dissents. I thought, without the third party intervention the application would probably have been declared inadmissible, or there would have been a seven to zero judgment against Mr Fretté. I advised Mr Fretté not to request a referral to the Grand Chamber but to pass the baton on and, in the next case that went to the Court on this issue, *E.B. v France,* I submitted a third party intervention.

The first lesson I learned from *Fretté* was not to go to the Court alone, as an NGO working on LGBT-I human rights, because it creates the impression that you are pleading for a judgment that will benefit a special interest but not address a mainstream human rights issue. So every subsequent intervention, starting with *Karner v Austria* in 2002, has involved a coalition of NGOs. At the time of *Karner,* the law in the UK had not changed and unmarried same-sex couples were not treated like unmarried different-sex couples, especially with regard to housing succession. Three NGOs collaborated in that case: ILGA-Europe, Liberty and Stonewall. I think a coalition is important because it more or less says to the Court, we have heterosexual friends in the human rights community who think this is an important issue and you don't have to take it just from us. It strengthens the credibility of the intervention.

Some NGOs have the idea that their third party interventions are neutral, but I think that is ignoring reality. In most cases you're intervening on the side of the applicant, to try and level the playing field because the government has a huge legal department on its side. Occasionally you might propose an intervention to support the government, but only when you think the national decision is correct. Some NGOs take the view that they're entirely neutral and they don't have contact with the applicant or their lawyers. I see giving advice to the applicant's lawyer as a way of supporting the case, in addition to the intervention.

The only time I have known the applicant in a case for which I have submitted an intervention was in the Philippe Fretté case. In *E.B. v France*, I met the applicant at the hearing at the European Court. In other cases—*Oliari and Others v Italy, Vallianatos and Others v Greece, Karner v Austria*, and *X. and Others v Austria*—I never met the applicants. What's been more common is to have contact with the applicant's lawyer or other representative. In terms of interventions being welcome, applicants can't object to an intervention being made. I suppose you might get some applicants thinking that an NGO is politicising their individual case of injustice, but I haven't actually come across that. The European Court prefers to have as few interventions as possible, so they'll encourage NGOs to make one joint submission. If there's an obvious violation of the Convention they might say no to a request to submit an intervention. For example, leave to intervene was rejected in *Alekseyev v Russia* because it was such an obvious violation of the right to freedom of assembly that I don't think the Court thought they needed it.

My overall motivation for submitting third party interventions is to try and change the case law of the European Court. So I always have in mind the benefit for lesbian and gay individuals, and same-sex couples, across 47 countries, including the UK. As an academic lawyer, one way to try and change the law is by publishing and hoping that a practising lawyer will draw your publications to the attention of the court. What I decided to do was to cut the corner, or take out the middleman, and present my arguments, as comparative law research, directly to the Court. Often it's a question of trying to persuade the Court that there's sufficient European consensus to justify finding a violation. That kind of research is harder for an individual practising lawyer to do, so that's the added value of a third party intervention.

The cases I've tried to focus on are the family law cases, because they're the most difficult for the European Court. But there are other cases on violence, and refusing to register NGOs et cetera, which to me should be legally fairly straightforward for the Court, but an intervention might still help. In terms of ILGA-Europe's strategic litigation programme, they have been contracting out, so to speak, some of the interventions to other lawyers; I've not been doing all of them by any means, I would never have the time. Their programme has grown to the point where they've hired a litigation officer for the first time. I suppose ILGA-Europe has a sort of right of first refusal to take the leading role in cases, but other NGOs are now initiating interventions in sexual orientation discrimination cases. The International Commission of Jurists in Geneva now has a half-time sexual orientation officer.

The growth of this field is impressive and important, but it is still quite minor compared with the resources of the opponents—they generally have more resources to devote to third party interventions.

Those submitting third party interventions don't normally get to speak at hearings in Strasbourg. However, I've twice been given exceptional permission to speak on behalf of the intervening third parties. The first time was in *Schalk and Kopf v Austria* which, although the applicants didn't win, resulted in an important statement on family life and some useful words about Article 12, which can be interpreted in different ways. The second time was *Gas and Dubois v France*, which was another intervention that was unsuccessful. In both cases, I was given ten minutes to make arguments on behalf of the third parties, whereas if you were the lawyer for the applicant you get thirty minutes. In fact, it was very frustrating in the hearing on *Schalk and Kopf* because the lawyer for the applicants, who did not have any particular expertise on the Convention, sat down after ten minutes. I wanted to be able to make a motion to the Court that his twenty minutes be transferred to me! But that's what can happen when you have a non-specialist lawyer. And this is why the NGOs can really support applicants.

In terms of the experience of the applicants themselves, I think it's very difficult. If their names are being used in the proceedings then they're exposed to media attention. If they're trying to do as much as possible to change the law for others, they're more likely to consent to interviews, because that will assist with legislative change. Applicants don't know whether they'll win in Strasbourg, so media interviews can help contribute to the debate at the national level by putting a human face on the issue. There can be a lot of pressure involved in taking a case to the Court and it requires enormous patience, because of the length of the proceedings. It is a difficult process and that's why, in same-sex couple litigation, it's common to find several couples to share the burden. Also, you don't want to put all your eggs in one basket. That was the case *in Oliari and Others v Italy*, because if it had just been Mr Oliari and his partner, what would have happened if they'd broken up just before the judgment? That might mean the Court striking the case from its list, because the victim has disappeared.

I don't think applicants expect quick relief from the Court. If you're an asylum seeker and you're about to be deported, your lawyer can request interim measures from the Court, which means that the Court would ask your government not to deport you until your case has been heard. But, in most cases, something bad has happened and the applicant just has to get on with their life. Often the applicants themselves don't benefit. Take the lesbians and gays in the armed forces cases against the UK: were they reinstated, did they go back to their careers? The cases tend to be about trying to make sure this doesn't happen to someone else, trying to change the law for the future. If applicants sat down and thought about how long it's going to take, the risk of losing, and the very small compensation that's awarded, and if they were being completely selfish, they might think, it's not really worth it, I won't bother. So I think most of them are altruistic.

I think it would be a disaster if the UK withdrew from the Convention. I think LGBT applicants should be among the loudest voices opposing the current growth of the idea that we don't need the European Court anymore. We don't know what could change in the future, what traditional family values party could sweep through in elections. With the European Court, we will always have somewhere to go. So it's in our own interest to remain a part of the Convention. It's also about extending the equality we enjoy to Eastern Europe. Our example carries much more weight if we're a party to the Convention and a Member State of the Council of Europe. I care more about the Convention than the Human Rights Act. The Human Rights Act is also very important because it allows us to enforce the Convention in UK courts but, if they tinker with that, although I wouldn't like it, I could live with it more than not having the possibility of having errors corrected by the European Court.

The important point is that British judges are very good, but not infallible, and we, like everyone in Europe, benefit by having an international court where we can go to have mistakes corrected. The way I look at it, as a teacher in a university, is that the Court's use of European consensus means that the more progressive countries in Europe teach the less progressive ones. So, in effect, the example of the progressive countries is reflected up to Strasbourg, is noted as an emerging European consensus, and then is imposed down on the countries that have been lagging behind and who are told they have to catch up. That's what happened to the UK with LGBT human rights, from 1981 to 2002. We were lagging behind the rest of Europe, we were told we had to change, and we did. We didn't attack the Court and say this is outrageous, this is mission creep—the government's current term. We have an opportunity to teach other countries but we have to be willing to learn as well, when we are not keeping up.

In terms of unfinished business in the UK, we have the issue of marriage discrimination in Northern Ireland. This is a good example of a case where a UK court could quash or strike down part of the Marriage (Northern Ireland) Order 2003, under the Human Rights Act, because it's discrimination contrary to the Convention, and because it's not primary legislation. But there's no precedent of the European Court supporting that, and there's been ongoing debate about whether UK courts should get ahead of Strasbourg or not. So this will be a very interesting test. Let's say a case is rejected in Northern Ireland and goes to the UK Supreme Court. I think that a case would probably succeed there. But let's just say hypothetically that the UK Supreme Court says, no, this is a question for the legislature. The case could end up in the European Court and would raise an interesting question of whether you have to have same-sex marriage throughout your country. It would be *Dudgeon v the United Kingdom* all over again in that respect. Except, on the issue of marriage, we probably wouldn't have enough European consensus, so would have to come up with an argument that it was about consistency within one country.

PART 3
SOCIOLOGICAL ANALYSIS

Stories are very interesting.
Euan Sutherland

This part of the book provides an analysis of the oral histories contained in Part 2. The purpose of this analysis is to illuminate and examine patterns within the oral histories in order to provide an in-depth understanding of the process and experience of making a complaint to Strasbourg. Whilst each account of 'going to Strasbourg' forms, to some extent, a unique story—because of the specific social contexts and life circumstances of the applicants from which their complaints arose—a thematic analysis of the oral histories shows that there are significant elements of commonality (as well as difference) between them. The analysis focuses on the motivations and aspirations of the applicants, their relationships with non-governmental organizations and legal professionals, their experience of the media and publicity, their relationships with their families, their expectations of the Strasbourg organs, and the effect of making a complaint to Strasbourg on their day-to-day lives. In the final section, the applicants' views on the future of the relationship between the UK and the Convention system are examined. What emerges from the analysis is a rare insight into the process and experience of human rights litigation from the standpoint of those who initiate it.

6

Expectations, Motivations, and Outcomes

A Thematic Analysis of the Oral Histories

Context, Motivation, and Aspiration

An application to Strasbourg by an individual who complains about sexual orientation discrimination arises, in essence, from the individual's experience of the social and legal relations of the European society in which they are situated. Individual applications begin, therefore, with the lived reality of the applicant who—to put it in the terms of the European Convention on Human Rights—is a person claiming to be the victim of a human rights violation.[1] Whilst applications relating to sexual orientation discrimination always concern an issue that, as the European Court of Human Rights puts it, 'transcends the person and the interests of the applicant',[2] the primary purpose of the Convention system is to provide individual relief.[3] Therefore, although a decision or judgment of the Court may have implications that go far beyond an individual applicant and the State about which he or she complains,[4] it is, first and foremost, the experience of individual applicants that is the foundation of Strasbourg litigation.

The oral histories in this book clearly demonstrate that the personal experience underlying much of the litigation in Strasbourg is one of acute suffering. All of the applicants' accounts illustrate, in vivid terms, significant experiences of harm and pain caused by sexual orientation discrimination. Emma Riley, for example, describes how, as a result of her treatment by and discharge from the Royal Navy, she was 'massively distressed', 'immensely traumatized', and 'completely lost'. Duncan Lustig-Prean, who was subjected to similar treatment, speaks of suffering from which he only began to recover after a fifteen-year period. Moreover, Mary Simpson, who remained in her home following her partner's death whilst attempting to resist its possession by the local council, describes how:

[1] Convention for the Protection of Human Rights and Fundamental Freedoms (4 November 1950) ETS No 005, art 34.

[2] *Deweer v Belgium* (1980) Series A no 35, para 38.

[3] As recognized in *Karner v Austria* ECHR 2003-IX, para 26.

[4] The Court has stated that its 'judgments in fact serve not only to decide those cases brought before the Court but, more generally, to elucidate, safeguard and develop the rules instituted by the Convention, thereby contributing to the observance by the States of the engagements undertaken by them as Contracting Parties'. *Ireland v the United Kingdom* (1978) Series A no 25, para 154.

Going to Strasbourg: An Oral History of Sexual Orientation Discrimination and the European Convention on Human Rights. First Edition. Paul Johnson. © Paul Johnson 2016. Published 2016 by Oxford University Press.

the kids in the street found out I was gay and they broke every window in that house. They thought that was fun. Even the police couldn't stop it. Because being gay wasn't 'normal', was it? But I still stayed put. I had no electric; they cut the electric off. There was broken windows, toilet just worked, just a little drop of running water, it was a right mess. I still stuck it out ... I was holed up there until we went to court and it was horrendous.

These accounts demonstrate that these applicants were not complaining to Strasbourg about discrimination in abstract terms but, on the contrary, were seeking relief from the personally injurious consequences of discrimination. In all of the accounts, words such as 'fear' (Kevin Bazeley), 'scary' (Richard Desmond), 'terror' (Jeffrey Dudgeon), 'torture' (J.M.), and 'risk' and 'vulnerability' (Ralph Wilde) convey the personal privation at the heart of these cases.

The suffering experienced by applicants, as their accounts testify, was inflicted by a range of actors who, for the most part, acted on the authority of the State. Police officers, local authority housing officials, and revenue collectors are some of the officials who, empowered by law, subjected these individuals to detrimental treatment because of their sexual orientation. Yet, as the applicants' accounts also demonstrate, the broader social relations in which this discrimination took place exacerbated and compounded its effects. Will Parry describes those social relations as 'default homophobia' and, like other applicants, talks about his experience of living in a time when there was 'an awful lot of negative publicity and inference about being gay and almost nothing that was positive'. It is exposure to what Richard Desmond describes as 'intense homophobia' and its subjective effect that provides the broader context for most of the applications to Strasbourg discussed in this book. Therefore, although complaints to Strasbourg about sexual orientation discrimination always focus on a discrete and singular legal 'problem', they also address the social and cultural relations that underpin and sustain inequality.

Because applications to Strasbourg about sexual orientation discrimination are propelled by an individual's own experience of discrimination, it is unsurprising that one of the primary motivations of applicants is the desire to achieve personal redress for a detriment that they have suffered. William Nash describes the motivation of his 'deeply aggrieved' client (who had been subjected to a lengthy prison sentence for engaging in adult same-sex sexual relationships) for complaining to Strasbourg as being 'fairly obvious', and, to some extent, the obvious motivation of gaining relief from discrimination characterizes all of the applicants' accounts. The accounts show that applicants were seeking to address a problem in their 'personal situation' (Euan Sutherland), challenging those they feel should not 'get away with' (Graeme Grady) discriminating against them, and 'making a protest' in order to get the 'validation' (Emma Riley) that they had been wronged.

However, although applicants to Strasbourg are clearly concerned to address their own personal suffering, they are also often motivated to take action for another key reason, which is to alleviate the suffering of others in a similar situation. As Wena Parry put it:

In terms of my motivation, I was prepared to take the case because there were other people, other transsexuals, who had the same problem as me. I literally had to fight for them. I know how frightened you can get, when everybody turns against you … So I was doing it for other people, and for myself and my wife … I was not prepared to break up my marriage … I will fight for people's rights, even if I have to fight it for myself, because I am part of the human family.

The idea of going to Strasbourg in order to, as Andrew Courten put it, 'help all people suffering in my situation' is a common feature of the applicants' accounts. For example, when asked by his solicitor why he wanted to take a case challenging his discharge from the Royal Navy, Terence Perkins stated, 'I don't want anyone to have to go through this.' Graeme Grady, when challenging his discharge from the Royal Air Force, said that he decided:

Strasbourg's where I'm going to go, because I don't want it to be just about me, I want to try and change something for everybody else as well. That was my big thing; it wasn't just about me, it was something that could help other people as well.

There is no account by an applicant in this book that does not describe, to some extent, how a desire to help others was a motivation for them deciding to pursue litigation in Strasbourg.

What the applicants' accounts reveal is that empathy for the pain and suffering of other people forms, as Will Parry describes it, a 'prime motivation' for taking action aimed at ensuring that others will not have to 'face the same level of prejudice and ignorance' in the future. As Mary Simpson explains:

I kept thinking I've got to do it because if I don't do it nobody else is going to do it. Nobody else is going to say, 'Right, we've got to have some rights.' They'd just give up. I never give up … I did it for the freedom of being gay. Because there are a lot of people that are gay that won't admit it. In those days a lot of them never came out. They shut the door and kept the closet locked. But if you can just express yourself and say, right, I've done it for freedom… Freedom's a great thing. It's hard getting it, but it's a real good thing when you've got it … I will fight for my rights and I will keep on fighting until everybody gets their share of their rights, because it's not fair.

Mary Simpson's account clearly shows how a concern to address her own situation was inextricably bound up with an awareness of and concern for others in a similar position. Sociologists have long recognized that empathy is often a key factor that motivates an individual to undertake a course of action designed to 'overcome the inertia' of law, convention, and custom,[5] and such empathic motivation is clearly demonstrated by Duncan Lustig-Prean's account:

I certainly didn't leave the ship in mind to become a test case. I was acutely embarrassed, I was very private and I didn't feel comfortable talking about my own sexuality … It wasn't my inclination to scream and shout about it. I would have gone quietly … But I became involved with Rank Outsiders [and] [t]he final straw for me happened in October or November 1994, when I was asked to go down to the Tamar Bridge because of a sailor who

[5] Max Weber, *Economy and Society: An Outline of Interpretive Sociology* (University of California Press 1978) 321.

was there at two o'clock in morning, in the rain, surrounded by police, wanting to jump. That's when I decided, you have to stand up and say 'no' publically and it was the final persuader for me to take on the case. I felt, having shied away and being embarrassed about who I was, if I was worth the bloody commanders' rank, then I had to stand up for people like that. You cannot have people being hurt so severely that they are going to kill themselves at the age of nineteen just because they're gay. That was the final kick in the arse I needed.

Duncan Lustig-Prean's account shows that a profound empathic concern for others was foundational to his decision to pursue litigation in Strasbourg. It illustrates the way in which empathy generates a commitment to undertake altruistic action aimed at addressing both an individual and collective form of suffering.

It is clear from the applicants' accounts that, in making a complaint to Strasbourg, they often aspire to achieve outcomes that go far beyond addressing a problem in their own lives. One of the most common aspirations expressed by applicants is the desire to change the *law* in ways that will have widespread benefit for other individuals. Applicants describe wanting to 'change the ... law for all lesbians, gays and transgender people' (Graeme Grady) and how complaining to Strasbourg is a way of 'standing up in front of everybody and saying this law is wrong and we want to change it' (Will Parry). However, changing the law in ways that benefit other gay men and lesbians is also sometimes linked to an ambition to achieve broader *social* change. For example, Euan Sutherland describes how his complaint, which sought to promote the values of '[f]airness, dignity and respect', was something that 'seemed a very good thing to be doing for society'. Hugo Greenhalgh, in similar terms, describes how the aim of his complaint was to 'change society, to change people's opinions, and to achieve equality'. Central to some of the applicants' accounts, therefore, is an ambition to advance and promote the principle of social equality in ways that go beyond the confines of a specific concern with sexual orientation-related law reform.

It is notable that, when talking about their aspirations, the applicants rarely mention personal financial gain. Even when, as is often the case, applicants have suffered a financial detriment as a result of discrimination, they rarely refer to financial compensation as a goal of their complaint to Strasbourg. When the issue of 'money' is brought up, it is often within the context of an applicant explicitly dismissing this as an aim of the litigation. For example, as Emma Riley puts it, 'My motivation for contacting a solicitor was that I wanted to change the law ... To get to the point where the law actually changed was the golden goal. It wasn't about money; it never was, it never will be.'

Similarly, Terence Perkins states:

I didn't care about the money. After I left the Navy I went back to computing and I was being paid a lot more than I would ever have been paid in the Navy, even if I had been an officer. I wasn't interested in the money, that wasn't my issue at all.

These and similar sentiments are commonly expressed in the applicants' accounts. In this respect, Kevin Bazeley's account could be seen as atypical, given that he states, 'I will be totally honest and say, of course, there was a financial aspect to the case I was bringing.' However, he goes on to state, 'I did want things to change, because

I did not believe that it was right for anybody to be discriminated against', and it is clear, therefore, that, like the other applicants, the aspiration to achieve broader social change was also an element of his application to Strasbourg. Kevin Bazeley's reference to being 'honest' about the financial aspect of his case is, like Andrew Courten's account, best understood within the context of the financial hardship caused by discrimination. Put simply, for these applicants, going to Strasbourg was not a means to make money but a way to address a financial detriment created by State-sponsored discrimination.

The Role of Non-Governmental Organizations

Loveday Hodson's analysis of the role of non-governmental organizations (NGOs) in Strasbourg litigation shows the significance of 'single-issue group litigation' by 'LGBT rights' organizations.[6] Angela Mason and Nigel Warner's accounts clearly bear this out and demonstrate the centrality of LGBT rights organizations to Strasbourg litigation about sexual orientation discrimination. As many of the applicants' accounts show, LGBT-focused and other NGOs have often played a considerable role in their complaints to Strasbourg. In some cases, applicants were selected by an NGO in order that it could pursue 'strategic litigation' under the Convention. However, although NGOs have undoubtedly been central to Strasbourg litigation relating to sexual orientation discrimination, the accounts in this book show that there is considerable variability in the interaction between NGOs and individual applicants.[7] Whilst some applicants were significantly supported by one or more NGOs, other applicants had little contact with NGOs. What the accounts show, therefore, is diversity in the relationships between applicants and NGOs.

The applicants' accounts demonstrate that, in most cases, NGOs played some part in their respective complaints to Strasbourg. In some cases, the role of an NGO was minor. For example, Emma Riley describes how she initiated her application:

> in 1998, when I first spoke to Stephen Grosz, who became my solicitor. I'd phoned up Stonewall and they gave me his number and set me on the path to exactly where I needed to be ... I had no involvement with Stonewall other than that sole phone call and I didn't have any contact with any other organization, like Rank Outsiders. You would have thought that I would have done but, no, I was totally on my own. I didn't do the case as part of an organization. I didn't even think to align myself with something like that.

The only role played by an NGO in Emma Riley's case, therefore, was by Stonewall in facilitating contact between her and her expert legal representation.[8] This type

[6] Loveday Hodson, *NGOs and the Struggle for Human Rights in Europe* (Hart Publishing 2011) 138–9.

[7] For a general discussion of the role of NGOs in human rights litigation, see Tullio Treves, Marco Frigessi di Rattalma, Attila Tanzi, Alessandro Fodella, Cesare Pitea, and Chiara Ragni (eds), *Civil Society, International Courts and Compliance Bodies* (T.M.C. Asser Press 2005).

[8] For a discussion of the role of NGOs in facilitating contact between applicants and legal representatives, see Rachel A Cichowski, 'Civil Society and the European Court of Human Rights' in Jonas Christoffersen and Mikael R Madsen (eds) *The European Court of Human Rights between Law and Politics* (Oxford University Press 2011).

of support, although seemingly negligible, can sometimes be decisive. For example, William Nash notes, in respect of the first application to Strasbourg against the UK about sexual orientation discrimination, that '[t]his was not a case that was heavily backed or inspired by one of the gay organizations; it was very much [the applicant's] own effort. I don't think he had any particular links with any gay organizations.' However, William Nash also describes how the National Council for Civil Liberties had referred the case on to him after the applicant had contacted it. It was an NGO, therefore, that facilitated contact between the applicant and his expert legal representation. Further, as William Nash explains, although he was not 'a single-issue campaigner', he 'had links with the gay rights organizations that were around at the time' and was able to draw on their expertise in preparing the submission on the merits of the case. NGOs and gay rights groups therefore had an indirect involvement in the litigation.

Andrew Courten's account is the only account by an applicant which shows that NGOs played no part whatsoever in an application to Strasbourg. However, Andrew Courten did attempt to gain the support of an NGO—Stonewall—and was 'very disappointed that they had no interest in me at all' and felt 'left on my own'. For the majority of the other applicants, NGOs had direct and significant involvement with their Strasbourg cases. Jeffrey Dudgeon, for example, who, as his own and Nigel Warner's account demonstrates, took a very active role at all stages of his Strasbourg case, was directly supported by several organizations. Jeffrey Dudgeon's application to Strasbourg itself grew out of and was supported by his involvement with gay rights groups that were engaged in political campaigning for homosexual law reform:

> I came back to Belfast in 1974 and there was a Gay Lib Society at Queen's University. I joined a small but dynamic group of about twenty people. I had some earlier experience in political life in the Northern Ireland Labour Party and other left-wing groups, so I was probably the person who pushed for parliamentary law reform as much as gay liberation ... We started a local campaign to try and get the Assembly to address homosexual law reform ... About a year later, in 1975, I met up with Kevin Boyle, a law lecturer and barrister in the University, who said to me that we had a good chance with a case at Strasbourg.

Similarly, Wena Parry's application to Strasbourg developed from her involvement with Press for Change and her broader political campaigning activities. In these cases, NGOs were not responsible for initiating applications to Strasbourg, but they did provide a range of advice and expertise to the applicants that was necessary for them to 'steer' the litigation.

Some applications to Strasbourg, as is clear from the accounts in this book, were deliberately instigated by NGOs. Nigel Warner's account describes how many of the complaints to Strasbourg in the 1980s about sexual orientation discrimination in the UK were the result of contact between the individual applicants and Peter Ashman. This contact came about from Peter Ashman and Nigel Warner, under the auspices of the Campaign for Homosexual Equality (and later the International Gay Association/International Lesbian and Gay Association), actively finding applicants, through a variety of means, to pursue strategic litigation. Similarly,

Angela Mason's account details the ways in which Stonewall, in respect of its 'age of consent' campaign, advertised for applicants to enable it to pursue strategic litigation in Strasbourg. However, as the applicants' accounts show, even when they were 'recruited' by NGOs, they often played a significant role in the process of making a complaint to Strasbourg. This is not least because, in some cases, an applicant's involvement with Strasbourg litigation was bound up with their broader political commitments and activities relating to gay and lesbian human rights.

For example, Hugo Greenhalgh and Will Parry were both active campaigners on gay and lesbian human rights issues before they answered Stonewall's advert in relation to the age of consent campaign. Similarly, Ralph Wilde describes how being 'politically engaged' and 'wanting to change the world' encouraged him to get involved with the same campaign. Although Richard Desmond describes the London Gay Teenage Group, where he met Peter Ashman and Nigel Warner, as not being a 'politicized group', he notes how being 'in a very politicized family' encouraged him to complain to Strasbourg. It is clear that although these applicants were—to use a term that appears in a number of their accounts—acting as 'figureheads' for an application by an NGO to Strasbourg, their involvement in the litigation process was strongly linked to their pre-existing political beliefs and actions. For instance, Euan Sutherland 'knew this was not so much about me' and felt that he was 'an illustration being used to paint a picture', but his contact with Stonewall and involvement in the subsequent complaint to Strasbourg was the direct result of his own political campaigning (which took the form of communicating with his Member of Parliament).

It is important to acknowledge the 'activism' of these applicants in order to rescue them from any idea that they were passive puppets of NGOs. These applicants were not the 'silent partners' of NGOs, and, although their degree of involvement in the legal process and any accompanying public campaign surrounding it is clearly variable, they played an important role in shaping litigation. For instance, in Duncan Lustig-Prean's account, we see how he and the organization he worked for, Rank Outsiders, 'had to persuade Stonewall, under Angela Mason—herself coming from a left-wing, activist background—and their board, that this was a cause that was worthy of funding'. Hugo Greenhalgh's account similarly demonstrates the active role he took in litigation initiated by Stonewall and how this made the relationship between them 'fraught at certain times'. This fraughtness is something that Angela Mason recognizes:

> Working with the applicants was very exciting in lots of ways, because these were big cases, big trials. There were difficulties though, which I'm sure the applicants would talk about. We were interested in the cause and in building Stonewall through these cases. The applicants were, naturally, interested in their own circumstances. So there were some tensions … between what we were trying to do and some of the applicants' personal wishes.

Although tensions can clearly arise, a general trope of the applicants' accounts is that NGOs and gay rights groups provided the platform and support necessary for them to achieve their ambition to address and challenge discrimination. As J.M. puts it, 'The case going forward would never have happened without Liberty, because I didn't have the know-how, the knowledge or understanding. I owe everything to them. But they wanted me as a vehicle as well, and I wanted to be that.' This neatly summarizes the idea, found in several of the accounts, that the relationship between an applicant and an NGO is generally one of mutual support and dependency.

Interactions with Law and Legal Representatives

Everyday life in the UK is infused with and regulated by law. Yet, for most of the time, individuals tend not to think about law or, when they do, often imagine it as a 'magisterial, remote, and transcendent force governing human affairs from some high and distant plane'.[9] Although some gay men and lesbians, as a result of having been subjected to a range of discriminatory treatment by law, may develop a particular legal consciousness,[10] law still often remains a 'mysterious science'.[11] As the accounts in this book demonstrate, for many individuals law is experienced as an aloof, obscure, and inaccessible set of actions and practices. This is especially the case when individuals engage in litigation that requires them to interact with people and practices that they might not otherwise be exposed to. Such exposure can lead to encounters with 'judges with their robes on' talking in incomprehensible 'jargon' (Graeme Grady) inside 'a great big building' that is 'scary' (Mary Simpson). As the applicants' accounts demonstrate, interactions with law and legal representatives can sometimes be 'surreal' (Euan Sutherland) because they are outside of common experience.

The sense of law being divorced from everyday life can be heightened in the context of Strasbourg litigation. The geographical location of the Court, outside of the UK, can make it appear remote and distant. However, it is also this feature of the Court that has, at times, made it appear attractive to those who face problems in the UK that are not solvable by any domestic means. In such circumstances, the Court has often been imagined as an institution capable of 'rescuing' individuals from domination and tyranny by the nation state.[12] As Duncan Lustig-Prean describes it, in the 1990s '[t]here was huge hope in this country that the European Court was the answer to every gay problem'. The Court, as Hugo Greenhalgh puts it, 'seemed to offer a future model of democracy and freedom where rights were recognized and

[9] Patricia Ewick and Susan S Silbey, *The Common Place of Law: Stories from Everyday Life* (University of Chicago Press 1998) 15.

[10] Rosie Harding, *Regulating Sexuality: Legal Consciousness in Lesbian and Gay Lives* (Routledge 2011).

[11] Daniel J Boorstin, *The Mysterious Science of the Law: An Essay on Blackstone's Commentaries* (University of Chicago Press 1941/1996).

[12] Robert Wintemute, 'Strasbourg to the Rescue? Same-Sex Partners and Parents under the European Convention' in Robert Wintemute and Mads Andenæs (eds) *Legal Recognition of Same-Sex Partnerships: A Study of National, European and International Law* (Hart Publishing 2001).

equality was enshrined ... [It] represented hope for us ... [It] seemed this amazing, wonderful, shiny, beacon of equality and modernity.' Emma Riley encapsulates the spirit of this optimism in her description of how she viewed the Court 'as the defender of my soul'. It is clear from the applicants' accounts that the Court has often been imbued with considerable symbolic value and imagined in ways that possibly exceed the scope of both its legal function and practice. However, this is understandable given that the Convention has been styled as a 'beacon' of hope since it was first signed[13] and the Court has been described in grand terms as the 'conscience of Europe'.[14]

Whilst the applicants' accounts show that the Court might not be regarded as remote, they also show that the law under which it operates often remains obscure. Some applicants are candid about the fact that they never read the Convention (for example, Kevin Bazeley and Emma Riley) or that they only have a 'very, very basic understanding' of it (Graeme Grady). Some applicants view the Convention as 'too complicated' (Mary Simpson) and not something easily 'understood' (Richard Desmond). Ralph Wilde, a young man at the time of his application, acknowledges, 'I don't think I understood what international and European human rights law was.' By contrast, other applicants did read the Convention and develop an understanding of it. This is clear from William Nash's account of his client who 'obviously knew something about it because he'd put [the application] forward'. Similarly, Duncan Lustig-Prean had 'studied enough law' and 'immersed' himself in his case to be able to make informed decisions about which Articles of the Convention he wished to bring complaints under. The same is true of Wena Parry, who states, 'I read the Convention and I considered that it should be one hundred percent for me because it was about human rights and my human rights were being trodden on with hobnail boots.' Similarly, both Hugo Greenhalgh and Will Parry describe how they developed an understanding of the Convention during their case and of the rationale for complaining under particularly Articles. As Will Parry puts it:

> We definitely had a sense of the European Convention on Human Rights and a sense that the reason we were taking the case to Europe was because, at that stage, the Convention hadn't been incorporated into British law ... We certainly had an understanding of the contents of the Convention as a result of talking to Stonewall. I think I'd be lying if I said we had a sense of it when we first turned up at the Stonewall office. However, we spoke, we talked a lot, about the right to privacy, and the right to equality.

In sum, the applicants' accounts demonstrate variable knowledge and understanding of the Convention and how it is applicable to their Strasbourg case.

The applicants' accounts also demonstrate that, regardless of an applicant's level of knowledge and understanding of the Convention, it is common to engage a professional legal representative to submit the application to Strasbourg. Although an individual is able to submit an application to Strasbourg without professional

[13] Sir David Maxwell Fyfe, quoted in Human Rights Information Bulletin, *The European Convention on Human Rights at 50* (Council of Europe 2000) 47.

[14] John Coleman (ed), *The Conscience of Europe* (Council of Europe 1999).

legal representation,[15] this has not been—with the exception of William Nash's client—the practice of the applicants in this book. For these applicants, even those who take an active interest in Convention law, professional legal representation is seen as essential when preparing and submitting an application. This is summed up by Wena Parry's view that it would not be 'a wise thing' to make an application to Strasbourg without professional legal advice. For the majority of applicants, working with legal representatives—solicitors and barristers—is, therefore, at the heart of applying to Strasbourg.

The relationship between applicants and their legal representatives, as the accounts in this book demonstrate, takes different forms. One of the striking things about the accounts is the way they document the extent to which many applicants actively collaborate with their legal representatives in preparing submissions to Strasbourg. For example, as Duncan Lustig-Prean states:

> I didn't believe in being a client who sat idly by and allowed the experts to deal with the case. It was something I wanted to be intensely involved in … [I was] able to advise on military regulations. It was also important for me to be involved because, although I wanted to achieve an improvement in the services—a civilization in this one aspect which I thought the services had got wrong—I didn't want to end up in a situation where civvies interfered with something they didn't necessarily understand.

In Jeffrey Dudgeon's account, we see that a similar active engagement with the substance of the legal arguments being made in his case led to the breakdown of the relationship with his legal representatives:

> I'm not a lawyer, I'm a politically minded individual so, in terms of the Strasbourg application, I did the politics, as I thought best, and Kevin Boyle and the solicitor, Francis Keenan, did the legal stuff … They were doing Article 8, private life stuff, but, being a radical, I wanted to pursue Article 14 … With some reluctance, the lawyers did pursue that point but it created some tension and, after we won at the Commission, I changed lawyers because they weren't willing to pursue Article 14 hard enough … I switched to gay lawyers in London—a solicitor, Paul Crane, and a barrister, Terry Munyard—and a senior counsel, Lord Tony Gifford. Obviously, that was hard and it was sad in a way. I always felt a bit guilty and a bit annoyed that I'd had to do it … But pursuing Article 14 wasn't political unreality; we were going to win on Article 8, so why not push the boat out? It would have been neglectful not to.

Jeffrey Dudgeon and Duncan Lustig-Prean's experiences are outliers among the accounts in this book—in terms of the extent of their involvement in shaping the legal arguments in their Strasbourg cases—but many of the applicants' accounts document their active engagement with crafting the legal substance of their complaints. Wena Parry, for example, states that her barrister 'asked me about the Articles in the Convention', and 'I was very involved in making the application.' This type

[15] Rule 36(1) of the Rules of Court states, '[p]ersons … may initially present applications … themselves or through a representative'. According to Rule 36(2), following notification of the application to the respondent Contracting Party, the applicant 'should be represented … unless the President of the Chamber decides otherwise'. European Court of Human Rights, *Rules of Court* (1 January 2016).

of 'involvement' characterizes the experience of a number of other applicants, such as Euan Sutherland:

> In terms of the Strasbourg application process, I did feel involved. I remember sitting in chambers with Peter Duffy, Angela Mason, and with other people. I don't know if I was able to alter, adjust or change the arguments, but I was able to offer personal stories that would help make points in law.

What this and other accounts reveal is the collaborative enterprise at the heart of Strasbourg litigation. The majority of these applicants did not passively defer to legal experts but, to varying degrees, worked with legal representatives to co-produce applications.

Media Attention and Family Support

Applications to Strasbourg, particularly ones that are successful, often generate considerable public interest and result in sustained coverage in news and other media. Many of the people in this book talk about their involvement with the media and its effect upon them as being the most important aspect of their Strasbourg litigation. In some cases, this is unsurprising because an application may be just one element of what Ralph Wilde calls 'a full spectrum initiative to change the law' that involves 'doing interviews on television, in newspapers, [and] giving speeches in various places'. In cases where applicants have worked with NGOs—particularly Stonewall—interaction with the media has been regarded as an important means of raising public awareness of the litigation. However, it is clear from the applicants' accounts of these cases that media attention, as Hugo Greenhalgh puts it, can be 'extremely uncomfortable'. For some applicants, such as Emma Riley, the personal discomfort produced by unwelcome media attention—her 'Lady Diana experience of having a camera stuck in my face'—was the basis for her choosing to request anonymity in her Strasbourg application. Similarly, J.M. explains that she chose anonymity (and retains it) because she does not want 'someone to pick [the case] up' and 'be cruel'. However, as Jeffrey Dudgeon explains, his decision to relinquish anonymity was based on his realization of the need to 'become public to do the public advocacy'. What the accounts show is that applicants, for the most part, are ambivalent about media publicity.

The most common way in which applicants talk about media publicity is in terms of how it affects and shapes their relationships with family members. In some cases, as the accounts show, publicity causes tensions and problems between applicants and their families. As Will Parry explains:

> My mum was pretty old school … One thing that made her very unhappy was the fact that we were making a fuss about it, were going on TV … I remember one incident when I had gone back to hers for Sunday lunch and suddenly, out of the blue, she said, 'I don't know why you're doing this, it's so embarrassing for me, you're making such a fuss about this, and I just don't understand, why are you doing it?'

Graeme Grady had a similar experience with his mother:

> I'd said to my mother, 'I'm going to take this to court', and she said, 'It's not going to be in the papers is it?' I said, 'Oh god, no, nothing like that.' … And then there you are, that first day, on the tube, seeing your photo splashed on the *Evening Standard*, and the next day, on every newspaper … My mother struggled with it big time … So the publicity didn't worry me, but it did worry other people.

It is clear that parents, for various reasons, have concerns about their child, as Mary Simpson's mother put it, 'sticking [their] neck out'. This is sometimes linked, as the accounts show, to a parent's dislike or disapproval of their child's sexual orientation and a desire to avoid the stigma or shame produced as a result of publicity of it. In this sense, it is the publicity surrounding an application to Strasbourg, rather than the application itself, that produces problems between applicants and their families.

By contrast, family members also often provide much needed support to applicants in respect of their interactions with the media. For example, Euan Sutherland, one of the youngest applicants to take a complaint about sexual orientation discrimination to Strasbourg, had 'family support' from his parents who were 'kind and supportive enough to partake in television, radio and newspaper interviews'. Duncan Lustig-Prean's father—his 'strongest supporter'—helped him deal with unwanted media attention: 'I've told them … I'll sue the arse off them.' Moreover, when press coverage exacerbated the persecution experienced by Wena Parry, her wife, Anita, provided considerable support.

It is clear from the applicants' accounts that media publicity often plays a significant part in complaints to Strasbourg. Even when an application is not, as Richard Desmond puts it, 'hugely public', most applicants are aware that they risk 'notoriety'. What the accounts demonstrate is that the experience of publicity often shapes relationships between applicants and their families in significant ways. What this shows more generally is that the 'right of individual petition' to Strasbourg is usually exercised within the context of a network of social relationships and that these relationships can play an important role in shaping applicants' decisions. Although, as Sir David Mawxell Fyfe argued at the time the Convention was being conceived, 'the general modern tendency of international law has been to emphasise the rights and duties of an individual as a subject of international law',[16] this fails to understand the ways in which the individual who is the subject of law is also a subject of the wider social relations in which he or she is embedded and, crucially, these wider social relations determine—to varying degrees—her or his interaction with law.

Expectations of Strasbourg

Those who make applications to Strasbourg about sexual orientation discrimination have differing expectations about the outcome of their complaint. Some applicants

[16] Council of Europe, First Part of the Second Session of the Consultative Assembly, Sixth Sitting (14 August 1950) in *Reports, Part 1, Sittings 1 to 12* (Council of Europe 1950) 174.

commence an application to Strasbourg with a strong expectation that they will win. Others are more ambivalent about their prospects, and some feel there is little chance of success. A range of factors influence an applicant's expectations about the chances of their case being successful. One factor, as Hugo Greenhalgh's account demonstrates, is how applicants 'calibrate' the substance of their complaint to Strasbourg with the wider social and political relations in which it is made:

> We would have won the case in Strasbourg ... Society was on the cusp of change, not just in the UK but across Europe as well. There was the rise of gay rights activism on a national and international level. The issue of gay rights, which of course had been going on for decades, became more an issue of human rights ... We witnessed the morphing of gay rights and human rights and I think, at that stage, although we were far, far ahead of public opinion, on a policy or parliamentarian level, we were almost there. So that's why we thought the European Court would almost certainly rule in our favour.

Hugo Greenhalgh's high level of certainty that his application would have succeeded had it progressed to the Court is born from a belief that a judgment from the Court would have reflected an emerging European consensus on 'gay rights'. In this respect, Duncan Lustig-Prean reached a different conclusion:

> The reality was that we ... had the fall of the Soviet Union. We had former Soviet bloc nations now joining the Convention and becoming members of the Court, still with very strong conservative social views on this issue ... To my mind, depending on the constitution of the final Court, it was not a sure bet that we would win.

What these two accounts have in common is that the applicants' expectations are shaped by the idea that the broader social and political relations of European societies determine the outcome of complaints to Strasbourg rather than a strict 'moral' interpretation of the rights and freedoms contained in the Convention. Andrew Courten encapsulates this succinctly by stating that, although he hoped that the question of 'right and wrong' would be important to the adjudication of his application, he recognized that, because the 'Council of Europe contained many homophobic countries', the outcome would be determined by 'realpolitik'. Although legal professionals and academics routinely engage in debates about the extent to which the Court's jurisprudence should reflect the social and political relations of European societies—for instance, by relying on an assessment of European consensus[17]—it is clear that a consideration of this issue also shapes applicants' expectations. Similarly, whilst legal professionals and academics continue to debate the legitimacy of the Court's use of the margin of appreciation doctrine when adjudicating disputes,[18] applicants, as Richard Desmond's account shows, also reflect on how Strasbourg jurisprudence is shaped by deference to Contracting States.

[17] For the most comprehensive recent discussion, see Kanstantsin Dzehtsiarou, *European Consensus and the Legitimacy of the European Court of Human Rights* (Cambridge University Press 2015).

[18] See, for example, Andrew Legg, *The Margin of Appreciation in International Human Rights Law: Defence and Proportionality* (Oxford University Press 2012).

Applicants' expectations about the chance of their application being successful in Strasbourg are also clearly influenced by their knowledge of relevant Convention jurisprudence. As Emma Riley explains, 'I'm not sure I knew what to expect from Strasbourg. At the beginning, I didn't think I'd win. As time went on, once Duncan Lustig-Prean and the others' complaints were deemed admissible and they won, I had more confidence that my case would follow that precedent.' What this and other accounts show is that applicants are aware that the chance of their complaint being successful in Strasbourg is not dependent solely on being able to show—as all of the applicants in this book obviously could—that they had suffered a detriment as a result of a difference in treatment based on their sexual orientation. Rather, they are aware of the ways in which, as Robert Wintemute's account shows, precedent can limit the chance of an application being successful because the Court is often reluctant to evolve its jurisprudence.

The Effect of Making a Complaint to Strasbourg

Making a complaint to Strasbourg, as the accounts in this book demonstrate, is no small undertaking. Rather, it involves considerable commitment and investment by an applicant. One of the major investments that applicants make is in terms of the amount of time they devote to the process. An application to Strasbourg can take five or more years to reach a conclusion, and, during that time, applicants will be required to undertake a range of activities with their legal representatives. In some cases, applicants may travel to Strasbourg. As a consequence of making a complaint, applicants often face a range of challenges and are required to deal with issues and problems that arise, sometimes unexpectedly, during the process. As a result of this, complaints to Strasbourg can have far-reaching and long-term effects on applicants' lives. Such effects, as the accounts show, can be both positive and negative.

The applicants' accounts demonstrate that a complaint to Strasbourg can produce a range of negative effects. One such effect is that applicants can experience the process as 'incredibly stressful' (Andrew Courten) and suffer considerable 'personal attrition' as a result of feeling 'naked and exposed' (Duncan Lustig-Prean). The process of making a complaint about sexual orientation discrimination can be, as Mary Simpson puts it, 'hard' at a time when 'being gay' is 'hard'. One particularly 'hard' consequence of making a complaint is the hostile reactions it generates in others. For example, Jeffrey Dudgeon's account shows the 'ordeal' he had to endure at work after his case was publicized on television and, further, the trouble he subsequently experienced at home: '[I]n 1983 and 1984 … [t]here were a series of attacks on my house, with breezeblocks through the window, and injuries and all that. That is very disturbing, to say the least, and lingers for years.' Similarly, Euan Sutherland describes his experience of receiving 'death threats':

> In 1996 … [a]t my home address—and also at the solicitor, Stonewall, and my college addresses—I received a series of really nasty, very descriptive, very believable death threats, which completely gave me a wobbly. It was scary. My godmother took me down to our local

police station in East Dulwich to log it. There was very little that they could do—I don't think they were ever able to trace anything or anyone—so it all fell by the wayside. The college were nice and supportive, but I had a complete wobble during my English exam. It was upsetting and worrying and distressing. It did throw me and worry me hugely, but it didn't put me off doing the case.

The significant antagonism that these applicants experienced is, perhaps, unsurprising given that their complaints to Strasbourg challenged a social status quo that a large proportion of their fellow citizens wished to see continued. However, it is not only the hostility of private citizens that applicants sometimes face but also the antipathy of State officials. For example, Hugo Greenhalgh and Will Parry's accounts detail how, as a consequence of being publically open about their sexual relationship, they were questioned by the police. As Will Parry explains, 'we were then facing a real risk that we could be prosecuted'. Similarly, Ralph Wilde knew that in undertaking his complaint he was 'choosing' to expose himself to a considerable similar 'risk'.

Further potentially negative consequences of making a complaint to Strasbourg may arise from the financial costs involved. One significant concern of applicants is the potential for adverse financial penalties to arise from the 'very long and costly process' (Andrew Courten) of exhausting domestic remedies in the UK courts. Graeme Grady's account of this is characteristically light-hearted, but it shows the level of financial risk involved in the pre-Strasbourg phase of litigation:

It was very disappointing when we lost in the different levels of the UK courts. I remember the Master of the Rolls saying, 'I'm sorry Mr. Grady, I have to award costs against you, however I would not expect the Ministry of Defence to follow you up for it.' It was £75,000 and I had a little laugh when he said that, and I thought to myself, where would I get that money? Then I thought, I'll say that I'll pay them a pound a week!

There is also the potential to incur financial costs in Strasbourg as a consequence of engaging specialist legal representation. For this reason, the applicants' accounts show that they often rely upon legal professionals undertaking work on a *pro bono* basis.

The applicants' accounts show that, because of the potential or actual negative consequences of making a complaint to Strasbourg, they often identify a number of 'personal characteristics' that they feel they possess. Being 'angry' (Jeffrey Dudgeon, Hugo Greenhalgh, and J.M.), 'pig headed' (Andrew Courten), and 'idealistic' (Ralph Wilde) are some of the personal characteristics that applicants identify as underpinning their resolve to pursue and see through a complaint. Mary Simpson describes herself in these terms:

They tried to knock me down but, although I'll get really down, I'll come back fighting. I've got an inner fight in me … Yes, it was frightening, but I kept thinking I've got to do it because if I don't do it nobody else is going to do it. Nobody else is going to say, 'Right, we've got to have some rights.' They'd just give up. I never give up … I don't care; I always put my neck on the block. That's me … I've got some type of inner strength, because I've been through so much in those thirty years. I've still got a fire in my belly.

This account describes the tenacity and fortitude that, to some extent, characterizes all of the applicants in this book. As the accounts show, an applicant's decision to challenge entrenched and systematic discrimination in the UK, in the face of the negative personal consequences that this could produce, often demands high levels of courage and determination.

However, despite the negative effects that a Strasbourg complaint can produce, the applicants' accounts show numerous positive benefits. Emma Riley talks of the 'empowering' nature of making her complaint to Strasbourg, and Will Parry describes how pursuing his complaint 'gave me a lot of self-confidence that I didn't have before'. One of the youngest applicants to take a complaint about sexual orientation discrimination to Strasbourg, Richard Desmond, describes being 'excited' by aspects of the experience. In addition, Ralph Wilde who, like Richard Desmond, took a complaint to Strasbourg as a young man describes his experience in similar terms:

> People say, 'Oh, you were so brave and courageous.' I think I was just wanting the adventure of doing something that was a step into the unknown ... It was a very efficient way—a sort of therapy session—to face up to everything that you spend your teenage years having problems with and transform that into something you're not ashamed of and, moreover, are going to fight for. I think that is incredibly empowering and it gave me a sort of confidence to do other things, afterwards. It's partly a class thing—I'm from a working class family and I'm the first member of family to stay at school after the age of sixteen—and I think it helped with that too. When you do something like that and it's a risk, when you draw attention to the greatest source of shame and vulnerability in your life and it ends up not being a disaster but ends up working out really well, I think that can give you a kind of confidence that transfers over to other things. I think that has stayed with me.

Both Ralph Wilde and Richard Desmond describe the various ways in which the process of complaining to Strasbourg exposed them to people and situations that were beyond their existing (working class) life experiences. Their accounts demonstrate how involvement in the process of Strasbourg litigation can disturb the hitherto bounded and delimited nature of an individual's 'experience' that is itself the result of their position in particular social and physical space. Such a disturbance is created because the individual is, to a certain extent, 'lifted out' of the routine social relations by the extraordinary act of going to Strasbourg. This may have a significant effect on an individual's 'habitus'—the 'systems of schemes of perception, appreciation and action' that individuals acquire from their position in and embodiment of the social world that enables them to 'perform acts of practical knowledge'.[19] Both Richard Desmond and Ralph Wilde describe such effects in positive terms.

Perhaps what is most striking about the applicants' accounts is how they describe, in almost universally positive terms, their feelings about having taken a complaint to Strasbourg. Applicants—whether they won or lost their case—reflect on their application as something they are 'pleased' (Andrew Courten and Kevin Bazeley) and 'proud' (Richard Desmond, Jeffrey Dudgeon, Mary Simpson, Will Parry, Terence Perkins, and Euan Sutherland) to have done. Making a complaint to

[19] Pierre Bourdieu, *Pascalian Meditations* (Polity Press 2000) 138.

Strasbourg generates 'immense pride' (Hugo Greenhalgh and Emma Riley), produces a sense of being 'incredibly privileged' (Ralph Wilde), and creates outcomes that are 'hugely pleasurable' (Duncan Lustig-Prean). It is clear that these applicants have—as some of them explicitly state—no regrets about making a complaint to Strasbourg but, rather, derive continuing and long-term satisfaction from having done so. The accounts also demonstrate that applicants often derive a degree of 'ontological security'—a form of personal and subjective security that is the opposite of 'existential anxiety'[20]—from having made their complaint. This results from an applicant situating their application to Strasbourg within the wider history of the development of lesbian and gay human rights. Emma Riley describes this as the 'integral part' she played in the 'journey' of social and legal change in the UK; and Richard Desmond defines it as 'my bit in the history of what has happened'. Graeme Grady puts it in these terms:

> This is going to sound bizarre, but for years I wondered, 'Why am I here, what am I here to achieve, what am I on this earth for, what do I do?' and then one day, I thought, oh my god, perhaps that's what I was here for, perhaps that's me done my bit, I can go, I can pass away, I've done my bit.

The Future Relationship between the UK and the Convention System

It is perhaps unsurprising that people who have experience of making a complaint to Strasbourg often have strong views on the future of the Convention system and the UK's relationship with it. These views are particularly interesting in the context of contemporary debates about whether the Court has developed 'mission creep', and if, therefore, the UK should renegotiate its commitments under or even withdraw from the Convention.[21] The applicants' accounts show considerable diversity of views on this question. For instance, Wena Parry, who was 'disappointed' with the Court and felt 'failed' by it when it declared her complaint inadmissible, argues that the Court 'could make a better job if each of the countries were prepared to give up control of their own human rights to Strasbourg'. Wena Parry's argument is, therefore, that the Convention system may be more effective if the UK ceded more responsibility and authority to Strasbourg. By contrast, Jeffrey Dudgeon, the first person to 'win' a sexual orientation discrimination case in Strasbourg, is 'quite critical of the Court today', and although recognizing it as 'hugely important', he

[20] Anthony Giddens, *Modernity and Self-Identity: Self and Society in the Late Modern Age* (Polity Press 1991).

[21] Conservative Party, 'Protecting Human Rights in the UK: The Conservatives' Proposals for Changing Britain's Human Rights Laws' (2014) 3. For a critical discussion of this, see Kanstantsin Dzehtsiarou, Tobias Lock, Paul Johnson, Fiona de Londras, Alan Greene, and Ed Bates, *The Legal Implications of a Repeal of the Human Rights Act 1998 and Withdrawal from the European Convention on Human Rights* (2015) <http://ssrn.com/abstract=2605487> (accessed 16 February 2016).

feels that it has 'moved away from a liberal position to maybe a radical one in some respects, which creates more difficulties in a complex Europe'. Jeffrey Dudgeon's account recognizes the 'crisis of confidence' that characterizes contemporary debate in the UK about the Court and the centrality of the Court's judgment on the 'prisoners' voting case' to this.

One striking characteristic of the applicants' accounts is the considerable value that many of them attach to the UK being a part of the Convention system. This value is principally found in the capacity of the Court to provide an 'objective' mechanism (J.M.) for examining human rights issues in the UK, to be a 'third party' that can offer 'an independent decision on the facts presented' and tell the UK 'hang on, that's not right, this is the right thing' (Kevin Bazeley), as well as being a means by which the UK can 'get [its] house in order' (Euan Sutherland). For these reasons, some applicants say they read with 'absolute horror' (Will Parry) and are 'very fearful' (Duncan Lustig-Prean) of proposals to weaken the relationship between the UK and the Court. However, it is also clear that even the strongest supporters of the Convention system are not uncritical of it. Graeme Grady, for example, who is sympathetic to criticisms of the Court's judgment on the disfranchisement of UK prisoners, provides a nuanced and subtle argument for continuing the UK's relationship with the Court:

> I think there is a good argument to keep the European Court of Human Rights there, so we have got somebody else that can say, 'No, you're actually doing this wrong.' I'd be totally against the UK pulling out because it would be like going back to the dark ages ... There are some cases in Strasbourg where you think, that is ridiculous. Prisoner voting, I'm totally against that. I think if you're in prison, you're there to be punished, so why should you have the right to vote? I know some people say it's all about rehabilitation, but I think you lose your right to vote as soon as you're locked up. But, to me, it defeats the object if you sign up to the Convention and you don't enforce it because you don't like the Court's decision. It's that catch twenty-two thing where, although I disagree with it, I think if we've signed up to it we have to do it.

Graeme Grady's account, like the accounts of other applicants, offers a powerful argument for the UK continuing to accept the jurisdiction of the Court and execute its judgments—even in respect of the most contentious cases—because the ultimate value of doing so is that it prevents the UK 'going back to the dark ages'. It is, perhaps, unsurprising that those who have benefitted from the Convention system would wish to see it continued. Nevertheless, what the accounts show is that those who argue in favour of the UK being a part of the Convention system do so on the basis of recognizing its overall value to people in the UK. The accounts show that the benefit of the Court is seen to be that it will 'live, breathe and develop' (Duncan Lustig-Prean) human rights jurisprudence in a way that does not simply reflect the 'institutional beliefs' (Kevin Bazeley) of the UK. The Court is able to do this because it is not 'country-related' (J.M.) and therefore transcends national legal systems. For those who suffer State-sanctioned discrimination, this is the tangible value of being in a State that is part of the Convention system. The ability to go to Strasbourg, as Nigel Warner puts it, offers individuals a 'lifeline'.

APPENDIX 1

A Note on Method

This note on method provides a short reflection on the process of carrying out the empirical research that resulted in the oral history accounts contained in this book. I discuss the formulation of the research questions, the sampling of participants, how the oral history interviews were conducted, and the process by which the final text of the accounts was produced.

The Research Idea

In November 2012, Gay's the Word bookshop in London held an event to launch my book, *Homosexuality and the European Court of Human Rights*. Richard Desmond, who I had not previously met, came along, and we discussed the complaint that he had made to Strasbourg in 1982 about the discriminatory 'age of consent' for male homosexual acts. During that conversation, Richard mentioned that in order to submit his application to Strasbourg he was required, because of his age, to obtain parental permission. He went on to describe the process, which is detailed in his account in this book, of how his mother came to 'sign the paperwork'. As a sociologist who had spent several years studying legal documents, I found this real-life account both refreshing and fascinating. I am profoundly grateful to Richard for that discussion because it provided the basis for the idea of carrying out research on the people 'behind' the Strasbourg cases concerning sexual orientation discrimination.

The initial idea for the research was propelled by my awareness that, in the vast majority of cases, very little information is publically available about the applicants who make complaints to Strasbourg. Decisions and judgments issued by the Strasbourg organs usually contain a short section called 'the facts', but this normally provides scant information about the applicant. Sometimes, Strasbourg cases are reported in the popular news media but this reporting often takes the form of reiterating or commenting on the contents of a decision or judgment. Given the potential effect of a judgment of the European Court of Human Rights on the lives of people living in European states, the value of gaining greater knowledge about the individual applicants seemed obvious to me. After all, the vast majority of people in European states who suffer violations of their human rights and fundamental freedoms do not make a complaint to Strasbourg. On this basis, I formulated a number of key research questions that I wanted to address, which were: from what contexts and circumstances do applications to Strasbourg arise; what are the motivations and aspirations of those who make applications; what is the role of organizations or groups in supporting applicants; what relationships do applicants have with legal representatives; and what are the effects and outcomes of 'going to Strasbourg' on applicants' lives?

Selecting and Finding the Participants

I decided at the outset to conduct qualitative interviews with individuals who had made an application to Strasbourg against the UK concerning sexual orientation discrimination.

Furthermore, I decided to focus only on those cases that had resulted in the Strasbourg organs issuing a publically available decision or judgment. The decision to focus solely on applications against the UK was based on two primary factors. First, concentrating on one jurisdiction has allowed me to produce an in-depth historical account of the socio-legal context from which applications arose. Secondly, as a native English speaker (with a limited ability to speak any other European language) conducting interviews with UK-based applicants has presented no language challenges. The decision to focus only on cases that resulted in a publically available decision or judgment was based on a strong desire to produce accounts by applicants that correspond with available legal documents. Specifically, I wanted to make available to legal practitioners—law students, lawyers, and judges—the accounts of the real people behind the mass of jurisprudence that they routinely read, study, and use.

Whilst social science researchers often have a large sample of people from which to select participants, the available sample for this research was small—it comprises the applicants in the cases that are listed in Appendix 3. Moreover, the available sample was further limited by the fact that some of the applicants in the earliest Strasbourg cases are deceased. For example, the applicant 'X.', who made the first complaint to Strasbourg against the UK about sexual orientation discrimination, died in 1979. The importance of this case, and the impossibility of obtaining a first-hand account of it from the applicant, gave me the idea of interviewing the applicant's lawyer, William Nash, and that created the further idea of including three other accounts by legal professionals and campaigners who have been closely involved with complaints to Strasbourg about sexual orientation discrimination.

In light of the small available sample, I approached the research with a degree of concern about whether I could actually find people. Aside from Richard Desmond, I already had contact with Jeffrey Dudgeon and was easily able to arrange an interview with him. All of the other participants, however, required some tracking down through a variety of means. The most challenging people to contact were those who had requested that their identity not be disclosed in any document made publically available by the Strasbourg organs. In the case of Emma Riley, who chose to relinquish her anonymity for the purpose of this book, I came across her name serendipitously when looking at some documents that another participant had given me to read in respect of his own case. In the case of J.M., who wishes to remain anonymous, it was her legal representative who facilitated contact between us.

I approached contacting all of the applicants with a number of ethical concerns. A key question in my mind was to what extent is it reasonable to contact people who may have experienced traumatic events and ask them to talk about it many years later? After all, even an invitation to participate in research can provoke memories that 'bring alive' experiences from the past. This dilemma—which is foundational to much social science research on so-called sensitive topics—can only be solved by making a judgment about whether the value of knowledge that may result from research makes 'intrusion' into an individual's private life justifiable. Or, as the European Court of Human Rights would put it, whether such an intrusion is proportionate to the aim pursued. I decided that, in respect of the people I contacted, inviting them to participate in the research was justifiable.

I did not attempt to contact every person that has made an application to Strasbourg against the UK about sexual orientation discrimination. Rather, I contacted particular individuals attached to a selection of cases that are representative of the range of issues that have been complained about and the times in which applications have been made. I also tried to represent, as far as possible, female applicants. Although this book does contain more oral history accounts by men than by women—and, in that sense, is unbalanced—women (for a number of reasons) have made far fewer applications to Strasbourg against the UK about sexual orientation discrimination than men have. Therefore, the male-to-female ratio of oral history accounts in this book might not be seen to underrepresent women in the context of the available sample of applicants. All of the individuals that I contacted, and who agreed to participate in the research, did so on the basis of providing their informed consent. Two people who I contacted, who initially agreed to take part in the research, subsequently decided not to participate. Two further people who I contacted, through a third party, declined to take part.

Conducting the Interviews

Social scientists—particularly sociologists—have been writing for decades about the practice of conducting qualitative interviews. Ongoing academic debates concern not only the 'technical' aspects of the qualitative interviewing process but also epistemological questions about the nature of the knowledge that is produced. I will not rehearse these debates here, but will reflect on a number of practical aspects of the oral history interview process.

One aspect of the interview process that is worthy of reflection concerns the nature of the relationship that I, as a researcher, formed with the participants. By its very nature, qualitative oral history research of this kind requires in-depth discussion of personal and, sometimes, painful issues, and it has often been argued, therefore, that the 'social proximity' of the researcher and the participant is of significant importance. A participant who feels 'at a distance' from a researcher because of perceived or actual social differences between them may be reluctant to 'open up' and, as a result, this inhibits the dialogic engagement that is the essence of qualitative research. In respect of the majority of the interviews I conducted, social proximity between the participants and myself was ensured, to some extent, by a shared experience of sexual orientation discrimination. People who identify as being gay (or, perhaps, it is more accurate to say people who do not identify as being heterosexual) often have a 'baseline' of shared experience of discrimination that, although they may otherwise be very different, facilitates a degree of familiarity between them. Euan Sutherland told me that at the time of his Strasbourg case it would have been possible to 'find thousands of teenagers around the country who would relate to the bare bones of [his] story' of discrimination and, having myself been a teenager at that time, I could certainly relate to Euan's story. My own biography and experience of living as a gay person in the UK meant that I could, to some extent, relate to the 'bare bones' of the stories of everyone I interviewed and this produced a degree of familiarity between myself and the participants.

That familiarity facilitated, in most cases, a form of empathic communication between the participants and myself. Many of the interviews were intensely emotional experiences for participants: some cried or fought back tears as they recalled painful events from the past; others remembered and, to an extent, relived feelings of anger and frustration. An inability to empathize with the participants—to be unable to both *understand* and *feel* what they have experienced—would have significantly hampered my capacity to produce the accounts published in this book. It is inconceivable that participants would revisit and recount painful experiences—often deeply buried and unspoken about for many years—if they did not feel that the person they were talking to could, to some extent, see the world from their standpoint. I make a case, therefore, not for my own skills as an interviewer, but for the importance of sociologically informed qualitative research, which, unlike other methods of data production, is founded on the express commitment of 'viewing events, actions, norms, values, etc. from the perspective of the people who are being studied'.[1]

[1] Alan Bryman, *Quantity and Quality in Social Research* (Routledge 1988) 61.

Sometimes social distance—and a concomitant lack of familiarity—characterizes the research encounter, and this was particularly the case in respect of the interview I conducted with Wena Parry. When I met Wena and we started the interview, it became quickly apparent—as her account in this books shows—that she is uncomfortable with homosexuality. Wena specifically told me that she would not ask me about my sexual orientation—which I took to mean she did not want to know if I was gay. Wena told me several times during our meeting that she is not, and never has been, gay. In addition, she talked at length about her negative feelings towards homosexuals. I didn't in any way mind listening to Wena's views on homosexuality—why would a professional researcher have a problem listening to anything a participant says?—but I felt that, for Wena, this issue put us at a distance and, as a consequence, social proximity between us was lacking.

Producing the Oral History Accounts

When a researcher takes what has been captured in a qualitative interview on a sound recorder and transcribes it into written words, he or she is involved in an act of transformation. There is no way of performing this transformation so that what is written down is a 'pure' representation of what occurred in the oral interview. As Pierre Bourdieu puts it, 'to transcribe is necessarily to write, in the sense of rewrite'.[2] From the moment the process of transcribing begins, therefore, the researcher is engaged in the practice of creative destruction and construction. For instance, deciding where one sentence begins and ends, and then punctuating it, is an act of interpretation. The idea that it is possible to produce 'raw data' in this way, free from 'contamination' by the researcher, is a positivist fantasy. It is in acknowledgement of this that I decided to involve the participants in the process of producing the written accounts so that they themselves could control and determine the content. To achieve this, I invited each participant to review and amend the text of his or her oral history account once I had produced a 'first draft' of it. All of the participants did this, and, through the process of discussing and incorporating changes to the text, we agreed the final version of each account that is published in this book.

Whilst the oral history accounts can be seen to have been 'co-produced' by the participants and myself, it is important to note, however, that the draft text which I invited participants to review had already been shaped by a number of my own editorial decisions. These decisions were taken as I transformed the full verbatim transcript of each interview (which I produced myself) into the oral history format. This involved following a number of editorial steps, which Linda Shopes helpfully summarizes as editing the text to create a narrative structure, cutting extraneous material from the text, refining the text to remove unnecessarily repetitions, and intervening in the text to ensure maximum clarity.[3] There was, in addition, a fifth step: editing out my own voice from the text. After going through these editorial stages, the text contained in each oral history account appears significantly different to the verbatim transcript on which it is based. It is therefore important to acknowledge the extent to which the form of the accounts, as well as their content, had been determined by my editorial choices prior to the participants reviewing and editing the text.

[2] Pierre Bourdieu, 'Understanding' (1996) 13 Theory, Culture and Society 17, 31.

[3] Linda Shopes, 'Editing Oral History for Publication' (2011) 31 Oral History Forum d'histoire orale, 1.

Although most oral historians will view my editorial interventions as uncontroversial, this will not be the case for those social scientists who continue to regard the verbatim transcript produced from a qualitative interview as sacrosanct. Indeed, during the preparation of the accounts in this book, I described my editorial approach to a friend—an anthropologist at the University of Exeter—who told me in no uncertain terms that, in her view, I was committing the grievous sin of 'imposing' myself on the data. That, of course, is true. But if such an imposition begins, as I argued above, with the process of transcribing the oral interview material, then it seems to me that a researcher's imprint is already firmly on the verbatim transcript. The editing of the verbatim transcript into the oral history format—so long as this is done in such a way that strives to preserve the essence of the participant's experience—is no more a form of contamination than the act of transcribing (or, indeed, the act of asking a participant a particular set of questions during an interview at the expense of others). The way in which I have attempted to guard against imposing my own values or beliefs on these accounts is to involve the participants as much as possible in the preparation of the final text. Although I am not unaware of the shortcomings of such a process—particularly because, in some circumstances, participants may be reluctant (for the reason that they are embarrassed or shy) to amend text prepared by a university academic—I have tried, as far as possible, to overcome such limitations. In short, I have sought to represent the lives of the research participants in a way that does justice to their experiences, feelings, and beliefs. It is my sincere hope that I have achieved this.

APPENDIX 2

List of Oral History Interviews

The following table gives details of the oral history interviews conducted by the author.

Name	Interview date	Interview location
Kevin Bazeley	22 December 2015	By video call
Andrew Courten	9 October 2015	Mr Courten's home
Richard Desmond	1 July 2015	Mr Desmond's home
Jeffrey Dudgeon	2 September 2015	Mr Dudgeon's home
Graeme Grady	16 September 2015	Mr Grady's home
Hugo Greenhalgh	7 August 2015	By telephone
J.M.	8 February 2016	A pub close to Ms M.'s home
Duncan Lustig-Prean	24 July 2015	A hotel restaurant close to Mr Lustig-Prean's home
Angela Mason	2 November 2015	Camden Town Hall
William Nash	23 July 2015	By telephone
Wena Parry	5 August 2015	A public library close to Ms Parry's home
Will Parry	18 August 2015	Mr Parry's home
Terence Perkins	9 September 2015	Mr Perkins' workplace
Emma Riley	16 October 2015	Ms Riley's workplace
Mary Simpson	6 July 2015	Ms Simpson's home
Euan Sutherland	28 July 2015	Mr Sutherland's home
Nigel Warner	6 October 2015	A café close to Mr Warner's home
Ralph Wilde	27 July 2015	By telephone
Robert Wintemute	12 October 2015	King's College London

APPENDIX 3

Chronological List of Decisions and Judgments of the Strasbourg Organs in Respect of Cases against the UK Relating to Discrimination on the Grounds of Sexual Orientation

This is a chronological list of published decisions and judgments issued by the Strasbourg organs—the European Court of Human Rights, the former European Commission of Human Rights, and the Committee of Ministers of the Council of Europe—in respect of cases against the UK relating to sexual orientation discrimination. The list also contains a small number of decisions and judgments in respect of cases that do not explicitly concern sexual orientation discrimination and, where this is the case, a note of explanation is added. The list does not contain information about cases relating to sexual orientation discrimination in which an application has been declared inadmissible by the Strasbourg organs in circumstances where no decision has been made publically available.

The date(s) given for each case refer to the following: (D) Decision of the Court or former Commission; (J) Judgment of the Court; (M) Decision of the Committee of Ministers; (R) Report of the former Commission; and (S) Judgment of the Court on just satisfaction.

Details are given of the Articles of the Convention for the Protection of Human Rights and Fundamental Freedoms considered in each case.

The key issue given for each case is not an exhaustive description but, rather, a means by which cases may be conveniently grouped together.

Details in the 'Decision/judgment' column refer to the ultimate outcome of each case.

Date	Name	App. no.	Articles of the Convention invoked in the case								Key issue	Significance	Decision/judgment
			2	3	8	10	11	12	14	other			
04/04/74 (D) 30/09/75 (R) 07/12/76 (J)	Handyside v UK	5493/72				X			X	1,7,9, 13, 1 of P1	Freedom of expression (obscenity)	The case did not explicitly concern sexual orientation discrimination, but it was the first case transmitted to the Court involving an issue relating to homosexuality	No violation
07/07/77 (D) 12/10/78 (R) 12/06/79 (M)	X. v UK	7215/75			X	X			X		Minimum age of sexual consent	First complaint about sexual orientation discrimination deemed admissible by the Commission	No violation
03/03/78 (D) 13/03/80 (R) 22/10/81 (J) 24/02/83 (S)	Dudgeon v UK (originally X. v UK)	7525/76			X	X	X		X		Criminalization of private sexual activity	First successful complaint relating to sexual orientation discrimination	Articles 10 and 11 inadmissible; Not necessary to examine Articles 14+8; Violation Article 8
07/05/82 (D)	X. Ltd. and Y. v UK	8710/79				X			X	7, 9	Freedom of expression		Inadmissible
03/05/83 (D)	X. and Y. v UK	9369/81			X						Discrimination in immigration law	First complaint about sexual orientation discrimination in respect of 'family life'	Inadmissible

Date	Name	App. no.	Articles of the Convention invoked in the case								Key issue	Significance	Decision/judgment
			2	3	8	10	11	12	14	other			
12/10/83 (D)	B. v UK	9237/81			X				X		Criminalization of private sexual activity (military law)	First complaint about sexual orientation discrimination in the armed forces	Inadmissible
07/05/84 (D)	R.D. v UK	9721/82			X				X		Minimum age of sexual consent	First complaint about the 'age of consent' by a person younger than the minimum age	Inadmissible
14/05/86 (D)	Simpson v UK	11716/85			X				X	13, 1 of P1	Discrimination in housing provision	First complaint about sexual orientation discrimination in respect of housing	Inadmissible
17/07/86 (D)	Johnson v UK	10389/83			X				X		Criminalization of private sexual activity	First complaint about the criminalization of 'group sex'	Inadmissible
13/07/87 (D)	W.J. and D.P. v UK	12513/86			X				X	1	Discrimination in immigration law		Inadmissible
09/10/89 (D)	C. and L.M. v UK	14753/89			X			X	X		Discrimination in immigration law	First complaint about sexual orientation discrimination in respect of 'the right to marry and to found a family'	Inadmissible
10/02/90 (D)	Z.B. v UK	16106/90			X				X	13	Discrimination in immigration law		Inadmissible

(Continued)

Continued

Date	Name	App. no.	Articles of the Convention invoked in the case								Key issue	Significance	Decision/judgment
			2	3	8	10	11	12	14	other			
08/03/94 (D) 10/01/95 (R) 25/11/96 (J)	Wingrove v UK	17419/90				X					Censorship of homoerotic imagery on grounds of blasphemy		No violation
18/01/95 (D)	V., W., X., Y. and Z. v UK	22170/93			X				X		Criminalization of private sexual activity (sado-masochism)		Inadmissible
18/01/95 (D) 26/10/95 (R) 19/02/97 (J)	Laskey, Jaggard and Brown v UK	21627/93 21826/93 21974/93			X				X	7	Criminalization of private sexual activity (sado-masochism)		Articles 7 and 14 inadmissible; No violation Article 8
19/01/95 (D)	Wilde, Greenhalgh and Parry v UK	22382/93			X				X		Minimum age of sexual consent		Struck off list
21/05/96 (D) 01/07/97 (R) 27/03/01 (J)	Sutherland v UK	25186/94			X				X		Minimum age of sexual consent	Commission finds different 'age of consent' for male homosexual acts to be a violation of Article 8 in conjunction with Article 14	Struck off list
20/05/97 (D)	Fleming v UK	33987/96		X	X				X	13	Discrimination due to partner's employment in the armed forces		Inadmissible

Date	Name	App. no.	Articles of the Convention invoked in the case								Key issue	Significance	Decision/judgment
			2	3	8	10	11	12	14	other			
23/02/99 (D) 27/09/99 (J) 25/07/00 (S)	Lustig-Prean and Beckett v UK	31417/96 32377/96			X				X		Prohibition of homosexuality in the armed forces	First successful complaint (along with Smith and Grady v UK) about sexual orientation discrimination in the armed forces	No separate issue under Articles 14+8; Violation Article 8
23/02/99 (D) 27/09/99 (J) 25/07/00 (S)	Smith and Grady v UK	33985/96 33986/96		X	X	X			X	5, 13	Prohibition of homosexuality in the armed forces	First successful complaint (along with Lustig-Prean and Beckett v UK) about sexual orientation discrimination in the armed forces	Articles 5 and 5+14 inadmissible; No separate issue under Articles 14+8; Not necessary to examine Articles 10 or 10+14; No violation Articles 3 or 3+14; Violation Article 8; Violation Article 13
16/03/99 (D) 31/07/00 (J)	A.D.T. v UK	35765/97			X				X		Criminalization of private sexual activity	First successful 'group sex' complaint	Not necessary to examine Article 14; Violation Article 8
21/03/00 (D)	Craig v UK	45396/99			X				X	6, 13	Discrimination arising from court order in respect of parental rights		Inadmissible

(Continued)

Continued

Date	Name	App. no.	Articles of the Convention invoked in the case								Key issue	Significance	Decision/judgment
			2	3	8	10	11	12	14	other			
05/09/00 (D) 22/10/02 (J)	Perkins and R. v UK	43208/98 44875/98			X				X		Prohibition of homosexuality in the armed forces		No separate issue under Articles 14+8; Violation Article 8
05/09/00 (D)	Cardoso and Johansen v UK	47061/99		X	X						Discrimination in immigration law		Struck off list
05/09/00 (D) 22/10/02 (J)	Beck, Copp and Bazeley v UK	48535/99 48536/99 48537/99		X	X	X			X	13	Prohibition of homosexuality in the armed forces		No separate issue under Articles 14+8; Not necessary to examine Articles 10 or 10+14; No violation Articles 3 or 3+14; Violation Article 8; Violation Article 13
23/01/01 (D)	Young v UK	56276/00			X				X	13	Prohibition of homosexuality in the armed forces		Struck off list

Date	Name	App. no.	Articles of the Convention invoked in the case								Key issue	Significance	Decision/judgment
			2	3	8	10	11	12	14	other			
23/10/01 (D) 10/12/02 (J)	Waite v UK	53236/99			X				X	5, 13	Recall of prisoner on license to prison, which involved a complaint about discrimination created by the minimum age of sexual consent	The Court, although finding violations of Article 5, rejected the complaint about sexual orientation discrimination	No separate issue under Article 13; No violation Article 14; No violation Article 5(1); Violation Article 5(4); Violation Article 5(5)
27/11/01 (D)	Morris v UK	31701/96			X				X		Minimum age of sexual consent		Struck off list
08/01/02 (D)	Connell and Others v UK	43495/98			X				X		Criminalization of private sexual activity		Struck off list
15/01/02 (D)	Goddard v UK	57821/00		X	X	X			X	13	Prohibition of homosexuality in the armed forces		Struck off list
04/06/02 (D) 29/07/03 (J)	Brown v UK	52770/99			X				X	13	Prohibition of homosexuality in the armed forces		Struck off list
27/05/03 (D) 10/02/04 (J)	B.B. v UK	53760/00			X				X	5,13	Minimum age of sexual consent		Articles 5, 8 (partly) and 13 inadmissible; Violation Article 14 in conjunction with Article 8

(Continued)

Continued

Date	Name	App. no.	Articles of the Convention invoked in the case								Key issue	Significance	Decision/judgment
			2	3	8	10	11	12	14	other			
22/06/04 (D)	F. v UK	17341/03	X	X	X					5, 6	Deportation of asylum seeker		Inadmissible
13/12/05 (D)	Love and Others v UK	4103/04 5498/04 10617/04 14557/04 27313/04		X	X	X			X	13	Prohibition of homosexuality in the armed forces		Inadmissible
28/11/06 (D)	R. and F. v UK	35748/05			X			X	X	13, 17, 1 of P1	Recognition of same-sex marriage following gender reassignment	No explicit consideration of sexual orientation	Inadmissible
28/11/06 (D)	Parry v UK	42971/05			X			X	X	9, 13, 1 of P1	Recognition of same-sex marriage following gender reassignment	No explicit consideration of sexual orientation	Inadmissible
06/02/07 (D)	MacDonald v UK	301/04			X				X	13	Prohibition of homosexuality in the armed forces		Struck off list
13/02/07 (D)	Leathart v UK	10590/05		X	X				X		Prohibition of homosexuality in the armed forces		Struck off list
18/09/07 (D)	Ford v UK	10557/05		X	X				X		Prohibition of homosexuality in the armed forces		Struck off list

Date	Name	App. no.	Articles of the Convention invoked in the case								Key issue	Significance	Decision/judgment
			2	3	8	10	11	12	14	other			
11/12/07 (D)	Anderson v UK	40039/03		X	X	X			X	13	Prohibition of homosexuality in the armed forces		Partly inadmissible and partly struck off list
11/12/07 (D)	Wheeler v UK	1591/04			X				X	13	Prohibition of homosexuality in the armed forces		Partly inadmissible and partly struck off list
11/12/07 (D)	Blakemore and 41 Others v UK	10471/05 et al.		X	X	X			X	13	Prohibition of homosexuality in the armed forces		Struck off list
11/12/07 (D)	Boden v UK	10476/05		X	X	X			X	13	Prohibition of homosexuality in the armed forces		Partly inadmissible and partly struck off list
11/12/07 (D)	Chambers v UK	10540/05		X	X	X			X	13	Prohibition of homosexuality in the armed forces		Partly inadmissible and partly struck off list
11/12/07 (D)	De La Maziere v UK	10549/05		X	X	X			X	13	Prohibition of homosexuality in the armed forces		Partly inadmissible and partly struck off list
11/12/07 (D)	Day v UK	10545/05		X	X	X			X	13	Prohibition of homosexuality in the armed forces		Partly inadmissible and partly struck off list

(Continued)

Continued

Date	Name	App. no.	Articles of the Convention invoked in the case: 2	3	8	10	11	12	14	other	Key issue	Significance	Decision/judgment
11/12/07 (D)	Fitzgerald v UK	10555/05		X	X	X			X	13	Prohibition of homosexuality in the armed forces		Partly inadmissible and partly struck off list
11/12/07 (D)	Garford v UK	10561/05		X	X	X			X	13	Prohibition of homosexuality in the armed forces		Partly inadmissible and partly struck off list
11/12/07 (D)	Garnham v UK	10563/05		X	X	X			X	13	Prohibition of homosexuality in the armed forces		Partly inadmissible and partly struck off list
11/12/07 (D)	Griggs v UK	10569/05		X	X	X			X	13	Prohibition of homosexuality in the armed forces		Partly inadmissible and partly struck off list
11/12/07 (D)	MacDonald v UK	10600/05		X	X	X			X	13	Prohibition of homosexuality in the armed forces		Partly inadmissible and partly struck off list
11/12/07 (D)	O'Keefe v UK	10610/05		X	X	X			X	13	Prohibition of homosexuality in the armed forces		Partly inadmissible and partly struck off list
11/12/07 (D)	Self v UK	10615/05		X	X	X			X	13	Prohibition of homosexuality in the armed forces		Partly inadmissible and partly struck off list

Date	Name	App. no.	Articles of the Convention invoked in the case								Key issue	Significance	Decision/judgment
			2	3	8	10	11	12	14	other			
11/12/07 (D)	Stinton v UK	10617/05		X	X	X			X	13	Prohibition of homosexuality in the armed forces		Partly inadmissible and partly struck off list
11/12/07 (D)	Walton v UK	10621/05		X	X	X			X	13	Prohibition of homosexuality in the armed forces		Partly inadmissible and partly struck off list
07/10/08 (D)	Greig v UK	10567/05		X	X				X		Prohibition of homosexuality in the armed forces		Struck off list
07/10/08 (D)	Hocking v UK	40160/03			X				X	13	Prohibition of homosexuality in the armed forces		Struck off list
21/10/08 (D) 23/06/09 (J)	Hunt and Miller v UK	10578/05 10605/05		X	X				X	13	Prohibition of homosexuality in the armed forces		Partly inadmissible and partly struck off list
04/11/08 (D)	Courten v UK	4479/06							X	1 of P1	Discrimination in taxation		Inadmissible
02/06/09 (D)	Small v UK	7330/06			X				X		Minimum age of sexual consent		Struck off list
23/06/09 (D)	M.W. v UK	11313/02			X				X	1 of P1	Discrimination in social security benefit		Inadmissible

(Continued)

Continued

Date	Name	App. no.	Articles of the Convention invoked in the case								Key issue	Significance	Decision/judgment
			2	3	8	10	11	12	14	other			
28/09/10 (J)	J.M. v UK	37060/06			X				X	1 of P1	Discrimination in child maintenance		Not necessary to examine Articles 14+8; Violation Article 14 in conjunction with Article 1 of Protocol 1
31/05/11 (D)	D.B.N. v UK	26550/10	X	X	X				X	13	Deportation of asylum seeker		Struck off list

Index

ECHR = European Convention on Human Rights
EComHR = European Commission of Human Rights
ECtHR = European Court of Human Rights